What Makes Writing Academic

Also Available from Bloomsbury

Content Knowledge in English Language Teacher Education: International Experiences, edited by Darío Luis Banegas

Essentials for Successful English Language Teaching, by Thomas S. C. Farrell and George M. Jacobs

On Writtenness: The Cultural Politics of Academic Writing by Joan Turner

Pedagogies in English for Academic Purposes: Teaching and Learning in International Contexts, edited by Carole MacDiarmid and J. J. MacDonald

Researching Language Learning Motivation: A Concise Guide, edited by Ali H. Al-Hoorie and Fruzsina Szabó

Successful Dissertations: The Complete Guide for Education, Childhood and Early Childhood Studies Students, edited by Caron Carter

Teaching English-Medium Instruction Courses in Higher Education: A Guide for Non-Native Speakers, by Ruth Breeze and Carmen Sancho Guinda

The Value of English in Global Mobility and Higher Education: An Investigation of Higher Education in Cyprus, by Manuela Vida-Mannl

What is Good Academic Writing?: Insights into Discipline-Specific Student Writing, edited by Melinda Whong and Jeanne Godfrey

Writing a Watertight Thesis: A Guide to Successful Structure and Defence, by Mike Bottery and Nigel Wright

Writing the Research Paper: Multicultural Perspectives for Writing in English as a Second Language, by Philip M. McCarthy and Khawlah Ahmed

What Makes Writing Academic

Rethinking Theory for Practice

Julia Molinari

BLOOMSBURY ACADEMIC
LONDON • NEW YORK • OXFORD • NEW DELHI • SYDNEY

BLOOMSBURY ACADEMIC
Bloomsbury Publishing Plc
50 Bedford Square, London, WC1B 3DP, UK
1385 Broadway, New York, NY 10018, USA
29 Earlsfort Terrace, Dublin 2, Ireland

BLOOMSBURY, BLOOMSBURY ACADEMIC and the Diana logo are trademarks of
Bloomsbury Publishing Plc

First published in Great Britain 2022
This paperback edition published 2023

Copyright © Julia Molinari, 2022

Julia Molinari has asserted her right under the Copyright,
Designs and Patents Act, 1988, to be identified as Author of this work.

For legal purposes the Acknowledgements on pp. xii–xiii constitute an extension
of this copyright page.

Cover image: © Carlos Sanchez Pereyra/Getty Images

Bloomsbury Publishing Plc does not have any control over, or responsibility for,
any third-party websites referred to or in this book. All internet addresses
given in this book were correct at the time of going to press. The author and publisher
regret any inconvenience caused if addresses have changed or sites have ceased to exist,
but can accept no responsibility for any such changes.

This work is published open access subject to a Creative Commons Attribution-
NonCommercial-NoDerivatives 4.0 International licence (CC BY-NC-ND 4.0,
https://creativecommons.org/licenses/by-nc-nd/4.0/). You may re-use, distribute,
and reproduce this work in any medium for non-commercial purposes,
provided you give attribution to the copyright holder and the publisher
and provide a link to the Creative Commons licence.

A catalogue record for this book is available from the British Library.

A catalog record for this book is available from the Library of Congress.

ISBN:	HB:	978-1-3502-4392-7
	PB:	978-1-3502-4396-5
	ePDF:	978-1-3502-4393-4
	ePUB:	978-1-3502-4394-1

Typeset by Integra Software Services Pvt. Ltd.

To find out more about our authors and books visit www.bloomsbury.com
and sign up for our newsletters.

To Felia

Contents

List of Figures	viii
Foreword	ix
Acknowledgements	xii
List of Abbreviations	xiv
Letter to My Reader	1
1 Troubling Academic Writing: Problems and Implications for Higher Education	17
2 How Did We Get Here? A Selected History	45
3 What Makes Writing Academic: Learning from Writings 'in the Wild'	73
4 Critical Realism: Re-claiming Theory for Practice	99
5 Foundations for a Future Writing Pedagogy	131
Signing Off	163
Afterword	169
References	174
Index	199

Figures

1	A critical realist conception of academic writing	105
2	Sousanis (2015, p. 66 © Harvard University Press)	131

Foreword
Chrissie Boughey

Critical realism is a philosophy of being that accommodates the relativism of individual experience and practice as well as the existence of an ultimate reality independent of human thought and action. For those of us who draw on critical realism, understanding reality as layered and emergent means looking at the world with different eyes and never understanding it in the same way again. It involves asking questions such as 'What must the world really be like for my experiences and observations of it to be possible and for my experiences and observations to be different to those of others around me?' As we try to answer these questions, the potential is opened for the explanations offered to contribute to social justice.

One place where the need for social justice is often overlooked is higher education. In the last fifty or so years, higher education systems across the world have expanded and, as they have done so they have come to accommodate ever more diverse groups of students. Most of this expansion has been driven by discourses privileging the role of higher education in the production of 'knowledge workers' for the global economy. From this perspective, what can be wrong with the universities? How can they be unjust? More and more young people get to study in them and gain qualifications that will allow them to gain highly paid employment. Isn't this all for the social good?

What this sort of thinking masks is the fact that access to and success in higher education is socially differentiated. Who gets to attend the most prestigious universities? Who gets the best marks, the best degree classifications? Equally important are questions about who gets to thrive in universities. Whose ways of being, whose ways of expression do they privilege and whose do they undermine? Does every student go to university in order to gain better employment? Don't some students study to fulfil their own intellectual aspirations however they might imagine them?

As Julia Molinari argues in this book, what is usually referred to as 'academic writing' influences the answers to these questions in myriad ways. Dominant assessment practices continue to privilege particular ways of learning and of demonstrating that learning that favour some and exclude others. Rather than looking at the way dominant practices exclude the possibility of diversity, the response of most universities is to support the 'industries' associated with the production of 'acceptable' forms of demonstrating knowing in the form of writing courses, units and centres focusing on 'student development' and, even, attempts to police plagiarism. The result of all this is that those who do not produce the performances sanctioned, either because they have not yet mastered them, because they are alien to them or because they do not want to produce them, are 'pathologised' in a process that simultaneously ensures that the industries themselves are sustained and those who most reap the benefits of a higher education continue to do so.

Molinari's powerful text draws on critical realism to show how academic writing, the form of demonstrating knowing privileged in the universities, came to be reduced to a series of 'transferable mechanical skills'. These 'skills' are, of course, the raw materials of the industries used to sustain dominant forms of academic expression. In order to do this, she examines the way 'writing' came to be conflated with the alphabet and so-called 'higher order thinking' at the expense of oral and visual means of expression. In critical realist terms, this involves exploring the 'the world' that exists independently of our apprehension of it, the world of relatively enduring structures and mechanisms that led to the emergence of events over centuries in time and our experiences of those events. For those concerned with social justice, this exposition of the way things 'came to be' offers the potential to see how things could be changed.

Essentially, this book is about writing pedagogies and more specifically about the development of writing pedagogies as 'levers for change'. Historically claims have been made for other pedagogies to do this. Approaches to developing writing that saw the need for students to be socialized into a set of practices were seen as a means of opening access to students. What they offered, however, was access to an unchanged order of things. By identifying the multiplicity of literacy practices, researchers such as Brian Street and Shirley Brice Heath allowed us to see how some practices were more powerful than others and how some had more access to those practices. The problem, though, was that the acknowledgement of multiplicity did not necessarily entail ensuring that power was challenged and often this work was used simply as a means of understanding why some people found it more difficult to master performances of knowing than others.

The use of critical realism allows Molinari to identify texts as emerging from the interplay of enduring structures and mechanisms at a level of reality that cannot be accessed empirically. Understanding this interplay allows us to see what contributes to the experience of these texts as 'academic'. Molinari's location of scholarship as lever for change at this level of reality is important for a number of reasons not least because of the role of common-sense discourses in constraining action. She notes that writing has to have 'content', that it has to be *about something*. This leads to an argument for the use of interdisciplinary approaches that ensure that novice writers have something to write about. The trouble with interdisciplinary approaches is that those in the disciplines then draw on common-sense discourses to claim that they are not writing teachers, that their role is not to 'teach English'. The identification of scholarship as a mechanism that can be drawn upon to challenge academics' understandings of themselves as experts in the disciplines rather than teachers of writing is therefore key to change. Molinari's powerful arguments offer the potential to guide that scholarship regardless of the forms it takes.

Other mechanisms identified by Molinari as needing to be brought into play include indigenous knowledge systems and indigenous languages, long denied a place in the 'academic' world. At the centre of critical realist thinking is the idea that we should never conflate 'what is' with 'what can be known', a phenomenon termed the 'epistemic fallacy'. Language is a resource for making sense of the worlds around us and different languages allow us to do this in different ways. Requiring students to use English, or any other dominant language, requires the adoption of a form of sense making that may be foreign, enhancing the alienation they may feel from having to draw on the theories and principles that deny them the understandings that have sustained their lives before entering a university. If higher education truly is to contribute to social justice, how can we deny that 'what is' may be much more than what we can know by drawing on epistemologies and ontologies developed in the Global North?

In identifying these mechanisms at a level of reality that normally escapes us and in calling for others to engage in the enquiry necessary to recognize others, Molinari is not outlining a pedagogy in itself but rather the potential for the emergence of pedagogies that will contribute to change. This is what makes her book important. It is not a 'how to' manual. It does not advocate any one particular approach. Rather it opens up the possibility for the emergence of an array of pedagogies and approaches that will take account of the myriad different contexts in which students and teachers live and work. In doing this, the book offers hope and the excitement of seeing what can emerge as we work to make what can be counted as knowing and as manifestations of knowing more socially just.

Acknowledgements

The 2020–21 have been years of hostile environments; two painful years, exacerbated by COVID-19, climate emergencies, BREXIT, flood and wildfire devastation, political divisiveness, personal loss and heartache. The collective aftermath is still being felt and it will be long-lasting. Somehow, I managed to squeeze this book through the cracks of lockdown, trapped at home, and fortunate to not only have a home but to have one with 'a room of my own'. It was my best friend Felia, to whom I dedicate this monograph, who insisted: 'if not now, then when?' I am indebted to her dogged insistence, over forty years of friendship, that I 'do something' with these ideas! Thanks, Fe x.

I would be lost without Luay and Robs. They've had to endure the years of the PhD and now this, more hours at my computer, absent-mindedness in all matters domestic, last-minute and random decisions about what to eat or what to do on a weekend. Between the eye-rolls and theatrical yawns as they listen to me droning on about academic writing and how *it could all be so different*, they have never stopped repeating 'I am so proud of you' and 'Brava mamma'. I love them with all my being.

This monograph germinated and grew from the generous conversations, kind mentoring and vigilant supervision of Professor Patricia Thomson and Professor Andrew Fisher. I am beyond grateful to them, along with my examiners, Professor Gina Wisker and Dr Ian James Kidd, for believing there was something in the way I think about academic writing, both educationally and philosophically, that was worth teasing out. Pat and Andy, you'll recognize most of what we did for the thesis in here (including the stuff you probably weren't so keen on!) but there are also omissions and additions. I could have done more and better, but for now, and given the circumstances, it's the best I could do.

Also key to my thinking have been the three people involved in either reviewing the initial proposal or writing the foreword and afterword to this first book. Professor Chrissie Boughey, Dr Fiona English and Professor Suresh Canagarajah, all of whom are luminaries in their fields and have significantly shaped the ways in which I think about academic writing. They are creative, innovative and courageous intellectuals who have stood up for marginalized students and academics throughout their academic trajectories. Thank you for endorsing what I am trying to say and for generously giving up your time to do so. An anonymous reviewer also dedicated their energies to reading the whole manuscript and I hope that I have done some justice to your kind comments and suggestions.

Never in a million years would I have expected Bloomsbury to agree to publishing this, yet here I am, one of their authors! Who would have thought! Maria, Evangeline and Anna (my editors), and their teams, have been kind and patient and so encouraging at every step of what is a brand-new process for me. I am especially grateful for the early support and suggestions that I received, especially when I expressed the desire for the book to be available Open Access.

Several critical friends and colleagues have stood by me over the years. Two, in particular, stand out: Dr Alex Ding and Dr Sally Zacharias. This is because of the many hours we have spent talking each other's ideas through, constantly and generously looking for synergies in how we think about language, literacy and writing, differing on some aspects, but ultimately pushing each other to think through the implications of some of our more controversial positions. Please let's keep talking.

I now take full responsibility for anything that is good and everything that is bad in here.

Abbreviations

DBIS	Department for Business, Innovation and Skills (UK)
EAP	English for Academic Purposes
EDI	Equality, Diversity and Inclusion
EV	Epistemic Virtue
HEI	Higher Education Institution
HESA	Higher Education Statistics Agency (UK)
IELTS	International English Language Testing System
SAP	Socio-Academic Practice
SoTL	Scholarship of Teaching and Learning
TC	Threshold Concept

Letter to My Reader

Dear Reader,

I am assuming that if you have chosen to read this book, it is because you either teach academic writing as a tutor, lecturer or supervisor and/or you are an academic writer yourself, maybe a student who has to write essays, a doctoral researcher who needs to make choices about how to represent your knowledge or a writer of academic journals, maybe even books, who continues to question what shape and form your writing should take. If you are any of the above, then there should be something in here for you, maybe a reference you hadn't come across before or an idea for how you could write your next academic text, teach a writing lesson or advise a doctoral researcher. Note my use of 'how *you could*' – this gives a clue as to what this book is about. It is about possibilities for writing, not prescriptions on how *you should* write. How you should write is a question of opportunities and constraints that are so specific to your unique contexts that I would need to be the proverbial fly on the wall to glean the knowledge to advise on what you should do. No, this isn't a 'how to write' book. It is a book about the knowledge work that academic writing does and the forms that (dis)allow writing to do its job as a 'knowledge worker'. It is a book about possibilities for how academic writing could be.

By 'forms' I mean genres, understood throughout this book at their most basic level of 'conventionalised ways of acting and interacting by exhibiting regularities and shared understandings of how language is used' (Devitt, 1996; Hamilton & Pitt, 2009). I will be using 'form' and 'genre' somewhat synonymously and interchangeably rather than in any technical or specialized sense. This is because the book isn't about genre *per se* but about how academic writing comes to be classified as 'academic' in the first place. An IELTS essay, a traditional PhD monograph, a poem and an academic journal article are all examples of genres because they communicate knowledge by arranging words and sentences in ways that readers expect to find them. The reason genre is so important to understanding what makes writing academic is that academia is somewhat territorial and defensive of its writing traditions: as soon as anybody disrupts conventionalized ways of writing – breaks the rules, subverts the standards – the academic literacy wars erupt, students fail, articles get rejected and the almighty wrath of the guardians of the academic temple descend on their victim, a writer who may simply have been exercising their intellectual and creative right to communicate complex knowledge differently or grappling with the universally shared challenge of finding the right words to say what needs saying. Either way, messing around with genres, with form, is seriously frowned upon in academia.

As you can probably tell, I have started this book as I mean to continue it, by doing just that, by messing around a bit with genre. This is meant to be a serious 'academic' monograph based on my PhD research about academic writing, no less! Yet, here I am, informally chatting away, seemingly digressing as if you were here, in the same room or on the same screen as me (forgive me, I write this having been in lockdown for over a year because of the Covid-19 pandemic, I haven't been with people in a long time and the unexpected comforts that the informalities of lockdown have generated – from teaching in loungewear to lecturing from the kitchen table – may be wreaking havoc with my writing!). Well, this is a serious book, it is an academic book and what makes it academic is the knowledge it deals with, the references it draws on, the research that has gone into it and my identity, my right to be a writer who is present in her text. Le Ha (2009) did this too and she got published in an academic journal, as did Richardson (1997), so I tentatively, wholly deferentially, take my cue from them by giving myself the licence to be both academic and have a personality, to take a risk in negotiating institution and intuition, structure and agency, convention and voice. Some may not like this style, but others will, just as some don't like the zombified prose and predictable patterns of formal academic writing, but others feel reassured by the authority of its clinical, monotone and passive voice. If nothing else, it is the differences in taste about style that unite us because, at some stage, we all have to trudge through text that sends us to sleep or irritates us. And this again is the whole point of the book. There are different ways of communicating academic knowledge and I hope that if you do make it to the end (there may be some unfamiliar technical jargony hurdles to get over, but I do my best to explain), you will see that what makes writing academic is actually quite simple and has nothing to do with using the passive voice or avoiding personal pronouns.

What also gives me the licence to mess around a bit with my language and tone, with genre, is that what makes writing academic emerges from socio-academic and historical practices rather than conventionalized stylistic, linguistic or syntactic forms. What this means in practice is that academic writings are and can be varied. They don't all have to fit the mould of convention. Using a critical realist lens as my theoretical framework, the book re-imagines (I re-imagine) academic writings as twenty-first-century open systems that change according to affordances perceived by writers. In so doing, the book offers opportunities for re-imagining how, which and whose knowledge emerges. This matters because academic communication hinges on us all being able to write in certain forms but not others, which risks excluding knowledge that may lend itself to alternative forms of representation. Moreover, because academic ability tends to be misleadingly conflated with writing ability, limiting how the academy writes to a relatively narrow set of forms (such as the essay or thesis) and a single modality (such as language) may be preventing a range of academic abilities from emerging.

Standardized forms require abstracts, introductions, main bodies and conclusions. They are also predominantly monolingual and monomodal. One troubling shortcoming of this kind of standardization is that it can narrow, distort or flatten epistemic representation. A related shortcoming is that standardization is exclusionary and this can lead to a range of epistemic losses and gains. Drawing on the history of academia, socio-semiotic research, integrational linguistics and studies in multimodal and visual thinking, the book proposes that academic writings be re-imagined as multimodal artefacts that harness a wider range of epistemic affordances. It further highlights that even if writing were to remain the preferred academic mode, it needn't be so standardized. Old and new genres ranging from dialogues, chronicles, manifestos, blogs and comics can also be academic.

(I hope I just sounded academic enough).

My purpose in writing this book is threefold: (1) to provide students, teachers and supervisors with reasons (and a licence) to re-imagine academic texts; (2) to extend established academic writing scholarship by introducing critical realism as a conceptual framework for justifying plural, democratized, multimodal, diverse and inclusive forms of academic writing; and (3) to develop a philosophy of change that lays a foundation for diversifying writing pedagogies. Overall, I draw extensively on previous scholarship, extending its theoretical reach by providing a socio-philosophical perspective that explains how and why change is needed for socially just writing practices. I go beyond describing different approaches to writing academic texts and instead advance a social philosophy of change that provides a rationale for sustained innovation and diversity. I situate my book more firmly within the broader conversation on educational social justice by arguing that what makes writing academic are its epistemic virtues, namely what knowledge is valued, for what purpose and by whom. Epistemic virtues (and vices) affect how academic texts are written and who sets the standards by which they are deemed 'academic'. By situating my book in this way, I provide a rationale for diversity that is hinted at in several similar books, but not made fully explicit.

There are three further underlying reasons for writing this book. Firstly, UK universities, the context with which I am most familiar, are increasingly diverse spaces attended by up to 50 per cent of the UK's eligible population (ONS, 2019) representing a range of socio-economic and cultural demographics. This widened participation amongst home students brings with it a range of educational, linguistic and literacy backgrounds (for example, 90 per cent of students are from state-funded schools [HESA, 2020b]), abilities and motivations. Moreover, approximately 20 per cent of the UK university student body is 'international' with a further 20 per cent accounting for mature students (DBIS, 2016; HESA, 2020a; Tuckett, 2013). In Europe alone one in seven people of working age (fifteen to sixty-four) identify as disabled (EUROSTAT, 2019); yet, disabled people frequently face barriers when it comes to participating equally in many aspects of society, including education. The diversity that characterizes university students and that HEIs (Higher Education Institutions) boast of in their promotional literatures as hallmarks of their inclusive provision rarely manifests itself as diversity in academic writing practices. Rather, university literacy practices are designed to cancel differences, to homogenize and standardize to norms and templates that don't reflect or respect or explore the literacies and languages students bring with them. Yet, as Canagarajah (2021) reminds us in a recent online lecture, we can actually 'have it both ways' because norms can be negotiated; they can change because literacy and language are not fixed. Academic texts can be part of a rich and varied ecological landscape which acknowledges, for example, that there is no such thing as 'standard English':

> Standard English is not a 'thing'. It doesn't have a life of its own outside. We created 'standard English'. Standard English has words from so many languages, from Swedish, Norwegian, Tamil, lots of languages. How did this come to be treated as pure, normative, standard English? It's purely ideology. It's not something ontological. Language doesn't exist out there, in one state, in one stage and then start.

Canagarajah goes on to remind us that standards are merely 'approximations' whereby diversity can co-exist alongside the norms and whereby writers, understood as agents, can participate in norm changes. Diversity is possible because writers and readers recognize that patterns remain fairly stable over time: variation within those patterns does not threaten the unity of the pattern but it can provide writers with opportunities to take part in changing the norms that constitute the overall pattern.

The second underlying reason for writing this book is that movements to decolonize universities, educate online and question neoliberal higher education practices further highlight transformative trends that raise concerns about social justice, including who or what universities are for. As Boughey reminds us in the foreword to this book, diverse students bring diverse literacies and if universities are to be sites for inclusion, diversity and knowledge transformation, writing practices need questioning. And finally, my motivation for writing this is to index that what makes writing academic is evolving, emerging and contestable: it has evolved over time; it emerges as a practice that transcends its forms; and it remains contested, as academic disciplines revisit how best to represent the ontologies and epistemologies of their fields of knowledge. This matters at a point in history, now, when the crisis of representation endures: how should knowledge be communicated and in what forms in an era of instant social media, bite-size and click-bait broadcasting, fee-charging universities, widening participation, climate emergencies, six-minute or long reads, open access, posthuman technology and crowd-sourced wisdom?

The book begins by contextualizing academic writing within two particular fields of study: UK EAP[1] or EGAP (English for General Academic Purposes) and American Composition Studies (also referred to as Rhetoric and Composition or WAC (Writing across the Curriculum). I start my focus in these areas because they are the areas with which I am familiar as both a teacher and a researcher and because pedagogic programmes such as these are highly influential in shaping discourses about academic writing. As such, they have a responsibility to educate students and practitioners about the evolving purposes, forms and possibilities for academic expression. I then subject academic writing to an interdisciplinary (educational and philosophical) analysis in order to argue that what makes writing academic are its socio-academic practices and values, not its conventional forms. It is this argument that allows me to gradually re-think the theories that academic writing pedagogies traditionally draw on – such as genre theory and cognitive and applied linguistics – and to propose the inclusion of

---

[1] Presessional EAP courses in the UK enable access to undergraduate and postgraduate courses for which students, typically international students, have an offer that is conditional on passing an EAP course. These are different to insessional courses which offer EAP support alongside study on degree programmes. Both presessional and insessional courses provide academic communication support to international and home students.

a new one – critical realism – so that writing practices can be transformed into more inclusive methods of enquiry and of epistemic representation.

The norms taught by traditional, often commercial, academic writing programmes tend to be those associated with what has been called the 'scientific paradigm' (Bennett, 2015; Turner, 2010, 2018). EAP, for example, teaches this paradigm and in so doing is presenting a particular form and ideology of academic writing that is not representative of all disciplines. Asking students to replicate norms and conventions leads to uncritical syllabi and assessment practices that do not require knowledge of the broader educational process of understanding why these norms prevail, what they can and cannot afford, who benefits and what the implications of adopting these norms might be for them as learners and writers and for the academic knowledge communities they will be contributing to. Given that writing is the preferred mode of academic assessment, as evidenced by the 'essay' remaining the default genre in the humanities and in many of the arts and social sciences (Womack, 1993), it is not surprising that it is student writing that receives a great deal of attention in higher education and EAP. This has been shown in Nesi and Gardner (2012) and Andrews (2003). As a consequence of the centrality of writing, the focus on norms mentioned above is also to be found in how academic writing is approached. This is despite a shift, in the last twenty years or so, from a narrow focus on text and its linguistic norms towards more multimodal forms of communication (Andrews, 2010, p. 93; Andrews et al., 2012; Paré, 2018; Roozen & Erickson, 2017). This shift has seen literacy practices (such as informed rhetorical choices about style and multimodality), as opposed to skills (such as the decontextualized and transferable mechanics of writing, like paragraphing), come to the fore in several areas of research writing, including Kamler and Thomson (2006) and A. Archer and Breuer (2015). EAP, however, has been slow to catch up with or even embrace this trend, a trend that indexes the richness and possibilities academic writing practices afford so that it can fulfil a range of academic purposes. Such purposes include preparing students for the multimodal communication needed in the twenty-first century (Andrews et al., 2012; A. Archer & Breuer, 2016; Mcculloch, 2017; Paré, 2017), respecting and celebrating the diverse literacies, values and identities that students bring with them to academia (Canagarajah, 2019; Roozen & Erickson, 2017; Sperlinger, McLellan, & Pettigrew, 2018; Williams, 2017) and educating about writing so that students are empowered to make informed choices about what is possible and why it is possible as well as about what is expected (Downs & Wardle, 2007; Mays, 2017).

To answer my research question – what makes writing academic – I have chosen an interdisciplinary approach which draws on educational, sociological and philosophical theories. This allows my research to be explorative rather than exploitative (D'Agostino, 2012), meaning that it aims to 'discover and innovate' within the realm of what is possible, rather than 'add details and fill in gaps' (Krishnan, 2013, p. 19) within the boundaries of what already exists. In this sense, it fulfils the socio-academic practice of being imaginative about 'future possibilities' (Barnett, 2012, 2013). In the process of introducing a new theory to inform pedagogic practices, I reject dominant discourses that frame academic writing as a transferable skill which can be reduced to conventional forms. Instead, I show that academic writings are varied and evolve alongside changing writer agencies and textual environments. This accounts for the emergence of a diverse academic writing landscape that enacts diverse socio-academic practices and that does not reduce writing to the predictable static surface features that genre approaches to academic writing tend to get reduced to. My methodology resists traditional disciplinary classifications and is in line with the reflective and interpretative approaches associated with the humanities. Rather than 'filling a gap' in academic writing research, I see my role as a researcher as one that challenges existing writing conventions by questioning their underlying assumptions and highlighting the implications they lead to.

My approach further aligns with the kind of 'problematisation' discussed in Alvesson and Sandberg (2013), who also object to the uncritical adoption of the default 'gap-spotting' approach to research on the grounds that it posits an incremental, or 'additive', approach to academic enquiry that can leave unchallenged the underlying ontological, epistemological and ideological assumptions about what and whose information is missing and why it might be missing in the first place. Gap-spotting is problematic for a host of other reasons, too, as Canagarajah pointedly explains in the Afterword to this book and as Pat Thomson (2021) eloquently reminds us in her blog post. Rather, my aim is to unsettle assumptions about academic writing because (Barnett, 1990, p. 155)

> a genuine higher learning is subversive in the sense of subverting the student's taken-for-granted world, including the world of endeavour, scholarship, calculation or creativity, into which he or she has been initiated. A genuine higher education is unsettling; it is not meant to be a cosy experience. It is disturbing because, ultimately, the student comes to see that things could always be other than they are.

Monodisciplinary approaches to knowledge can lead to assumptions remaining unchallenged, allowing them to seem 'objective' and to then 'settle' into established, arguably complacent, ways of knowing. Such disciplinary objectivity and complacency have their challengers, though. For example, there exists a plurality of different conceptions of objectivity. This has been documented historically by Daston and Galison (2007) who trace the etymological trajectory of epistemic virtues. They locate the naming of the epistemic virtue of 'objectivity' (understood as a mechanical conception of reality that does not require the subjective interpretation of a knower) within the mid-nineteenth century (2007, pp. 17 and 31). Although they concede that etymology does not, in and of itself, bring reality into existence or deny it (i.e. naming something does not negate its previous existence), they nevertheless question the importance that etymology is given in the history of 'Western' knowledge because it can result in conflating how we come to understand the nature of knowledge. For example, they argue that the 'Western' scientific paradigm of conflating objectivity with epistemology is misguided. They claim that 'objectivity and epistemology do not coincide' because the history of epistemology, namely of the ways in which we have come to know and interpret reality, has drawn on other epistemic virtues that are not 'objective'. These include the virtue of 'truth-to-nature', which is an essentialist and universal *subjective* representation of reality whereby scientist and artist work together to represent, as well as distort, what they see (cf. early-eighteenth-century botanical drawings) and the virtue of 'trained judgment', whereby scientists, i.e. *subjects*, make judgements about and interpret data. History can thus unsettle our epistemic complacency by reminding us of the contingencies that have led to how and why things have come to be the way they are.

The socio-feminist theories of the twentieth century have further broadened the range of what counts as an epistemic virtue. Feminist philosopher of science Harding (1995), for example, has argued that disciplinary assumptions that seem to be 'objective' are only so from the particular 'standpoint' of the researcher. Standpoint theory has been described as a 'political and social epistemology' and explicitly positions the knower as a legitimate source of epistemic justification (Wylie, 2003), especially when oppression and other social injustices are prevalent. This indexes a further epistemic virtue, namely one in which 'insider knowledge' (such as being a black female maid in a white household) affords explanatory power not necessarily available to an outsider (such as a white male researcher investigating racism) and one where subjectivity is not only valued but is an epistemological precondition for understanding social phenomena.

Moreover, from a specifically interdisciplinary perspective, epistemologist D'Agostino (2012) recognizes that disciplinary classifications can and do advance knowledge. Because of this epistemic pursuit, 'disciplinarity' could be said to count as an 'epistemic virtue'. Yet, for D'Agostino, what actually binds traditional disciplines is their 'shallow consensus' rather than the epistemic virtue of 'objectivity', for example. This 'shallow consensus' can be understood as a broad and abstract disciplinary assumption (or agreement), such as 'democracy is worthwhile' in the discipline of Politics. However, a 'shallow consensus' can go unchallenged when more fine-grained, technical analyses within disciplines – such as *which* countries can be classified as democratic or *which* electoral systems are more conducive to democracy – prevent researchers from questioning their initial assumptions, such as whether democracy is indeed a universally worthwhile pursuit. When academic communities syphon into specialized and technical sub-fields about *how* to implement democracy, for example, they are less likely to question their initial assumptions, namely the value of democracy itself. Such syphoning then avoids abstractions, inhibits non-specialist communication and encourages incremental approaches to knowledge that can mask deep-rooted and potentially erroneous assumptions. All of this points to what Wiley recognizes as 'epistemic trade-offs' (2003, p. 34), namely that the objectivity-making properties of epistemic virtues cannot be 'simultaneously maximised'. What this means is that in the process of ascribing objectivity to the specialist knowledge that disciplines afford (e.g. when we claim that a voting system based on proportional representation leads to more democratic outcomes), we can lose sight of or stop questioning the bigger picture, so to speak, such as whether democracy is a desirable outcome in the first place, or for whom it might be a desirable outcome and in what circumstances. So, to remain with the democracy example and to paraphrase Wiley, the commitment to maximize specialist understandings requires a trade-off of empirical depth against value judgements about democracy.

An equivalent shallow consensus in EAP might be that 'academic writing is formal' or 'objective' or 'linear'. Fine-grained approaches to how to teach such formality then syphon EAP into its own sub-fields of discipline-specific writing, academic grammar and academic corpora, leaving the original assumption about whether academic writing is formal, objective and linear unchallenged and, in doing so, denying students the opportunity 'to see that things could always be other than they are'. The epistemic trade-off here consists in a commitment to maximize specialist knowledge about academic genres, grammars and vocabularies against the value, or even the possibility and meaning, of academic writing being formal, objective and linear in the first place. What this looks like in EAP is a 'piling up of highly similar textbooks and resources' on how to write an academic essay, for example, that 'resist' the challenge that might come from other disciplines, such as Composition Studies (Tardy & Jwa, 2016), Writing Studies (Adler-Kassner & Wardle, 2015), Academic Literacies (Scott & Lillis, 2007), Multimodality (A. Archer & Breuer, 2015), post-Colonial Literacies (Thesen & Cooper, 2013) and Philosophy and Sociology (Judd, 2003). An example of one such challenge might be that academic writing might be better described as 'recursive' rather than linear, as argued by Palmeri (2012), who belongs to both the Composition and Multimodal Writing Studies tradition. What he means by this is that when academic writing is seen through the lens of composition and multimodality, we notice recursive patterns of voice, argument, rhythm, pathos, logos and ethos that the attribute of 'linearity' fails to capture.

EAP is a fairly well-established field (it has its own journals, professional networks, conferences, publications and all the trappings of what constitutes a field of study) and, as such, it, too, boasts its own shallow consensus and fine-grained specialisms, from building lexical corpora to analysing discipline-specific genres. Rather than add further to the process of disciplinary specialization and incremental technicalization, I have chosen to take a step back, to 'zoom out' as Mays (2017) might say and challenge some of the shallow consensus that binds EAP with regards to the social complexity of academic writing. I do this by asking a deceptively simple question: what makes writing academic, given its diversity and contingent history and given that what can seem to be academic may not be academic at all (as in the case of academic hoaxes)? I have chosen Philosophy, broadly understood as a form of enquiry into the nature of things, or as an 'under-labourer', to quote Roy Bhaskar, as the main approach for my argument because it allows me to step back from the traditional disciplinary specialisms and standpoints of EAP and engage more freely in considering alternative conceptualizations of academic writing. For example, research into academic writing might benefit from resisting, or momentarily suspending, disciplinary and methodological classification. This is because researching writing has led me to raise broader questions that require educational and philosophical responses. Instead of deciding where I stand on any particular (specialist) theory of writing, by identifying putative gaps and limitations, I take a step back to look at writing as a broad and abstract social phenomenon and then try to clarify questions regarding its nature, such as 'what is writing' and 'what makes it academic'. This steers me more towards advancing a theory of academic writing which may then have repercussions for pedagogies that influence 'how to write'. I discuss these in the last chapter.

An analytic approach allows me to address the epistemological and ontological dualism that underlies EAP's approach to academic writing. This dualism manifests itself as a binary between skills, which tell us how to achieve something, namely procedural knowledge, and practices, which are claims about what is the case, namely propositional knowledge (Fantl, 2017; Knorr Cetina, Schatzki, & von Savigny, 2001). Writing instruction in EAP, for example, makes knowledge claims such as 'writing is formal, objective and linear' that collapse claims about how to write some academic texts (procedural) with what all academic writing is (propositional). Similarly, critics of American writing instruction, such as David Russell and Mike Rose, have highlighted the failure of what they call the 'myth of transience', namely the mistaken belief that writing skills, once learnt, can be 'transferred' to any writing context: the myth of transience is a myth precisely because it lures teachers and students into thinking that procedural knowledge about certain genres (such as the five-paragraph essay or the 'create a research space' gap-filling approach to research writing (Swales & Feak, 2012)) can be collapsed into propositional knowledge about academic writing in general. Such erroneous generalizations from the particular to the universal are seductive because they are easy to standardize, to teach and to learn. But, equally, these same generalizations run into trouble and become increasingly difficult to unlearn when academic writers move across contexts, negotiating new academic purposes and discovering the affordances of diverse ways of representing their knowledge. Academic writing instruction collapses epistemology into ontology by conflating some of its basic constitutive elements (which are by no means exhaustive), such as its putative formality, with its characteristics as a whole: the fact that one academic text is formal does not mean that all academic texts are formal. The mistake of collapsing epistemology (how we come to know something) with ontology (what something actually is) occurs when we generalize what academic writing is (as a whole) on the basis of some of its features (its parts). The fact that I have come to know academic writing as 'formal, objective and linear' does not tell me what academic writing is because there could be other kinds of academic writing that do not share these characteristics. In fact, as I show throughout the book, there are plenty of reasons to *not* describe academic writing as linear, objective and formal. In this sense, EAP conflates how it has come to *know* and then *define* academic writing with what academic writing is. This amounts to an epistemic fallacy, discussed in Chapter 4, whereby 'how we come to know the world' from a monodisciplinary and particularist position gets equated with the way the world is or could be. That this fallacy is problematic can be evidenced by how, for example, definitions of IQ or literacy differ according to the methods of enquiry used to establish their ontologies: for example, a child will be deemed illiterate if my definition of literacy reifies the prescriptivist standards of a Latin-inspired grammatical tradition or of monolingualism over the socio-communicative skills of descriptive grammars or of multilingual literacies. Similarly, prescriptive approaches to academic writing tend to single out particular forms and standards of academic writing and then reify these to the status of universal standards. A student whose academic literacies may be more complex, varied or epistemologically and ontologically nuanced will inevitably be disadvantaged when assessed against standards that reduce the academicness of writing to the shallow consensus of linearity or objectivity rather than frame this academicness as a recursive or disciplinary social and historical phenomenon (whereby what counts as 'objective' becomes a matter of disciplinary contentions and epistemic virtues rather than a matter of the surface features of the text).

EAP is a field of writing instruction that has a responsibility for educating students *about* academic writing just as much as it has a responsibility to teach them how to write particular genres. Yet, it often falls foul to universalizing a particularist version of academic writing at the expense of other ways of writing academically, as I show in Chapters 1 and 3. Moreover, EAP has been known to make further misleading ontological claims, such as 'composites are nothing more than the sum of their basic constitutive elements' (Beckett & Hager, 2018, pp. 138–40), thus compounding the perception that learning to write academically is about learning to master a set of discrete, finite and transferable skills. This deeply troubling reductionist framing of academic writing underscores many mainstream and commercial approaches to EAP writing. It is this framing that I challenge throughout the book.

My analytic approach exposes these epistemological and ontological conflations by proposing a generative model of academic writing that accounts for change in how instances of academic writing come to be classified in the first place and for what academic writing is and could be: the former requires empirical and inductive observation and includes a range of methodologies such as ethnography and corpus analysis to show how varied academic writings are. The latter demands a conceptual shift that does not conflate what something is composed of with what it is as a whole. This means that whatever our inductive observations tell us about what academic writing looks like may not be sufficient to determine what makes writing academic. Rather, what I am proposing in this book is that what makes writing academic – its academicness – emerges from a complex stratified ontology of structures and agencies. Because of this emergent nature, academicness cannot be reduced to any defining feature or variable, such as its grammar or vocabulary or style. Instead, academicness can be thought of as 'multiply realizable' (Fodor, 1974, 1997), a position that is compatible with systems theory (Ball, 2004; Mays, 2017) and its implications for the philosophy of mind and sociology (Sawyer, 2001). Similarly, the multiple and emergent realizability of academic writing has important implications for understanding writing as an evolving social academic practice rather than as a static genre.

The book is divided into five chapters. Chapter 1 is concerned with explaining what academic writing is in EAP and how EAP can misrepresent it. Chapter 2 delves into the history of writing and literacy to tease out the ideologies shaping writing practices. Chapter 3 showcases a range of academic writings that challenge conventional understandings of what makes writing academic. Chapter 4 proposes a macro-theory of academic writing that can inform academic writing pedagogies. This theory is critical realism. It is a socio-scientific philosophy that allows us to re-imagine academic writing within a non-linear, emergent and complex social open system. Conceptualizing academic writing as an open system allows us to shift our thinking away from describing writing as a reductive and mechanistic 'transferable skill' that can be deployed across all writing contexts. When re-imagined as an open system, change and diversity in academic writing practices become not only possible, but inevitable. The final chapter proposes a foundation for a future pedagogy of academic writing as an open system that can continue to change. It highlights ways in which writers and teachers of academic writing can enact their agencies to effectuate change in their teaching and writing practices. When conceptualized as an open system, diverse genres can emerge.

Notes on Style

You may be pondering the same question I am often asked when I present my work to others at conferences, staff meetings and workshops: doesn't the genre that I have chosen to communicate my knowledge undermine my argument for diversity, multilingualism and multimodality in academic literacy practices (even my examiners asked me that)? The short answer is – no. My argument is not that we should all stop writing linear, passive and impersonal prose. My argument is that we shouldn't all have to. The whole point of acknowledging diversity by pluralizing and democratizing academic expression and communication is exactly that, to acknowledge the diversity (Horner & Lu, 2013). That includes my own preferred style as the style that falls within my (cap)abilities, my background and my education. I wouldn't know where to start drawing or rapping my research and even if I could, I am not sure what the rationale would be. Scholars who represent their research in modalities other than language or multilingually have compelling reasons to do so and, unlike those of us who write in the conventional canon, they shoulder the added intellectual labour of having to persuade others of why they need to transcend language and traditional genres. But if my reasoning on this still doesn't persuade you, then have a look at *Playing with #acwri* by Molinari (2021), where I used the genre of the dialogue to enact a play about these very same issues.

What you *will* notice about my style is that because of the interdisciplinary (e.g. philosophy, education, history, sociology) readings that I have drawn on to write my research, there is some stylistic heterogeneity in my academic prose as well as some inconsistency. As an academic writer and regarding stylistic variations, although I have been mindful of what voice to project in my writing, the book reflects the heteroglossic (Bakhtin & Holquist, 1981), multimodal (A. Archer & Breuer, 2015) and theoretical (Besley & Peters, 2013; Peters, 2009) discourses that have informed my thinking. By 'discourses' I mean the different ways that language is used in the different disciplines and in the social practices that they enact (Fairclough, 1992). This means that I swing between encyclopaedic tones, especially when trying to relay key historical events that have shaped writing, to ones that are didactic (when providing examples), analytic (when trying to convey key notions in philosophy) and simplistic (when trying to retain a macro stance that glosses over micro analyses). Since I have also drawn on historical and archival methods to advance my arguments, the reader will also notice that I defer some knowledge to footnotes – a literary device that is frowned upon in the academic writing circles I inhabit. But once more, I take my cue from others who do this and who have actually devoted an entire book to the footnote on the grounds that the rhetorical use of footnotes in the field of History functions as 'the humanist's rough equivalent of the scientist's report on data: they offer the empirical support for the stories told and arguments presented' (Grafton, 1997, p. vii). In my own writing, footnotes also serve a rhetorical function: they disrupt the faux linearity, orchestrated sequentiality and perceived clarity that 'polished' academic prose is designed to conceal, further affording the reader-researcher nuggets of knowledge that store the potential to germinate into something new and unexpected.

Regarding multimodality, the book is a manifestation of the skills and practices I am familiar with, of negotiations with editors and informed choices about expectations. It reflects my agency in relation to the textual environments that have shaped me. What I advocate here is that academic writers should be writing, drawing or dancing their PhDs or other texts according to their (cap) abilities, in line with epistemological and ontological rationales and in relation to what is structurally possible and institutionally negotiated with(in) the textual environment (see Figure 1, p. 105). I am not advocating that writers engage in acts of 'arbitrary or radical defiance' (Sousanis, 2016), but that they be respected as agents who have a degree of freedom and knowledge to enact unique ways of expressing themselves academically. This book represents my (cap)abilities in re-shaping (Bazerman, 1988) and transducting (i.e. translating from one mode to another) (Bezemer & Kress, 2008) the knowledge that I have developed through research and which came to me in the form of words, images, quotations, personal anecdotes, conversations with students, colleagues and critical friends, social media interactions, blog writing and conference presentations. My own multilingualism and literacies (English, Italian, Venetian and French) will be manifest in my text through idiosyncrasies in signposting, sentence structures and linguistic choices (including multilingual choices and possibly some malapropisms that may have slipped through unwittingly). Some readers will find these odd or unexpected or unclear whilst others who share my cultural backgrounds and who know me will find these perfectly consistent and will probably not even notice them since they will seem perfectly normal to them. These idiosyncrasies have become part of my style of writing and just as others have styles that are not always familiar to me or that I find difficult to read, I hope my reader will be as charitable and cooperative in understanding how I express my ideas as I try to be when reading others.

Enjoy, as my best friend says,
Julia
26 July 2021, Buxton, UK

1

Troubling Academic Writing: Problems and Implications for Higher Education

Introduction

> It is ironic that some educational institutions … militate against the very higher-order thinking that they are supposed to encourage.
>
> (Andrews, 2010, p. 53)

In certain circles, English academic writing has developed a troublesome reputation. Its genres, jargons, grammar, syntax and overall forms have been pejoratively described by writing scholars as straightjackets, chains, pigeonholes, frauds and hoaxes. It has also been branded as discriminatory, elitist, exclusionary, colonial, dull, zombified and confusing. Far broader indictments are that academic writing's privileged status within the academy compounds the perception that alphabetic and monolinguistic texts are superior to other forms of knowledge communication, such as multimodal and multilingual texts. These are hefty value judgements on something that is so crucial to academic life at all levels, from undergraduate study onwards.

This chapter lays the foundations for the rest of the book by exposing some of the ways in which academic writing is (mis)understood and by highlighting some of the consequences of this confusion. In doing so, my intention is to show why academic writing is troublesome. I draw mainly on the context of EAP writing instruction in the UK, with which I am most familiar, but also refer to the US tradition of Rhetoric and Composition, especially where there are parallels. After some brief remarks about epistemology and ontology to establish the foundations for this and the ensuing chapters, I go on to trace the roots of the trouble to the ways in which academic writing has been reduced to a series of transferable mechanical skills. I then expose some of the implications. My staging of the problem will require even further background to do it justice and this I provide in Chapter 2, where I situate the trouble within its historical legacies.

The 'Ologies'

An early, but swift, distinction between an epistemological and an ontological conceptualization of writing is necessary because it is the binary that seams the book: most of the time it keeps to the margins, but occasionally, it will take centre stage, particularly in Chapter 4, where I propose critical realism as a theory for explaining what makes writing academic.

The problem with academic writing, as I have come to know it, is (mis) understandings around *what* it is and *how* it gets taught. This begs further questions about what it means for something to be academic in the first place. At the root of these (mis)understandings are inconsistent ontological and epistemological distinctions between what academic writing is (its ontology) and what it does (its epistemology). Eliding this distinction has consequences.

Simply put, ontology is the study and classification of *what* things are. Epistemology is the study of *how* we make decisions about what things are. This matters for how we then classify things as being one thing rather than another. Epistemology is therefore associated with the methods and methodologies used to generate findings, whereas ontology is associated with what those findings are then classified as. Ontology and epistemology are co-extensive, meaning you cannot understand one without the other. For example, I can't classify an apple as a fruit (ontology) until I have investigated what counts as a fruit and to what extent an apple fits in to that classification (epistemology). Similarly, I can't classify writing as academic until I have investigated what it means for something to be academic and how writing fits in to that classification.

Here is a hopefully accessible, albeit caricatured, way of explaining this in relation to academic writing.

Popular textbooks have traditionally classified academic writing as *something* that is formal, objective, impersonal and so on (see, for example, Stephen Bailey (2006)). Other, less popular textbooks have classified academic writing as *something* that allows us to transform knowledge (see, for example, Lillis et al. (2015)). These are ontological classifications, each of which has implications for classroom instruction. If I classify academic writing as 'impersonal', I am likely to teach students to write certain kinds of texts, for example, ones that have features associated with being *impersonal* (such as the passive voice). On the other hand, if I classify academic writing as a transformative practice, I am likely to teach a student to do something that *transforms knowledge*: in the first scenario, the student is more likely to form the belief that what makes writing academic are its impersonal forms and that for something to be 'academic', it needs to be impersonal. In the second scenario, the student is more likely to form the belief that what makes writing academic are a wider range of features, since there are many ways of transforming, or re-configuring, knowledge (see, for example, work by Fiona English (2011, 2015)).

Each ontological classification is the result of an epistemological finding. If what makes writing academic are its impersonal forms (ontology), this assumes that being impersonal is what it means to be academic because academia has been found to be the kind of place where impersonal claims are made (epistemology). If, on the other hand, we posit that what makes writing academic are its powers to transform knowledge (ontology), this assumes that transforming knowledge is what it means to be academic because academia has been found to be the kind of place where knowledge is transformed (epistemology).

Here is a sense of the confusion generated when these distinctions are elided in writing instruction. Sam is a semi-fictionalized but real UK university student whose words I have anonymized to protect their identity but to also signal that they represent the familiar refrain of many such students.

> I got 48% in my essay and I don't understand why. I got distinctions in my Access course and when I was writing this essay, I thought it was good. I put in references, avoided personal pronouns, I looked at different aspects of the research question, my friend, who is really good academically, advised me to start with some context and give some definitions, but my tutor said I had too many ideas and they weren't really connected to the main question. I also don't really know what a paragraph is or how long it should be and what should go in the introduction and conclusion? Is the conclusion just a summary? I need to start writing my second essay and I just don't know where to start now. I want to do it right, but I don't know how. How do you write an academic essay? How is it different to what they taught me on my Access course? I know people who have done A-Levels and they also say it is completely different to an A-Level essay.

Sam is a casualty of misunderstandings about what makes writing academic. By asking *how do you write an academic essay*, they put their finger on the problems introduced above. These were that, firstly, academic writing cannot be ontologically reduced to its characteristics, such as being impersonal or having paragraphs. There is no such thing as a 'standard' academic essay because there are several kinds. The reason there are several kinds of writing is that academic writing is doing and achieving different sorts of things. In fact, a far better designation for referring to the writing that takes place in the academy might be to use the plural form of 'academic writings' (exemplified in Chapter 3). Sam has formed the belief that an academic essay is a 'certain kind of thing' (ontology) that can be transferred across contexts. Had they been taught that academic writing is a method for representing knowledge, they might have been more open to understanding it epistemologically. An epistemological understanding of academic writing is more likely to have prepared Sam for the seemingly confusing feedback they had received because if writing is understood for the epistemological work that it does, it becomes easier to recognize that it will vary in its forms according to its purposes.

Having introduced the distinction between ontological and epistemological understanding of academic writing, I now highlight another dualism intended to further trouble what makes writing academic.

Enduring the Legacy of Skills versus Practices

Academic writing – how it is taught, talked and written about and then experienced – is dualistic. This dualism broadly consists of framing academic writing as either a *skill* (Hyland, 2006, p. 17) or as a *social practice* (Lea & Street, 1998, p. 159; Lillis & Curry, 2010a, p. 19), a distinction that has important implications for how academic writing is taught. References to this dualism resonate throughout the literatures in which writing is discussed from a UK EAP/Academic Literacies perspective (e.g. Hocking & Toh, 2010; Lea & Street, 1998; Scott & Lillis, 2007; Wingate & Tribble, 2012) and a US Composition Studies perspective (e.g. Anson & Moore, 2016; Downs & Wardle, 2007; Russell & Cortes, 2012). A 'skill' can be understood as the mechanical ability to turn, for example, an active sentence into a passive one. This ability requires *knowing how* to use grammar, regardless of context, purpose or audience. By contrast, a 'social practice' is *knowing that* the use of a passive or plural can be inappropriate. Skills can be further understood as being transferable to other academic contexts whereas social practices are less straightforwardly transferable because they are concerned with protean human activity that changes according to socio-academic contexts, purposes and intentions.

Distinctions between skills and practices are premised on broader sociologies of knowledge that differentiate between 'knowing how' to do something (for example, how to spell a word) and 'knowing that' (for example, that words can have different meanings in different contexts). Skills thus become equated with 'technical knowledge' and social practices with 'practical knowledge': the former concerns knowledge of rules and techniques; the latter 'consists of organised abilities to discern, judge and perform that are ... rooted in understanding, beliefs, values and attitudes .... Practical knowledge is acquired by living within the organised social world' (Hirst, 1998, p. 152). Specifically, this dualism maps on to the distinction between procedural knowledge (knowing how to do something) and propositional knowledge (knowing that something is the case), whereby skills are examples of the former and practices of the latter (Fantl, 2017).

The roots of this dualism run deep and have evolved from translations of the ancient Greeks' distinction between *epistêmê* (science/theory) and *technê* (craft/practice). As such, the dichotomy of skills and practices characterizes 'Western' thinking and it is traditionally traced to Aristotle's ethical theory. Aristotle describes as *poiesis* those human actions that require a form of knowledge he called *technê*, which has been translated as a rule-governed 'ability to make' an artefact, such as a pot. Because *poiesis* requires the maker to know in advance what the result of their activity will be, it is not the same as *praxis*, which is an action aimed at 'doing' some morally worthwhile 'good'. Within the Aristotelian tradition, political, social and educational activities fall under *phronesis*, meaning wisdom and deliberation and, as such, they are aligned with *praxis*, not *poiesis* (Carr, 1998; Hogan, 2015), because of their open-ended reflective and explorative nature.

The legacy of this dualism survives in current philosophical, sociological and educational discussions about how theory relates to practice. However, to make matters confusing, current understandings of 'theory' are probably closer to what Aristotle meant by *praxis* (i.e. reflection and deliberation), whereas *poiesis* is possibly closer to the idea of what we now call 'practice' (as in the repetition of a skill to achieve an outcome known in advance, e.g. a painting or riding a bike). The sematic slipperiness of these terms might explain why misunderstandings arise from their usage. For example, modern-day understandings of 'skills' are associated with practical and technical abilities (*poiesis* and *technê*) rather than theoretical dispositions (*praxis*); yet, each shares attributes of the other: a joiner is both skilled in a technical sense and is reflective in a theoretical sense because they need geometrical knowledge to deliberate that a range of practical possibilities for shaping the wood is available. American educationalist Mike Rose (2005) has endeavoured to blur these distinctions in his sociological accounts of the tacit propositional knowledge (knowing that) needed to perform the highly skilled labour of 'American workers'; writing scholars Graff and Birkenstein (2006) do the same when they encourage the use of 'know how' templates as a way to 'demystify' the practice of academic writing; and Warner (2018, p. 20) goes further by subsuming 'skills' under 'practices' alongside 'knowledge', 'habits of mind' and 'attitudes'.

Whilst I acknowledge the confusions underpinning the skills-practice divide (such as the fact that propositional and procedural knowledge cannot be seamlessly prised apart; that skills are needed for practice and vice versa; and that both theory and practice guide human actions), in theorizing about whether academic writing is a skill or a practice and what any of this has to do with what makes it academic, I have deliberately chosen to foreground a particular view. This view is that academic writing instruction, in both the UK and United States, has, historically, erred on the side of skills, understood as technical abilities associated with knowing how to do something (*poiesis*). Along the way, the conflation of academic writing with a skill has generated misunderstandings about what makes writing academic. It has done this by proposing templates as 'formulaic devices … that encourage passive learning or lead students to put their writing on automatic pilot' (Graff & Birkenstein, 2006, p. xxii). In this sense, skills are more readily seen as 'limitations' that encourage 'mere habits' (Dewey, 1916). Such negative framings of skills as habit-forming underscore several literatures that critique the ways in which academic writing is taught to university students (see, for example, Yun & Standish (2018)). Skills-based approaches to writing can be further understood with reference to what anthropologist and New Literacy scholar Brian Street (1984) called the 'ideological and autonomous approach'. This model 'encourages a transparency approach to language and transmission understanding of language pedagogy' (Fischer, 2015, p. 83). What Fischer means by 'transparency' and 'transmission', respectively, is that the meaning of words is treated as unequivocal (i.e. clear) and that this meaning can be taught and learnt (i.e. transferred) without the need to interpret why the words are used, by whom and in which contexts. As such, the autonomous model frames academic writing as a cognitive skill that exists independently of its contexts and which, for example, 'does not recognise that learning rests on the integrated development of both writing and reading within the disciplinary discourse' (Turner, 2018, p. 134). Zamel (1998a, 1998b) has similarly argued that the autonomous model presents the learning of language in essentialist terms, namely as a skill that is decontextualized from the 'intellectual work' that it has to do. For example, learning how to compose a paragraph (a skill, closer in meaning to *poiesis*) is not the same as understanding the 'intellectual work' that paragraphs do (a practice, closer in meaning to *praxis*), which is to cumulatively build arguments (Thomson, 2018a): it is for this reason that there can be no template for writing them. A paragraph can vary in length and structure because it is part of an argument that forms a broader deliberation (Hayot, 2014), a fact that was not made clear to Sam, my semi-fictional student.

In EAP, the skill–practice dichotomy reveals similar binaries. On the one hand, it foregrounds an atomistic and technical understanding of what makes writing 'academic'. It does this by conflating skills-based approaches with the teaching and learning of discrete but tangible textual items, such as lists of 'academic words' (Coxhead, 2011; Paquot, 2010) or rules for 'paragraph structures' (Bailey, 2006). A skills-based approach becomes problematic because, for example, it remains silent on the more elusive academic practice of developing an 'academic voice' (Elbow, 1994; Matsuda & Tardy, 2008) or on cultivating an awareness of readership (audience) (Richardson, 1990b). On the other hand, the more 'holistic', reflective and complex understanding of literacy associated with the social practice approach can lose sight of the particulars needed to make a text 'academic'. For example, a social practice approach will typically downplay the centrality of linguistic 'accuracy' or question what is meant by an appropriate 'academic style' on the grounds that these vary or that they embody exclusionary ideologies that ignore a writer's purpose and the experiences they bring with them (Holbrook et al., 2020; Lillis, 2001; Scott, 2013; Thesen & Cooper, 2013; Turner, 2018). In this sense, both approaches – skills-based and social practice – are problematic as neither is satisfactory in pinning down what makes writing academic. By isolating textual and linguistic features from the wider social practices of having purposes and audiences, skills-based writing pedagogies and assessments (such as IELTS) weaken the academic credibility of the resulting written text (see Moore and Morton (2005) and Warner (2018)). Moreover, emphasizing skills (knowing how) at the expense of practices (knowing that) can lead to 'hollow' and 'stilted' expressions aimed at displaying language instead of thought. This trade-off, combined with weak and unsupported arguments, can result in 'bad writing' (Helms-Park & Stapleton, 2003). Yet, despite there being no evidence that correlates grammatical and lexical accuracy *per se* with good academic writing,[1] prescriptive, skills-based, straightjacket (Hamilton

---

[1] This is a controversial claim that I do not develop in this book. Suffice to say that I am aware of a vast body of literatures on this controversy. Hyland, K. (2016). *Teaching and researching writing* (3rd ed.). Abingdon: Routledge., Rose, M. (1989). *Lives on the boundary: the struggles and achievements of America's underprepared*. New York: Free Press. Collier Macmillan Publishers., Warner, J. (2018). *Why they can't write: Killing the five-paragraph essay and other necessities*. Johns Hopkins University Press., including ongoing debates about editorial bias with regards to standards of accuracy in academic writing. Politzer-Ahles, S., Girolamo, T., & Ghali, S. (2020). Preliminary evidence of linguistic bias in academic reviewing. *Journal of English for Academic Purposes*, 47, 100895. https://doi.org/https://doi.org/10.1016/j.jeap.2020.100895, Politzer-Ahles, S., Holliday, J. J., Girolamo, T., Spychalskae, M., & Harper Berksonf, K. (2016). Is linguistic injustice a myth? A response to Hyland (2016). *Journal of Second Language Writing*, 34, 4–8. https://doi.org/http://dx.doi.org/10.1016/j.jslw.2016.09.003.

& Pitt, 2009) approaches that focus on grammatical accuracy – often referred to pejoratively as 'essayist' literacies – have dominated the EAP approach to writing. Reasons for such a skills-based ontology of academic writing vary and are well documented. They range from the ubiquity of commercial assessments, whose imperative is to standardize testing, to the over-reliance of pedagogy on commercial textbooks (Bennett, 2009; Feak & Swales, 2013; Harwood, 2005; Leung et al., 2016; Tribble, 2015; Turner, 2004, 2018).

However, when standard forms of academic English are questioned and disrupted, for example, by being re-genred[2] (English, 2011) or translanguaged[3] (Wei, 2016), this raises concerns about where, how and whether we can draw boundaries between what counts and does not count as 'academic' (cf. Canagarajah & Lee (2013); Scott (2013)). Chapters 4 and 5 focus on theoretical and pedagogical approaches to overcome the muddles generated by the skills *versus* practices dualism, but, before we get there, more needs to be said about each to further appreciate their influence on academic writing instruction.

Skills-based approaches can be further said to encourage and perpetuate the 'myth of transience' (Russell, 2002). The 'myth' consists in the mistaken belief that writing can be taught in transitory, temporary and isolated ways without an authentic purpose. It further suggests that whatever skills are learnt in a writing class can be seamlessly transferred to all other contexts: Sam's confusion can, therefore, be explained by the myth of transience. Such approaches reflect the widespread perception that writing instruction can be outsourced and learnt separately from the disciplines, a phenomenon that has been criticized by American educationalist and writing scholar Mike Rose (1985, p. 355): 'The belief persists in the American university that if we can just do x, or y, the problem of poor student writing will be solved … and higher education will be able to return to its real work [of teaching disciplinary content].' Rose (1989) has lamented the conflation of learning to write with the acquisition of cognitive skills (such as memorizing rules). He claims that when we collapse the process of writing into the acquisition of skills, we risk sidelining attitudes and dispositions that may be more conducive to developing writing abilities. These include the

---

[2] 'Re-genring' is a term used by English (2011) to describe the process of re-working an essay by using a different genre, for example, from prose to a dialogue. This allows 'students to introduce new perspectives, debate new issues and show a greater sense of ownership over the topic than was apparent in their original essays' (2011, p. 1) and develops critical thinking in ways that are not text-centred.

[3] 'Translanguaging' is a term used by several sociolinguists, including Canagarajah (2011), Wei (2016) and Leung et al. (2016) to describe the multilingual practice of communicating by drawing on one's full linguistic repertoire to re-appropriate or re-define meanings. Translanguaging is viewed as a positive practice and signals a departure from framing 'interference' from other languages as negative.

need to nurture everyday exploratory and personal literacies (as also argued by Williams (2009); Williams and Zenger (2012)) and to cultivate the imagination and a sense of 'wonder'.

Rose traces the conflation of skills with writing ability back to the early-twentieth-century writing curriculum which was influenced by studies in psychology. These were used to inform pedagogies based on 'memory and drill' and the mechanics of grammatical 'dos and don'ts'. He labelled this approach to literacy as 'essentialist' and 'exclusionary', further claiming that it assumes the meaning of words is straightforwardly accessible i.e. 'clear' to all. Instead, argues Rose, it excludes learners who do not share its underlying conceptual frameworks. What better explains students' misunderstandings of academic discourse is often not their lack of 'academic' vocabulary but their ignorance of the 'semiotic reach' of academic words and of the conceptual frameworks and disciplinary traditions they belong to. His poignant example of a student, Lucia, is illustrative. Lucia, whose brother's mental illness drew her to a psychology degree, abandoned her course because her first-hand experience of psychological trauma differed from the academic depictions of it. The university's response to Lucia's difficulties was to remove her from the psychology class and send her to language lessons that would 'fix' and 'remedy' her lack of understanding. Rose's contention is that 'remedial' approaches to developing academic literacy that are removed from their disciplinary discourses are unlikely to help students become writers because Lucia is not so much 'suffering from a lack of specialist vocabulary' as she is ignorant of the histories of concepts that this vocabulary refers to (Rose, 1989, pp. 192):

> The discourse of academics is marked by terms and expressions that represent an elaborate set of shared concepts and orientations: alienation, authoritarian personality, the social construction of the self, determinism, hegemony, equilibrium, intentionality, recursion, reinforcement and so on. This language weaves through so many lectures and textbooks, is internal to so many learned discussions, that it's easy to forget what a foreign language it can be. Freshmen are often puzzled by the talk they hear in the classrooms, but what is important to note here is that their problem is not simply one of limited vocabulary. If we see that problem as knowing or not knowing a list of words, as some quick-fix remedies suggest, then we'll force glossaries on students and miss the complexity of the issue.

Learning any discipline requires access to 'scholarly conversations' (Healey et al., 2020) that have a semiotic reach extending far beyond lists of academic vocabulary. Moreover, since these remedial approaches are also frequently associated with skills-based approaches (see Anson & Moore, 2016; Myers Zawacki & Cox, 2014; Russell, 2002), skills also become enmeshed in the language of medicalization (*diagnose problems, drop-in clinic*) and failure (*fix, correct*), further contributing to a deficit approach to the teaching of academic writing. This indicates that skills cannot be understood outside the discipline by decontextualized rote learning and grammatical drills or gap-fills. The 'myth of transience' thus raises questions around what makes writing academic in the sense that if Lucia's first-hand experience of psychology, a phenomenon that is as much a personal experience as it is an academic discipline, is not reflected or recognized in academic representations of psychology, then what does it mean to study psychology, or any other domain of human knowledge, at university? We know from standpoint theory that knowledge is also 'situated knowledge'. This situated epistemological stance re-centres the knower, in this case Lucia, as a legitimate source of knowledge in virtue of her 'insider knowledge' (Wylie, 2003). Removing this insider knowledge from the domain of academic knowledge therefore serves to compound, rather than hold to account, epistemic hierarchies that de-legitimize what counts as knowledge and whose knowledge counts. And since academic writing is both a method of knowledge enquiry (Richardson & St. Pierre, 2005) and knowledge representation (Atkinson, 2013; Thomson, 2018c), then how does Lucia's knowledge come to be represented in writing if it is excluded from the outset? In Chapter 5, I suggest ways to answer this question.

So far, I have been implying that a skills-based approach to academic writing is insufficient to determine what makes a text academic. This is because skills-based approaches encourage the conflation of some characteristics of what it means for something to be academic (such as 'formal' academic lexis) with what academic writing is at the expense of other characteristics (such as situated knowledge and its related language). I now explain what is meant by 'practices' in relation to writing and conclude that this approach, too, is insufficient to determine what makes writing academic.

As discussed in Knorr Cetina et al. (2001), practices can be broadly understood as 'arrays of human activity' (2001, p. 11) organized around 'patterns', 'relations' and 'interdependencies' that cannot be reduced to the micro-activities of the individual. Rather, since they are part of our propositional knowledge (knowing that), they can guide and monitor our actions, including our procedural knowledge (i.e. the 'knowing how' of skills), without which practices could not be enacted. Practices are also closer to the classical meaning of *praxis* and involve reflection and deliberation.

Practices are generally viewed more favourably than skills by literacy theorists (Scott & Lillis, 2007), by philosophers (MacIntyre, 1985) and by progressive educationalists (Dewey, 1916). They are seen as *activities* that require reflection and thought, social interaction and a sense of purpose that changes to suit the aims, beliefs, values, experiences and choices of, in this case, writers (Scott, 2000; Williams, 2017). For sociolinguist and literacies scholar Theresa Lillis (2013, pp. 78),

> practice signals two key principles: an empirical commitment to observe and explore what, where and how people read and write, including their perspectives on what they do, as well as their values and interests; a theoretical interest in seeking explanations for the nature and consequences of what people do, including a focus on issues of power and agency drawing on notions from sociological and critical discourse theories.

The spirit of Lillis's sociological, ethnographic and normative understanding of practice resonates with the following claims by moral philosopher Alasdair MacIntyre (cited in Hogan, 2015, pp. 372):

> By a practice I am going to mean any coherent and complex form of socially established co-operative human activity through which goods internal to that form of activity are realized in the course of trying to achieve those standards of excellence which are appropriate to and partially definitive of, that form of activity, with the result that human powers to achieve excellence and human conceptions of the ends and goods involved are systematically extended.

MacIntyre's views on the role played by 'human powers', 'agency', 'activity' and 'purpose' in 'social activity' echo those of Lillis, who unequivocally foregrounds the role that 'people' have in shaping practices through their values, interests, experiences and agencies. This did not happen in Lucia's case because her experience and situated knowledge of psychology were not valued or deemed relevant to the academic discipline of psychology – as a consequence of her knowledge not being valued, the way that she expressed it in writing was not deemed to be academically appropriate. What MacIntyre's understanding of practice further indexes is its *processual* and *complex* nature whereby the standards of excellence in any given practice, such as the practice of writing academically, are relative to the practice itself, not to any specific token (product or artefact) of writing, such as an essay or 'academic' vocabulary: a skill thus becomes a means to an end, that end being a practice that human agents can 'extend'. As we shall see, this has important implications for what makes writing academic.

Drawing on the practice of farming as her example, Fitzmaurice (2010, p. 47) illustrates what MacIntyre meant by 'practice' and the 'standards of excellence' needed to achieve it. Specifically, Fitzmaurice is concerned with the practice of teaching and with teachers' agencies in transforming their practices. She argues that teaching requires human dispositions, values, virtues and qualities (*standards of excellence*) that transcend the application of techniques (or skills). If practices are understood as the ends of human activity, then when these ends change, so must the skills required to achieve them:

> The planting of crops is not a practice, but farming is, as are the enquiries of physics, chemistry, biology and the work of the historian, the musician and the painter. A practice involves standards of excellence and to enter into a practice is to accept these standards and to judge one's own performance against them. The goods internal to a practice can only be had by involvement in that practice unlike external goods such as money, status, prestige, which can be achieved in many ways.

A similar argument can be mobilized for writing. When academic writing is understood as a practice, it too requires an understanding of a range of *standards of excellence* that are internal to it. These might include specific disciplinary ways of representing knowledge or understanding how to re-purpose a text for different audiences, but they may also include more elusive qualities such as 'writtenness', discussed in Turner (2018). 'Writtenness' refers to qualities of 'good writing' that are difficult to pinpoint, that can be achieved in different ways and that experienced writers simply 'recognise' (Becker, 1986). The practice of writing is also the practice of writing in and for institutional framings, constraints and policy, where *standards of excellence* vary (recalling feminist epistemologist Sarah Harding (1995) on 'strong objectivity') and where communities of scholars are required to reach agreements about what counts as disciplinary writing (see, for example, research by Alvesson et al. (2017); Mcculloch (2017); Tusting et al. (2019)). Different genres also serve different purposes, with some, like the PhD thesis, possibly no longer being fit-for-purpose (Paré, 2017, 2018). Specifically, Paré argues that the traditional 'big book format' of the PhD requires skills that are obsolete, such as the ability to work alone, when much of academia and other professions require collaboration, co-authorship and versatility (Carmichael-Murphy, 2021; Thomson, 2018b). As such, the thesis understood as a *practice*, rather than as a skill, requires *standards of excellence* that adhere to the activities of research and enquiry, rather than to the skills required to achieve these standards, such as referencing: clearly, these skills are necessary, but they are simply means to achieving the practice; they are not the ends of writing a PhD thesis (or other academic text). Since they are means to an end, they are more likely to change because they are external to the practice of achieving a PhD, which is driven by internal standards of excellence that could evolve and be achieved by deploying new skills. These new skills may not even include writing, as I showcase in Chapter 3, but will always be instrumental to upholding the standards of excellence that inhere to the academic practice of research and enquiry.

In my endeavour to rethink dominant academic writing theories for practice, MacIntyre affords me an opportunity to signal something that will become important in understanding the theory of critical realism that I propose in Chapter 4, namely the importance of human agency in transforming practices. It is humans, MacIntyre reminds us, who have the 'powers' to be the agents of change that mobilize 'transformations' in any given practice (1985, pp. 193, emphasis added):

> What is distinctive in a practice is the way in which conceptions of the relevant goods and ends which the technical skills serve – and every practice does require the exercise of practical skills – are *transformed* and enriched by those extensions of *human powers* and by that regard for its internal goods which are partially definitive of each particular practice or type of practice.

What this entails for thinking about academic writing is that when writing is conceived as a practice, it is the writers (*human powers*), not the skills, who through reflection, deliberation and understanding (*by that regard for*) drive transformations and determine what writing could be. Clearly, institutional constraints and expectations influence the degree of agency that writers have but, as sociologist and critical theorist Norman Fairclough also reminds us, subjects have the capacity 'to act individually or collectively as agents' in opposing [ideological] practices (Fairclough, 1992, pp. 72–3; 80).

As mentioned at the start of this section, an over-emphasis on writing as a practice raises troubling concerns about the standards of excellence that are internal to the practice and about who sets these standards. When we foreground the importance of agency in determining standards, we run the risk of undermining the rules and conventions that have accrued over time (arguably, for good reasons) and of *praxis* being so open-ended that it loses its practical reach of each purpose. Laurel Richardson dramatically captures this tension in her book *Fields of Play: Constructing an Academic Life*, where she reflects on the academic field of sociology and on how sociological knowledge is represented in the academic literatures of her discipline. In one of her semi-fictionalized dialogues, Richardson disrupts standard written representations of sociology by publishing her research as poetry instead of prose, much to the consternation and hostility of her fellow conferees. In the edited extract quoted below, Richardson is the fictionalized *Professor Z* addressing other eminent scholars of sociology at a conference (1997, pp. 197–206):

> Professor Z: Why prose? Prose, I submit, is not the only way to represent sociological understanding. Another way is through poetic representation
> …
> Conferee 1: Where is the f———-king validity?
> Conferee 2: What about reliability?
> Conferee 3: Truth? Where's truth?
> Conferee 4: And reality?
> Conferee 1: You have lost your f———-king mind!!!
> Professor Z: (takes field notes)
> …
> Lundberg: (returns to the stage) Oh ye of little memory and less imagination: Sociology is what sociologists do … If a sociologist writes and publishes poems in a sociology journal, the poems are sociology.
> … Professor Z: I know why these people are so threatened. They fear that if any rule is violated, all rules might be violated. They fear lack of control not only in their professional but in their personal worlds. The subtext of the question, "But is it sociology," is their silenced fear: "If poetry is sociology and I can't do it, what happens to my identity, my prestige, my status – my place in the pecking order – ME? … Me, me …"

The tensions that this ignites about standards of excellence and the skills needed to achieve these standards (in this case, whether to represent sociological knowledge using poetry or prose) in order for the discipline of sociology to be recognized as 'sociology' are mirrored in the questions I am raising when I ask what makes academic writing 'academic'. At the heart of Richardson's concerns is a disagreement about which skills are considered to be internal and which are considered to be external to the practice of sociology (and who has the agency to decide). Richardson's reason for choosing poetry over prose to represent sociological knowledge is that the rhythms of poetry seem to be attuned to re-presenting the embodied and situated voices of the women whose stories she is re-telling. The standard academic prose of disciplinary sociology would not have captured the richness of these stories and would therefore have missed the meanings and emotions of Richardson's interlocutors. Richardson's use of poetry to enact the practice of sociology can be understood in terms of what MacIntyre calls skills that are 'external' to the practice of sociology: prose, poetry, drawings, animations and any number of modes of representation are methods for representing sociological knowledge that are external to the disciplinary practice of sociology because they can be understood as skills that are deployed elsewhere, i.e. they are not inherently sociological (another way of understanding the distinction between internal and external skills is in terms of essential and non-essential). Her fellow conferees, however, objected to her use of poetry on the grounds that they perceived prose to be a skill that is 'internal to the practice' of sociology and to achieving its standards of excellence. The use of the passive or active voice in academic writing and any number of markers of standard academic prose generate similar tensions because they are seen to be inherent in the practice of academic writing. Who determines what counts as an internal or external skill creates tensions between agency and structure, namely the extent to which, on the one hand, academic writers, at all levels, are required and expected to follow the rules and, on the other, the extent to which they are able and enabled to define what the standards of excellence are and what skills are needed to achieve them. The philosophy and sociology of critical realism attempt to reconcile these tensions. Before then, more needs to be said about the specific consequences of reducing the practice of academic writing to a set of finite skills.

Implications of Reductive Approaches to Academic Writing

In addition to the problem of deciding which skills are internal or external, there are undesirable, possibly unintended, consequences of reducing academic writing to a set of prescriptive transferable skills. I describe these consequences in turn as aesthetic and socio-ethical.

Aesthetic Implications

In a book on the difficulty of being (*La difficulté d'être*), French writer, dramatist, poet and film director Jean Cocteau made a fleeting reference to the nature of writing that illustrates what I am calling the 'aesthetic' problem. His words are thoroughly lost in translation so I will quote them in French first and then translate them (Cocteau, 1957, p. 151):

- Écrire est un acte d'amour. S'il ne l'est pas, il n'est qu'écriture
- My translation: *Écrire* (writing) is an act of love; when it is not, it is simply *écriture* (script, also writing).

Cocteau's distinction between *écrire* (to write – verb and process) and *écriture* (writing – noun and product) captures how academic writing instruction, such as EAP, has tended to represent academic writing, namely as *écriture*. By conceptualizing it as a formulaic product stripped of love, emotion and feeling, cleansed of the impurities of the 'difficulty of being' and of the inherent 'messiness' of ontological representation (Law, 2004), academic writing instruction teaches students to write scripts, not write.

Understood as a product, or script, a piece of text rather than a process, academic writing as *écriture* becomes an object of standardized convention, structure, formality, clarity and logic, or, in the words of political philosopher Jonathan Wolff, nothing but 'a dull read' that leads to 'literary boredom' (Wolff, 2007). Wolff further laments the genre's obsessive focus on 'clarity' and on 'making every move explicit', an act, he says, which kills suspense, removes surprise and saps joy. Such joylessness is inherent in what the reader will recognize as familiar attributes of academic writing: formal, logical, linear, clear, concise, balanced, more 'algorithmic than human', as Warner might describe it (2018). These characterizations are common in EAP teacher feedback and their origins can be traced to popular textbooks and manuals on how to write academically as well as to university and library web pages with advice on study skills and 'how to write essays': as a student reading this, you may be familiar with advice and feedback that tells you to structure your argument 'logically'. As a teacher reading this, you may recognize what is arguably shorthand for your lack of comprehension or knowledge, namely a comment in the margin of a student script about their 'lack of clarity' (as opposed to your incomprehension). Significantly, none of these characterizations suggest that academic writing is being either written or read as an *act of love*.

The distinction evoked by *écrire* and *écriture* is exemplified in the context of American academic writing instruction, specifically in controversies around who is responsible for teaching academic writing (Rose, 1989, p. 207):

Anything longer than the sentence (even two or three sentences strung together) is considered *writing* and the teaching of writing shall be the province of the English Department. Anything at the sentence level or smaller (like filling words and phrases into a workbook) is to be considered grammar review and that falls within the domain of the remedial programme.

Here, Rose could easily be likening the writing taught by English departments with the more prosaic beauty of *écrire* and the writing taught to students such as Lucia (the psychology student who was sent to remedial classes) as *écriture*. Along with several other educationalists concerned with literacy, social justice and access to higher education (Judd, 2003; Lillis, 2001; Russell, 2002; Sperlinger et al., 2018), Rose laments the disciplinary and institutional divides that create binaries between 'writing' as prose (*écrire*), taught by professors of English literature, and 'writing' as a mechanical skill, as *écriture*, taught by writing tutors in 'corrective' writing centres, library services or separate language units. Units that serve the academic disciplines in this way have been described as 'butlers' (Raimes, 1991) who are not integral partners in the shared endeavour of communicating knowledge.[4] In this sense, academic writing instructors are the 'underlabourers' (Bhaskar, 1989) of the disciplines, just like philosophy is to the disciplines, invisibly working to keep the academic show on the road, but rarely invited to dine at the disciplinary table where ideas are questioned and norms are challenged. Indeed, from a UK perspective, academic writing scholar Ken Hyland has described these 'remedial' units as 'handmaidens' and highlighted the way in which EAP practitioners (2006, p. 34)

> have generally been seen as inhabiting the less glamorous, low rent neighbourhoods of the academy and this is particularly true of those concerned with English for Academic Purposes, which is generally regarded as a handmaiden to those 'proper' disciplines which are more directly engaged in the serious business of constructing knowledge or discovering truth. EAP, in fact, has come to be regarded as an almost mercantile activity and attracted to itself negatively evaluative concepts such as pragmatic, cost-effective and functional, untroubled by theoretical issues or questions of power as it merrily seeks to accommodate students to the faceless and impersonal prose of their disciplines.

There can be little beauty in 'faceless and impersonal prose', but the dullness lamented by Wolff is potentially more insidious because it indexes deeper

---

[4] For a nuanced account of why this segregation endures in the UK, see Ding, A., & Bruce, I. (2017). *The English for academic purposes practitioner: Operating on the edge of academia* (P. Macmillan, Ed.).

epistemological and ontological consequences. To appreciate these consequences, we must briefly return to the skills–practice dualism.

The tension between academic writing as a skill and academic writing as a social practice re-emerges when framed by likening the skills-based approach to the 'servant' metaphors invoked above by both Raimes (*butler*) and Hyland (*handmaiden*) and the social practice approach to what Hyland has elsewhere referred to as 'transgression'. In the literatures on writing as a social practice, writing is described as 'transformative' rather than 'transgressive', but, connotations aside, what the transformative/transgressive metaphor signals is that the academy is a site of learning, creating and transforming knowledge (Bereiter & Scardamalia, 1987). What this means is that university students are expected to engage critically with knowledge by simultaneously learning it and critiquing it. Since the purpose of EAP is to facilitate access to the academy, it follows that EAP should be a site for *both* learning and transforming knowledge. Arguably, therefore, in addition to ensuring learners become knowledgeable about received norms for writing academically, EAP has a responsibility to prepare students for transforming this knowledge. This transformation, or 'transgression', might include becoming knowledgeable about norms that exist beyond those that are 'received', such as knowledge about who sets these norms and why; about the epistemological and ontological consequences of choosing to follow some norms rather than others; about the risks and ethical implications of choosing to follow prescribed norms; and about student agency in transforming these norms.

Knowing why some kinds of English academic writing have evolved to be 'faceless and impersonal' (and to be valued as such) and why other kinds have not can help students, like Sam, make sense of the confusing writing feedback they receive, but it can also help teachers provide nuanced rather than prescriptive feedback. Knowing, for example, why different supervisors, different disciplines and different editors have differing norms regarding the use of personal pronouns and other grammatical choices can empower writers to make, accept, reject and generally negotiate their writing styles with their teachers and assessors, including their publishers. For example, knowing that the convention to avoid personal pronouns in English academic writing is not universally shared, that it is historically contingent and relative to disciplinary orientations is likely to raise writers' consciousness and assuage their confusion. Conceptualizations of English academic writing, particularly the version of academic writing that is popularized, are 500 years old. They owe their imaginaries to the legacy of a Cartesian and then Lockean worldview which assumes that language and therefore writing are a reliable and unique proxy for representing the world (Bennett, 2015; Turner, 2010). In academic writing instruction, this legacy translates into linguistic prescriptions to sound 'objective' 'clear' and 'transparent' and encourages students to favour some linguistic forms over others. These include choosing the passive form over the active; third person pronouns over first; and nominalized sentence constructions that reduce the number of main verbs (because main verbs require subjects that can make the writing sound 'subjective').

Together, these prescriptions make for rather dull *écriture*.

Socio-Cultural and Ethical Implications

A further implication of EAP's reductive approach to writing is that it standardizes to a textual monoculture that makes academic writing look the same across the disciplinary spectrum, regardless of who has written it and why. This has broader socio-cultural and ethical repercussions.

Advocates of multimodal and multilingual approaches to literacy question the supremacy of the alphabet and of English-only texts and remind us of the socio-semiotic affordances of writing texts that draw on a range of modalities to create meaning. Palmeri (2012), Canagarajah (2018), Blommaert and Horner (2017) and Archer and Breuer (2015) are just a few of the literacy scholars who regularly remind us that conventions both endure and are flouted chronotopically (across time and space). They also warn that universalizing standards and rules thwarts multiculturalism (Björkvall, 2016, p. 28):

> In unstable social environments conventions disappear ... convention is actually an expression which comes from a period of relative semiotic stability where the exercise of power, not normally even noticed because it is very subtle, leads to a kind of agreement to do things in a certain way. But in a deeply multicultural world – a hugely diverse world – there are no such agreements. And, as you know, in Anglophone Ph.D. s in many places you can now use the first person, 'I', which you could not do 25 years ago.

Pedagogically, there is a commonly held assumption that conventions are necessary rather than contingent and that second language learners need to 'learn the rules before they can break them'. This forms the basis of what has been called the 'deficit model' of academic writing (see, for example, Bennett, 2009; Hathaway, 2015; Turner, 2004; Wingate & Tribble, 2012), whereby writers are told they must 'take themselves out of their writing and never use

"I'" (Parker, 2017; Rodríguez, 2017) or that the five-paragraph essay (Bernstein & Lowry, 2017) sets the standard for what counts as academic writing (see Sowton (2016), whose model 'academic' texts are five-paragraph essays and the ubiquitous 250-word IELTS essay). Yet, this approach is chained to ancient history. It is entirely modelled on the classical spoken and then written rhetorics of Aristotelian and Quintilian literacy practices. These posited that what counted as *argument* in the public fora of ancient Rome could be narrowed down to five parts: the *exordium* (the introduction), the *narratio* (the events in question), the *confirmatio* (the argument/claims), the *refutatio* (the counter-argument/claims) and the *peroratio* (summary) (Andrews 2010). As will become apparent in Chapter 4, arguments are by far more varied, especially when expressed multimodally (Molinari, 2021).

Interestingly and in relation to the question of what makes writing academic, the familiar form of the five-paragraph essay is considered to be a sign of 'bad student writing' for US Composition Studies, 'whereas in the EAP program the same form is considered "an extremely serviceable template"' (Tardy & Jwa, 2016). Tardy and Jwa explain the predilection for having standard models as follows: 'Students and teachers … desire a tool that can quickly and easily be applied to immediate writing needs' (2016, p. 59). The fact there are also significant inconsistencies in the advice given by academic style guide books should further alert us to engage critically with what and whose purposes these rules serve. On the one hand, guide books tell writers to avoid colourful words and the use of the personal pronoun 'I'; on the other, they encourage the use of vivid language and avoidance of the passive (Sword, 2012). Similarly, as shown in Ball and Loewe (2017), the very existence of unqualified, or 'bad', writing advice should suffice to undermine uncritical acceptance of what the rules of good writing are and who has the authority to break them. Indeed, with regards to the common refrain that one must 'learn the rules before one can break them', Canagarajah (2021) replies 'you can have it both ways' because there is no such thing as 'standard' English. The norms of a social practice like academic writing can be discussed, negotiated, chosen to fit the purpose, and re-created. When it comes to what makes writing academic, it seems that we actually can have our cake and eat it!

What is emerging from the discussion so far is that socio-cultural norms, however deeply embedded in tradition and however pedagogically reasonable, can be questioned and are, as such, questionable. Uncritical assumptions about 'rules being learnt before they are broken' can be challenged because, quite simply, these rules are not universally shared. And in virtue of not being universally shared, they are 'not the only possibility' (Sousanis, 2015). Opening up possibilities for academic writing is important because if higher education remains dependent on and reduced to monolingual (i.e. English) and monomodal (e.g. language) standards of writing proficiency, measuring academic success against language proficiency alone and against a narrow variety of this proficiency, it will encourage a deficit-model approach that judges students' diverse repertoires as 'deficient' rather than as resourceful: multilingual, multimodal, dyslexic, autistic, artistic and multicultural students have wide-ranging and diverse literacies that could be harnessed as resources instead of straightjacketed into anachronistic norms, or even cancelled. Standardization based on contingent and outdated norms becomes at best disingenuous and at worst exclusionary because it ignores the diverse identities of writers. Epistemically, it is also self-defeating, since knowledge is best arrived at via multiple representations.

A further problem with reducing writing to a monoculture is that if we agree that language is an expression of diverse socio-cultural identities (Evans, 2014; Holmes, 1992), then by insisting on linguistic homogeneity in academic writing, we are also insisting on 'cultural and social' homogeneity. By requiring everybody to write and speak in the same way, just as was once the case with RP (Received Pronunciation), English-speaking universities are creating the conditions for a homogenized academy that communicates via a monoliteracy modelled on *écriture* rather than *écrire*. I would further contend that this encourages the conditions for what sociologists Collyer et al. (2019), drawing on the work of African philosopher Paulin Hountondji (1995), call 'academic dependencies' and 'extraversion', the phenomenon whereby universities in the Global South model themselves on those of the rich North. A standardized monoliteracy culture, that conveniently also happens to be the literacy of the dominant universities, is likely to orient 'knowledge workers' on the peripheries of the academic 'metropole' towards a dependency on the 'techniques' of the dominant elites. These techniques include academic writing practices that favour norms shown to be unjust and exclusionary (Lillis & Curry, 2010a; Politzer-Ahles et al., 2016), such as publication bias (Politzer-Ahles et al., 2020).

When grammatical and linguistic norms, including disparate notions of what counts as 'accurate', become the focus of rule-learning, controversies further ignite around *which* standards and *whose* standards of 'good' English and writing are being privileged. Turner has compared controversies about what counts as 'good writing', an elusive quality that she calls 'writtenness' to the controversy of what counts as good pronunciation. But, unlike research on how accent and pronunciation are used to discriminate between 'good' and 'bad' spoken English

(Donnelly et al., 2019; Orelus, 2017), the socio-politics of *writtenness* have not received the same attention (Turner, 2018, p. 7):

> Writtenness is a cultural ideal, whose values are implicit rather than explicitly espoused. Indexed by evaluative tropes such as 'polished prose' ... and assumptions of precision, accuracy and stylistic elegance, it is saturated with ideological and cultural value. As such, it is similar to the position of RP (received pronunciation) in spoken language. However, unlike RP, whose ideological resonance has been extensively commented upon in sociolinguistics ..., the ideologies, social identifications and linguistic assumptions of written language have generated much less concern.

Deficit models signal that the knowledge which students bring with them is inadequate and needs to be replaced with the 'correct' conventions and rules so that the learner can be 'socialized' into their academic community (Lea & Street, 1998). Since the 'overall aim of an EAP course is to help students towards membership of their chosen academic community' (Alexander et al., 2008, p. 80), the assumption prevails that students are 'empty vessels' needing to be filled and becomes so normalized that it is hard to conceive how else it could be. This assumption, however, is fundamentally flawed, profoundly political and insidiously ideological. It signals troubling power asymmetries that sit uncomfortably with a participatory, emancipatory, democratic and dialogic progressive education. This has been shown by many, not least by Paulo Freire (2000), whose opposition to a 'banking model' of education captures the colonial ethical and educational agendas underlying deficit models. Whilst deficit approaches go largely unquestioned by most academic writing tutors, textbook writers and service providers, including the EAP sector, there are at least three reasons to challenge it.

Firstly, in a complex global (super)diverse higher educational context, diversity, not homogeneity, is the norm (Blommaert, 2013; Blommaert & Horner, 2017). Diversity is already manifest in the existing varieties of English academic discourse (such as blogs and reflective and graphic essays), in disciplinary diversity and in the multilingualism and multiculturalism that are already established in the academic landscape (Canagarajah, 2011). What are students being 'socialized into' if not a diverse but also mobile academic landscape? Yet, since academic writing instruction rarely exposes future generations of students to the broader academic writing landscape, it is unlikely that diversity can thrive if academic writing practices continue to converge towards a monomodal, monolingual and monocultural standard (Canagarajah,

2002a, 2013b, 2013c; Lillis & Curry, 2010a; Vertovec, 2007). Secondly, diversity provides higher education with opportunities rather than constraints in so far as it allows the academy to shift from a 'difference-as-deficit' model to a 'difference-as-resource' *consciousness* (Cox, 2014). This shift ensures students can bring their multiliteracies and identities to the classroom and create new ways of thinking, writing and representing knowledge (Thesen & Cooper, 2013). And thirdly, voice, originality and criticality – other qualities that contribute to the 'writteness' of good academic writing – are less likely to emerge when students' agencies are being corrected and 'socialized', with the intention of conforming to norms that are themselves also changing (Williams, 2017).

Deficit models have negative educational and academic repercussions because they risk eclipsing creativity (Robinson, 2001) and dismissing prior knowledge and experience, which a so-called 'progressive' education is said to value (Russell, 2002). In his seminal book *Democracy and Education: An Introduction to the Philosophy of Education*, associated with progressive and secular instruction (as opposed to authoritarian and religious), John Dewey defines education as 'the reconstruction or reorganisation of experience which adds to the meaning of experience and which increases ability to direct the course of subsequent experience' (Dewey, 1938, p. 76). If EAP and similar academic writing providers are genuinely committed to their higher educational ambition of helping students 'understand their disciplines and ... successfully navigate their learning' (Hyland & Hamp-Lyons, 2002, p. 1), then, based on a Deweyan understanding of education, they would need to foreground the experiences students bring with them, including their past and present literacies, at least as much as they foreground their mission to 'socialize' students into existing university practices. When academic writing instruction focuses entirely on socializing writers into existing writing conventions, it is training students to produce academic scripts (*écriture*) rather than educating them to write (*écrire*) academically and become writers. In this sense, student writers become de-humanized. Indeed, Dewey argues that training is the proper term for describing what we ask of (non-human) animals. Education, on the other hand, is what is proper to human beings. Training is the blind response to a *stimulus*, whereas education involves mental acts that respond to *meanings*. Training is 'less intellectual or educative' and can be understood as follows (1938, pp. 64–5):

> The more specialized the reaction, the less is the skill acquired in practising and perfecting it transferable to other modes of behaviour. According to the orthodox theory of formal discipline, a pupil in studying his [sic] spelling lesson

acquires, besides ability to spell those particular words, an increase of power of observation, attention and recollection which may be employed whenever these powers are needed. As a matter of fact, the more he confines himself to noticing and fixating the forms of words, irrespective of connection with other things (such as the meaning of the words, the context in which they are habitually used, the derivation and the classification of the verbal form, etc.) the less likely he is to acquire the ability which can be used for anything *except* the mere noting of verbal visual forms.

If we apply Dewey's reasoning to EAP, then when we over-specialize and focus on forms and conventions, we are training students rather than educating them. By *training* to write academically, we may be limiting students' ability to notice and make broader connections, such as how words that fall outside of academic word lists are used and how those that fall within it are not. The dangers of foregrounding routines and skills in discussions about education are that these lead to 'ineptitude' rather than understanding meanings and making connections (Dewey, 1938, p. 78):

> Routine action, action which is automatic, may increase skill to do a particular thing. In so far, it might be said to have an educative effect. But it does not lead to new perceptions of bearings and connections; it limits rather than widens the meaning horizon. And since the environment changes and our way of acting has to be modified in order to successfully keep a balanced connection with things, an isolated uniform way of acting becomes disastrous at some critical moment. The vaunted "skill" turns out to be gross ineptitude.

If academic writing instruction were as intent on educating *about* writing, i.e. explaining the diversity and mobility of writing genres and practices, as it is on teaching *how* to write some forms of writing at the expense of others, then it might avoid mechanistic 'routine actions that limit' the meaning-making potential that emerges from engaging with a far broader range of academic texts.

Some may argue that this is an unfair characterization of EAP, in particular. However, it is one that reflects the observations I have made throughout my thirty-year teaching and examining experience and one that seems to be shared by writing scholars such as Hyland (2016) and Jenkins (2016), both of whom have identified a mismatch between what EAP might be preaching in its scholarly publications and what it is actually teaching in its classrooms. For example, although some literatures claim that a wide range of academic genres are being taught by EAP practitioners, they also single out the academic essay as being the most prevailing (Nesi & Gardner 2012). This has likely compounded

EAP's privileging of developing a skill in 'a particular thing', namely the academic essay, over and above other genres. That Nesi and Gardner have also claimed that they are offering templates (2012, p. 2) for teachers to follow further betrays compliance with EAP's standardizing, rather than transforming, function within the university. By ignoring socio-semiotic and multimodal research on literacy development, for example, which approaches writing instruction as part of a complex educational ecology that cares about and integrates students' previous and current literacies into the acquisition of new ones (see, for example, Wardle (2017), Williams (2017) and Parnell (2012)), EAP projects itself as a perpetrator of functional transferable skills continually aimed at future 'target situations' (Ding & Bruce, 2017, p. 97):

> The notion of the gap between the present situation analysis (where students are now) and the target situation analysis – what students are required to know in the future in terms of academic language knowledge and skills – is an important concept that drives much of EAP and strongly influences pedagogy. Therefore, pedagogic goals in EAP tend to centre on the types of conventionalised communication – spoken and written – that students must process and master in university contexts.

That past and present literacies are so absent from the academic writing classroom is somewhat surprising because nurturing present literacies does not prevent future ones from emerging. On the contrary, valuing and harnessing the literacies students bring with them are more likely to nurture reflective dispositions that allow learners to make sense of new and diverse academic writing contexts. Since it is the students who will be inhabiting their own future 'target situations' long after their teachers and since their teachers can't know what these future target situations will require, students' future needs and capabilities (Robeyns, 2016) might be better 'served' by seeing past and previous literacies as conducive to learning and not as 'interference' (Bennett, 2010). This understanding of the writer-learner who *brings* experience in order to make sense of the future is echoed in Dewey (1938, p. 56):

> It is not a question of whether education should prepare for the future. If education is growth, it must progressively realise present possibilities and thus make individuals better fitted to cope with later requirements.

Ignoring the literacies, experiences, capabilities and agencies of individual writers fundamentally ignores what King (2010), arguing from a critical realist and humanist perspective, calls the 'dignity of the self' and what EAP scholar Bee Bond refers to throughout her book on *Making Language Visible in the*

University (2020) as the 'human' dimension of a university education. Dehumanizing students is a matter of great ethical concern and one that signals uncomfortable truths about the fairness and purpose of EAP practices overall, which include writing instruction. EAP is seen as a commercial sector whose imperative is to generate income by teaching transferable skills rather than to educate. This explains why it has been described in somewhat benign terms as a butler and a handmaiden, and in more pernicious ways as a 'cash-cow' (Ding, 2016) because of the way international students, in particular, are referred to behind closed boardroom doors. The unethical implications of this have not gone unnoticed by the media (Matthews, 2014):

> Global neoliberal trends ' ... have had astonishing success in creating markets for things whose commodification was once almost unimaginable: drinking water, body parts and social welfare among them' (Connell, 2013, p. 100). It is within this broader economic and political climate that the specifics of EAP commodification have attracted the attention of and also generated debate in the media by raising concerns around the ethics of taking money from foreign students who already pay significant amounts for their British degrees.

A systematic review of the unethical underpinnings of internationalisation can be found in Mulvey (2021). It seems urgent, therefore, to wonder what impact the commodification of EAP, discussed at length in Ding and Bruce (2017) and Hadley (2015), may also be having on the ethics of writing instruction. The assumption that all students wish to and should learn a standardized version of academic writing to the exclusion of all others seems unfair given the diversity of the student population. This population includes mature students who, for a range of reasons, may be unaccustomed to traditional academic writing and for whom traditional academic writing may even be obsolete (Grove, 2016); students who choose to or are expected to write creatively within the social sciences (Phillips & Kara, 2021) and to write multimodally (Palmeri, 2012); students with a range of abilities and backgrounds (Sperlinger et al., 2018); academic writers who communicate, or who might want to communicate and publish in English as a *lingua franca*; and students obliged to endure the high costs of learning a particular variety of English, which is arguably neither predictive of how students will cope with the language requirements of university study (Coleman et al., 2003) or a reliable indicator of linguistic competence (Leung et al., 2016), nor is it a measure of 'good' writing: indeed, Turner has pointed out that students who fail language proficiency tests, such as IELTS and, by implication, EAP courses that mimic the IELTS format, may be and go on to become able academic writers.

Yet, 'such students are being denied the opportunity to develop their academic writing, as well as their studies' (Turner 2018, p. 134) when they do not pass these courses. Entry exams such as IELTS and EAP, including the burgeoning textbook industry that supports them, are not only expensive but there is an increasing sense in which they are ineffective and exclusionary, too. This fuels the perception that they are socially unjust.

I close this chapter on reductive approaches to academic writing – whereby what makes writing academic is reduced to a finite set of transient skills – by raising one final, but no less troubling implication of standardizing academic writing in this way. Related to the ethical concerns decried above are the profits and injustices generated by profit-making essay writing services known as 'essay mills' and 'ghostwriters'. This phenomenon deserves a book in its own right, so, for now, I refer my reader to the growing debate and body of research on this phenomenon (Peters et al., 2021) whilst confining my own contribution to the following brief remarks. Writing templates, grammatical rules and conventions, standard phrases and genres, the outsourcing of writing instruction to 'service providers', such as EAP and Library Services – all the things that are associated with a skills-based approach to academic writing – can be replicated and reproduced, copied and sold, downloaded and programmed algorithmically (Collins, 2019; Introna, 2106). They can even be generated by computers as full-blown fakes that enter citation networks (known as 'farms') (Labbé & Labbé, 2012; Van Noorden, 2014). Standardization is both a cause and an effect of what Macfarlane (2021b) calls 'performativity',[5] whereby academic writers are taught to perform and display behaviours, including writing behaviours, that comply to the norm. This performativity includes forms of 'soft plagiarism' that are the result of 'symbolic citations' of scholarship that writers have never read and which lead to 'uncritical valorisations' of theories that are not understood. The use of essay mills (Aitchison, 2017; Medway et al., 2018; Peters, 2018) and the occurrence of academic writing hoaxes (Alvesson et al., 2017; Cuthbert, 2018) are symptoms of an academic writing culture that readily relies on the surface features of a genre in order to deem that a text is *bona fide* academic. I discuss hoaxes further in Chapters 3 and 4, but for now, my intention is to signal an ethics of academic misconduct that all too frequently places the moral burden on the student rather than on performative university practices that contribute

---

[5] The term 'performativity' has been used by scholars from a range of disciplines spanning critical theory, education and philosophy to mean a range of practices. In this book, I refer to 2 of its meanings: the first is as Macfarlane intends it to describe the hollowness and superficiality of academic writing forms. The second is as Lunsford (2015) intends it (see Chapter 3) to describe what academic writing can do and has positive connotations of action and agency.

to the conditions for misconduct (Molinari, 2014). One of the troubles with having a standardized, transient and reductive academic writing culture which also belongs to an increasingly commodified higher education sector is that writing is easily and readily monetized, plagiarized and disembodied from the humans who created it.

Conclusions

In troubling the way that academic writing is understood, taught and assessed by university programmes, such as EAP, my intention has been to foreground the predilection by writing service providers, including EAP, of reductive and standardized writing ontologies. These include the skills needed to produce a particular version of academic writing, one that is 'objective' and 'impersonal', monomodal, monolingual, and monocultural. Such reductive approaches have undesirable aesthetic, social and ethical implications, which include the denial a writer's humanity. The next chapter highlights some of the historical reasons that have led to the privileging of this version of academic writing and offers glimpses of how else it could be.

2

How Did We Get Here? A Selected History

Introduction

> The evidence has begun to accumulate that our beliefs about literacy are a blend of fact and supposition, in a word a mythology, a selective way of viewing the facts that not only justifies the advantages of the literate but also assigns the failings of the society, indeed of the world, to the illiterate.
>
> (Olson, 1994, p. 2)

This chapter highlights the contingency of human choices and shows that what counts as writing and, by extension, academic writing is a matter of human decision-making and ideology. I argue that 'Western' literacy has idealized 'higher order' thinking by arrogating and then conflating 'logical', 'linear' thinking with alphabet-based literacies. Throughout history, knowledge has been communicated via a range of script, alphabetic and non, each representing the values and purposes of people. Shining a spotlight on this range allows us to reflect on what was and what is. It further creates a space within which to consider why things are as they are and how we'd like them to be.

After some introductory remarks on why I use history to explain current practices, I suggest that the orthodox conflation of writing with the alphabet and with cognition is misguided and, because of this, writing should be re-positioned as *one of several* modes for communicating academic knowledge and thinking about it critically. I evidence some of the different ways that academic knowledge has been communicated to suggest that academia might reclaim some of this diversity. The final section of this chapter focuses on how the scientific paradigm of the European enlightenment and European colonial practices have imposed their own forms of literacy to the exclusion of others: this serves to remind us that writing practices are ideological, including those favoured by 'Western' academies (Canagarajah, 2021; Henderson, 2018; Lillis & Tuck, 2016; Russell, 2002; Street, 1984; Turner, 2010, 2018).

Using History to Understand the Present

History shows it could all have been different. In his *Representations of the Intellectual*, which document his 1993 BBC Reith Lectures, Palestinian critical theorist, secular humanist and historian, Edward Said (1994) claims that history, not God or similarly unaccountable entities, allows us to see why things are and how they could have been. In Said's thinking, humanism is a response to social injustices and is a way of 'speaking truth to power'. In this sense, 'humans are the measures of all things' and can therefore (Said, 1994, p. 45):

> Look at situations as contingent, not as inevitable, look at them as a result of a series of historical choices made by men and women, as facts of society made by human beings and not as natural or god-given, therefore unchangeable, permanent, irreversible.

Said identifies with the legacy of Giambattista Vico (1959 (1725, 1730, 1744, 1928)), the eighteenth-century Italian professor of Rhetoric whose seminal work *La Scienza Nuova* was a response to the rational hypothetico-deductive Cartesian philosophy of the time. Vico argued against Descartes's method on the grounds that 'it renders phenomena which cannot be expressed logically or mathematically as illusions' (Costelloe, 2018). Instead, Vico proposed that (Said, 1994, p. 45)

> the proper way to understand reality is to understand it as a process generated from its point of origin, which one can always locate in extremely humble circumstances.

More recently, critical theorist and historian Michel Foucault (1972a, p. 7) claimed that 'history is one way in which a society recognises and develops a mass of documentation with which it is inextricably linked'.

Our social practices – of which writing is one – are also 'located in extremely humble origins' and are 'inextricably linked' to our past, making the history of writing an inseparable part of understanding writing itself. With knowledge of why writing practices have evolved as they have, present and future practices can emerge from informed choices and possibilities, not templates, straightjackets or pigeonholes (Paxton, 2013). This allows us to *hold rules to account*, breaking, following and adapting them from a position of knowledge and openness towards change.

A Misguided Conflation: The Alphabet and Cognition

Historians of writing show that definitions of writing are as useful as they are redundant. None are univocal. Arguing from a philological and semiological perspective, Pettersson (1994) has claimed that attempts to provide core definitions of writing are fallacies doomed to failure. This is because of three interconnected reasons. Firstly, in order to decide what counts and does not count as writing, we would need to have a pre-agreed notion of what writing is before being able to recognize instances of it. But since we don't, as I discuss below, definitions remain elusive. Secondly, even if an antecedent definition were possible, countless problems would arise in trying to classify new instances that do not sit comfortably with the definition. For example, do non-alphabetical scripts such as pictorial rebuses or Chinese logographs count as 'writing' (DeFrancis, 1989; Harris, 1986)? And thirdly, by extracting a definition from an *ad hoc* classification based on 'uniquely identifying' features (such as a mark on a surface or an alphabet), we are, on the one hand, conflating what are contested defining properties with what is a *post hoc* classification and, on the other, begging a whole series of other questions such as what counts as a 'mark', a 'surface', an 'alphabet'. For example, history shows that writing is not exclusively alphabetic and that what has been labelled as 'writing' has varied in form, content, purpose and interpretation (Olson, 2001; Schmandt-Besserat, 2001; Woodard, 2001). Some argue that 'real writing' is unequivocally alphabetical, i.e. based on phonological representation, which explains why, over time, it has become conflated with 'literacy' (DeFrancis, 1989; Gelb, 1952; Havelock, 1976). Others, however, refute this conflation on the grounds that what counts as 'writing' very much depends on who is doing the counting and why, which leaves open the possibility to re-think what writing means (Coulmas, 1989; Harris, 1986, 2000). The debate over what counts as 'writing' further assumes that there was a key moment in time that separated non-writing communities from writing ones. It also rests on a contention concerning the purpose of writing: does it function as a *representation* of the objects it refers to or as a *symbolic correspondence* that 'stands for' something else? If it *represents* the objects it refers to, then what is the nature of this representation: a copy or replacement of its object, as the alphabet is said to graphically 'replace' the phonology of spoken language? If writing is *symbolic* in its correspondence to nature, who decides which symbol stands for its referent and how do they decide this?

Despite its problems, the representational theory of language has endured and forms the basis of influential theories that underscore modern-day structural linguistics (Harris, 2000; Harris & Taylor, 1989; Orman, 2016). Its origins can be traced to how Cuneiform 'writing' is said to have evolved during the early Mesopotamian era of 8000–3000 BC from the use of geometrically shaped counters to record the inventory of goods (such as grain) to incisions, or marks, on clay tablets that *re*-presented these goods functionally: clay tokens 'stood for' an object not a sound, as the alphabet is said to do. While representational theories of language may account for the one-to-one correspondence between a geometric token and the number of grains needed for a commercial transaction, they struggle to explain pictographic languages, such as ancient Egyptian hieroglyphs or ancient Chinese characters, because the use of pictograms, namely pictures representing ideas, is not concerned with one-to-one correspondence with an object but with symbolism. This linear (and highly compressed) history of how writing has evolved leads us to logographic writing (2600–2500 BC), of which both ancient and modern Chinese are examples. Here, a sign or mark is said to *re*-present or 'stand for' a sound or word, not an object. In philology, it is generally agreed that the emergence of logograms marks the shift from a visual representation theory of language, where a mark stood for an 'object', to an aural representation theory of language, where a mark now stands for a 'sound' (Schmandt-Besserat, 2001). Syllabic scripts, where signs represent syllables rather than whole words, are concurrent with logographic ones (Fischer, 2005). Current Indian, Japanese, Arabic and Hebrew are all examples of syllabic languages and are said to have converged in 2000 BC with the invention of what is commonly, but, as we shall see, problematically, referred to as the 'Greek' alphabet: this moment marks a seismic shift in how phonetic languages came to be represented in writing and in how 'Western' notions of literacy subsequently developed.

The alphabet is Proto-Sinaitic-Phoenician-Palestinian-Greek-Lebanese and dates to between 2000 and 1000 BC (Fischer, 2005; Goody, 1977; Harris, 1986, pp. 30–1; Schmandt-Besserat, 2001, p. 16623). Its designation as 'Greek' and as having been 'invented' at one moment in time, i.e. 2000 BC, is, therefore, inaccurate because of the vast geographical area where the alphabet developed and because it established itself over one thousand years. While it may seem pedantic to point this out, it is a reminder that men and women select which histories and whose accounts and approximations to refer to when they trace the genealogies of the phenomena they care about. By signalling that nationalistic claims to ownership of something as momentous as the origin of the alphabet are questionable, I am preparing the reader for what is to come.

Indeed, some linguists and historians of language (e.g. Harris, 1986) remind us that writing systems did not suddenly appear but they developed incrementally, synchronously and serendipitously alongside other writing systems. This suggests that it is misleading to reduce definitions of writing to alphabetic writing. This is because rather than having evolved in a linear and chronological fashion, from pictograms to ideograms to logograms, to syllabic representations culminating in the phonetic representations of the alphabet, writing systems are likely to have co-existed. And during this co-existence, they are likely to have borrowed and (erroneously) copied from each other, adapting these borrowings to specific needs (Fischer, 2005, pp. 296–7). If writing is thought of in this serendipitous way, then 'alphabetic' writing is just one of many kinds of writing.

Despite the possibility that writing can be non-alphabetic, the alphabet has become co-extensive with 'Western' definitions of 'writing', most likely because it now forms the basis of some of the world's writing systems, those that share an alphabetic genesis, such as Latin, Arabic, Hebrew and Cyrillic. Unlike pictographic and logographic forms of notation, the 'Greek' alphabet had twenty-two letters 'each standing for a single sound of voice, which, combined in innumerable ways, brought an unprecedented flexibility to transcribe speech' (Schmandt-Besserat, 2001, p. 16624): it is this flexibility that is said to explain why alphabetic script formed the basis of so many languages. Gradually, writing came to be defined by the alphabet because, unlike a picture, writing could 'record a linguistic utterance directly' (Woodard, 2001, p. 16633):

> The term 'writing system' specifically denotes a set of symbols which is used for the graphic (written) recording of language …. Forms of graphic expression which may have some semantic content – such as cave drawings, petroglyphs, icons and even sophisticated picture messages – but which do not or could not record a linguistic utterance directly, are thus excluded from the realm of writing.

The co-existence of pictorial and alphabetical symbols allowed philologists to create different categories with which to include and exclude different forms of graphic representations. These categories included distinctions between non-writing systems, as noted by Woodward, above, partial writing systems[1] and full writing systems (DeFrancis, 1989, p. 5):

> Partial writing is a system of graphic symbols that can be used to convey only some thought. Full writing is a system of graphic symbols that can be used to convey any and all thought.

---

[1] For DeFrancis, mathematics and rebuses are forms of 'partial writing' because they are not based on the sounds of speech.

To side-step the many difficulties generated by creating categories to include and exclude what does and does not count as writing (such as whether 'all thought' can be conveyed by any form of representation), others, such as Erard (2018), began framing writing in functional terms, not graphic ones. Erard sees writing as a 'layered' concept that has explosive effects. His conception challenges the idea that 'writing' can be defined by reducing it to any single form:

> I like to think of writing as a layered invention. First there's the graphic invention: the notion of making a durable mark on a surface. …. Then the symbolic invention: let's make this mark different from all other marks and assign it a meaning that we can all agree on. Humans have been doing this for a long time, too. Then there's the linguistic one: let's realize that a sound, a syllable and a word are all things in the world that can be assigned a graphic symbol. This invention depends on the previous ones and itself is made of innovations, realizations, solutions and hacks. Then comes the functional invention: let's use this set of symbols to write a list of captives' names, or a contract about feeding workers, or a letter to a distant garrison commander. All these moves belong to an alchemy of life that makes things go boom.

Olson (2001, p. 16640) and Harris (1986) have argued that, rather than an evolution from mark to picture to sound, changes in scripts reflect borrowings, errors and adaptations from several co-occurring scripts. A modern-day example of such borrowings is English spelling, a system which bears an erratic resemblance to its phonology because of its Latin, French and Anglo-Saxon influences, because of historical errors in transcriptions and because it has never been possible to systematize it via, for example, an Academy of Language. This mottled history explains why the English language has remained a porous and open system that can swiftly accommodate neologisms and changes in meaning (Barber, 1993; Crystal, 1988). Harris, Olson and others have argued that similar dappled borrowings and unsystematic uses are likely to have occurred in ancient times, too, especially over the course of the thousand years that culminated in the establishment of a 'Greek' alphabet. What this less linear account suggests is that the orthodox conflation of 'writing' with the alphabet may be unwarranted (Harris, 1986):

> Writing was originally merely a term designating the process of scoring or outlining a shape on a surface of some kind. (In this very broad sense, writing ought to include drawing and even the art of the silhouette. Nowadays, it does not, although that original use of the verb write survives in English as late as the sixteenth century). Ancient Egyptian had one word meaning both 'writing' and 'drawing'. Similarly, the Greek verb γράφω ('to write') originally meant in

Homer 'engrave', 'scratch', 'scrape'. The later restriction of such words to designate alphabetic writing hardly warrants the narrow perspective adopted by those historians of the subject who take for granted that graphic signs count as writing only when used for purposes which alphabetic writing was later to fulfil.

On Roy Harris's account, if 'writing' can include drawing, then, in principle, it can include other forms of representation. Indeed, both Harris (1986) and Halverson (1992) have argued that many enduring assumptions about how writing originated need challenging. In particular, Harris refutes the classical Aristotelian and De Saussurean thesis that the alphabet, understood as a precursor to writing, evolved as a substitute for speech, with each letter (*grapheme*) representing a sound (*phoneme*). Rather, since an alphabet cannot capture all the nuances of speech, writing can never be a full surrogate of speech (Harris, 1986, 1989, 2000). That the alphabet does not account for all forms of writing is evidenced by the existence of Chinese characters and script, an example of a writing system that can be processed semantically without an intermediate phonetic stage. Unfortunately, the reason Chinese was *not* considered to be a writing system by 'Western' standards has more to do with political ideology than it does with the putatively unique adeptness of the alphabet in capturing the sounds of speech. I discuss this later in the chapter, but before then, more needs to be said about why the conflation of the alphabet with writing is misguided.

Even if we grant that alphabetic writing is a representation of speech, it has become clear that it is inherently inadequate in this representation. This inadequacy is evident when we consider the vast range of non-alphabetic ways that humans have developed to try and compensate for the fact that the alphabet cannot fully represent speech (Olson, 2001, p. 16641):

> The history of writing is largely the history of inventing devices, such as punctuation and text structures, as well as rules for interpretation that have taken sometimes as long as millennia to develop.

If the alphabet, and by implication writing, cannot fully represent speech, then it becomes as (in)adequate as drawing in representing human thought. This is one reason why Harris (1986, 2000) and Coulmas (1989) see no difference between writing and drawing (Olson, 2001, p. 16641). In fact, for both Harris and Coulmas, semasiographic systems, such as road signs and mathematics, are systems of writing capable of representing meaning without relying on a prior link to spoken forms.

A final difficulty with reducing the function of writing to a representation of speech is that it assumes 'speech' is synonymous with 'language'. But this conflation, too, is problematic not least because of its exclusionary implications (see Evans (2014)). If 'speech' were equal to 'language', this would entail that deaf/mute people don't communicate linguistically. The fact that a deaf/mute person can read, write and understand alphabetic script suggests that it is meanings, rather than sounds, that are conveyed by the graphic sign, whether alphabetic or not: this is because there is nothing phonologically inherent in 'cat' that it needs to be heard or pronounced as /kæt/ to be understood as meaning 'cat'.[2] By undermining the conflation of the alphabet with writing, on the grounds that writing does not need to be heard to be understood (or seen, for that matter), we are more likely to accept that pictographic and logographic scripts convey meanings in ways that do not rely on alphabetic script or sound. Similar arguments are developed in Evans (2009) and Malpas (2002). They are important because, as we will see, the prominence given to the alphabet by 'literate' cultures has been used to discriminate against non-alphabetic cultures and against multimodal ways of communicating knowledge.

Notwithstanding the above critiques, influential historians of writing, like Gelb (1963), have defended the thesis that for a script to count as 'writing' it needs to be alphabetic. Gelb claimed that pictures cannot be considered part of writing because the urge to draw is aesthetic, not communicative (Pettersson, 1994, p. 131). This stance led him into several difficulties when attempting to 'lay a foundation for a full science of writing' (Gelb, 1963, p. 23 cited in Pettersson, 1994, p. 138). Not only did Gelb equate writing with the alphabet and therefore speech, but he also insisted that for writing to be considered 'writing' it had to consist of a 'mark on an object' rather than 'be' that object (as a token or a drawing might be). Significantly, Gelb's definition of writing would rule out Chinese script as a written form of its language,[3] because it is not alphabetic. Gelb

---

[2] An extreme example of how *unphonetic* the English language is illustrates this point further by showing that there is nothing phonologically inherent in the letters of the alphabet that they sound one way or the other: 'ghoti seagh' is a non-sensical phrase in English; yet, based on how the English language has evolved to represent the sounds of the alphabet, it can be pronounced as 'fish chef' (Fish: Gh pronounced as 'f' as in 'enough'; O pronounced as 'i' as in 'women'; Ti pronounced as 'sh' as in 'tion'. Chef: S pronounced as 'sh' as in sugar; Ea pronounced as in 'bread'; Gh pronounce 'f' as in 'enough').

[3] In an attempt to assuage the divisive polemic that has surrounded dismissive 'Western' attitudes to Chinese (cf. Jean-Jacques Rousseau and Joseph Priestley in Harris, 2000, p. 2), DeFrancis, J. (1989). *Visible speech: The diverse oneness of writing systems*. University of Hawaii Press has argued that although Chinese is not alphabetic, it is nonetheless 'phonetic' in the sense that the early pictograms and the later stylized signs of Chinese characters represent phonic elements (such as morphemes and syllables) or whole words. This, according to King, B. (1991). Reviewed work(s): Visible speech: The diverse oneness of writing systems by John DeFrancis. *Linguistic Society of America*, 67(2), 377–9. http://www.jstor.org/stable/415119, is, however, a trivial observation that can be applied to all written forms because they can all be pronounced whether they are alphabetical or not. In this sense, then, DeFrancis does little to extinguish the polemic. Rather, Chinese characters, whilst having originated as pictograms, have since become so stylized and far removed from their original pictorial depiction that Chinese cannot meaningfully be said to be a pictorial language any more. This is because the original representation can no longer be discerned.

therefore revised the definitions he gave in *A History of Writing* by omitting any reference to the alphabet (Gelb, 1980, pp. 21–2 cited in Pettersson (1994, p. 144)):

> The proposed new definition of writing is as follows: writing in its broadest sense is a recording system or device by means of conventional markings or shapes or colour of objects, achieved by the motor action of the hand of an individual and received visually by another.

This new, non-alphabetical definition of writing would now include picto/logographic languages but it remains problematic for at least the following reasons:

- 'conventional markings' would now cover the entire field of semiotics, including semasiography (whereby communication is achieved entirely without words, such as in road signs);
- the requirement for writing to be 'achieved by the motor action of the hand' would rule out Stephen Hawkin's 'writing' because he used eye movement and dictation software; and
- the condition that the marks be 'received visually by another' excludes braille from the definition.

What this cursory[4] overview has served to highlight is that there are reasons to challenge the conflation of writing with the alphabet as well as to question the motivations for this conflation. Since definitions of writing, literacy and cognition have been used to exclude and vilify forms of literacy that do not conform to the alphabetic canon, writing is as much ideological as it is a mechanical skill. Indeed, as noted by Olson in opening this chapter, being or not being 'literate' has implications for social inclusion and exclusion.

Many studies on 'Western' literacy assume a linear transition from an oral to a written culture. They include influential work by historian Havelock (1976, 1982), who has also dated the origins of 'Western' literacy to the Greek alphabet. I have

---

[4] Key linguistic theories of the twentieth century have been necessarily omitted because the scope of this chapter is to provide a very brief historical foundation for justifying the possibility, in principle, of diverse forms of (academic) writing. I am, however, aware of the complex and nuanced tradition of 'Western' linguistics, in particular De Saussure's structuralism, which distinguishes between writing and speech by drawing attention to the diachronic contingencies of the latter (*parole*) and the synchronic stability of the former (*langue*) Harris, R., & Taylor, T. J. (1989). *Landmarks in linguistic thought: The Western tradition from Socrates to Saussure*. Routledge, Saussure, F. d., Baskin, W., Meisel, P., & Saussy, H. (2011). *Course in general linguistics*. Columbia University Press and with Derrida's deconstruction of Western logocentrism, which de-centres language and meaning and re-positions them as differential relationships involving absences, differences and defferals. Derrida, J., & Spivak, G. C. (1976). *Of grammatology*. Johns Hopkins University Press.

already questioned the sweeping linguistic and geographical generalizations that underscore this view, namely that what is meant by 'Greek' is actually a vast geographical area that includes the modern-day Middle East. Indeed, the 'West' is far too readily accepted as a synecdoche that covers immense geographical and cultural areas which are not 'Western', as patiently shown, for example, by Appiah (2016a) in his Reith Lectures and by de Sousa Santos (2009) in *A Non-Occidentalist West*: both have challenged the mis-appropriation of 'Western' by the 'West'. When Havelock claims that the 'psychological and epistemological revolution' brought about by written, i.e. alphabetized, prose, 'inheres only in an alphabet' (Halverson, 1992, p. 151), he is clearly advancing, or at least assuming, a normative thesis about the superiority of the alphabet compared to other systems of thought and knowledge representation. This has cemented and perpetuated the collective dismissal of oral and visual cultures on the grounds that they restrict thought and lead to indoctrination, whereas written culture ('Western' written culture, specifically) frees thought from rote repetition. An obvious objection to this is that civilizations that are non-alphabetic, but nonetheless 'written', have also generated their own 'psychological and epistemological revolutions' – China's millennial history of medicine, philosophy and literature being a case in point (Van Norden, 2017) and the debunking of the myth that 'literate' minds are more conceptually 'agile and deductive' than non-literate ones, being another (Scribner & Cole, 1981).

Despite such objections, the shift from oral to written societies, where 'written' is equated with 'alphabetic', has been credited with developing a 'logical' mind because it has allowed us to 'see' language, enabling us to do what Havelock calls 'backward scanning', whereby we can reflect on how a text is organized, categorize the topics that it deals with and create logical ordering. This has allowed us to turn language into an object of study which has generated grammatical concepts such as 'clause' and 'sentence' (Olson, 1994). In addition to providing opportunities for reifying language as an object of study, the shift from oral to written has also freed us from the need to preserve cultural wisdom through repetition, proverbs and prescriptive metrics – associated with oral prose – so that we can create novel statements through writing. Havelock illustrates this shift through a detailed analysis of the socially unifying and culturally preserving function of Homeric prose, which used repetition, proverbs and prescriptive metrics as a way to preserve cultural wisdom. By having a writing culture, he argues, we are no longer bound by the need to memorize familiar ideas and to be 'indoctrinated'. In short, according to Havelock, 'the Greeks did not just invent an alphabet; they invented literacy and the literate basis of modern thought' (cited in Halverson, 1992, p. 152). This view has not only had negative repercussions on how the 'West' has treated non-Western civilizations, but it has led to the illogical and normative conclusion that alphabetically literate cultures are superior to non-alphabetic ones, rather than being simply different (Appiah, 2016b; Said, 1978, 1993).

Notwithstanding its widespread acceptance and influence, Havelock's account may also be misguided. Firstly, whilst it is true that writing has afforded the development of a systematized grammar, it does not follow that thinking in ordered ways would not have happened if alphabetical writing had not developed. This leaves open the possibility that other forms of representation, including images, also produce ordered ways of thinking. Secondly, according to Halverson, Havelock based his arguments that the Greek alphabet has shaped 'Western' thought on some unfounded assumptions about Homeric prose and about the primacy of orality over the written word. Indeed, there seems to be insufficient evidence to conclude that Homer's ballads were indeed spoken first and then transcribed: they could have been written and co-existed with an oral tradition. If Halverson is right, this would undermine the orthodox view that society transitioned from orality to writing and that the latter is a thought-structuring substitute for the former. If true, this would have significant implications: if writing did not substitute speech but co-existed with it instead, then the arguments that suggest writing is superior to speech are weakened indicating that writing and speaking simply allow us to think *differently*, not better or worse. And finally, even if it were true that writing was a precursor of logical alphabetical thought, this does not entail that writing *caused* logical thought[5] since, for example, logical thought was presumably already happening with Socrates before Plato transcribed him for posterity. In fact, because there is no conclusive evidence for the need to memorize spoken language in the first place, it is hard to see what role writing played at all. It is possible that alphabetic writing simply functioned as cuneiform writing in corresponding to and recording astronomical-mathematical observations or accounting. That new thoughts became possible because of the structures and societies that developed as a result of writing is not the same as saying that writing caused us to think 'better'.

Walter Ong (1982, 1986), another influential historian of literacy who continues the legacy of Havelock, is notoriously credited with the cognitive

---

[5] This is referred to as a *post hoc propter hoc* fallacy, namely the illogical conclusion that derives from stating that if an event precedes another it must have caused the event that follows it. Another way of thinking of this is in relation to the difference between correlation and causation.

theory that writing is, in fact, superior to speech because it raises consciousness by developing reasoning in ways that orality does not. Ong's most cited work, *Orality and Literacy* (1982), argued that the transition from speech to writing in literate societies had a profound impact on the ways in which people thought and argued. Ong makes the seemingly reasonable claim that the technological advent of writing simply makes us think *in a certain way*, suggesting that writing is comparatively, rather than qualitatively, different to other ways of communicating (1986, p. 24):

> Without writing, the literate mind would not and could not think as it does, not only when engaged in writing but even when it is composing its thoughts in oral form.

But Ong soon betrays value judgements that relate to the putative *superiority* of literate thinking (writing-influenced) over non-literate thinking (oral) (1986, pp. 29 and 32):

> We know that totally oral peoples, intelligent and wise though they often are, are incapable of the protracted, intensive linear analysis that we have from Plato's Socrates. ... Like other artificial creations and indeed more than any other, writing is utterly invaluable and indeed essential for the realization of fuller, interior, human potentials ... By distancing thought, alienating it from its original habitat in sounded words, writing raises consciousness. Alienation from a natural milieu can be good for us and indeed is in many ways essential for fuller human life. To live and to understand fully, we need not only proximity but also distance. This writing provides for, thereby accelerating the evolution of consciousness as nothing else before it does.

The above quote is revealing in several other ways. For example, the reference to 'alienation' and 'distance' signals that Ong considers detachment from context ('original habitat' and 'natural milieu') to be a virtue. This might explain why the characterization of academic writing as objective and impersonal has come to be accepted as an inherent epistemic virtue rather than a culturally determined attribute. Elsewhere, Ong also draws attention to the 'cool, analytic processes generated by writing', invoking Plato's shunning of the oral poets in *Phaedrus* (Ong, 1986, p. 29). He goes on to observe that writing has an impersonal quality because it 'separates the world from the living present' in a way that speech does not. Ong's references to writing being 'impersonal', 'cool', 'detached', 'distant' and as providing a 'full consciousness' very much echo in modern-day understandings of academic writing as autonomous, objective and impersonal.

The conflation of writing with the alphabet and with higher-order thinking (e.g. Emig, 1977) clearly has enduring historical and ideological roots and it explains why Turner has referred to it in terms of an 'ontological complicity' (2018, p. 181): it is a complicity because it assumes 'good' thinking cannot take place without 'good' writing and it is ontological because 'good' writing is equated with 'good' thinking. Notwithstanding its misguided legacy, this complicity remains largely unquestioned. Yet, as I have shown, there are reasons to question the assumed qualitative superiority of 'Western' written literacies over other forms of literary practices and to consider the affordances of non-standard, including non-written, communication for expressing higher-order thinking. I turn my attention to this in Chapter 3, after showing that academia itself, the institution of higher-order thinking *par excellence*, has a long tradition of communicating knowledge in a variety of formats, including poetry, a tradition which seems to have become lost in modern-day academic practices.

Varied 'Academic' Writings

One way of approaching a history of English academic writing is to locate it within the history of how universities have historically communicated knowledge. Unfortunately this lies far beyond the scope of this book, but, luckily, I can defer instead to historians of scientific and other academic writings, such as Bazerman (1988), Doody et al. (2012) and Taub (2017), who have painstakingly documented and analysed an impressive catalogue of written academic genres. These include the ancient world's tradition of communicating science via poems, letters, encyclopaedias, commentaries and biographies, to name a few and via modern-day understandings of 'essay'. My aim in this section is to draw on the wealth and breadth of this research to trace an account of how the modern-day imaginary of what makes writing 'academic' celebrates objectivity, linearity, some linguistic standards rather than others, prose and impersonality at the expense of other epistemic virtues, such as creativity, public and popular engagement (to democratize knowledge), recursiveness and composition, multilingualism and multimodality. A note of caution is that what I refer to as 'academic' genres are not necessarily texts that have been written at an academic institution, such as a university, as we now know it: universities as we now think of them have a varied history, and scientific and other knowledge, which we now associate with being generated at institutions of higher learning, has been equally developed within learned societies, such as research centres and royal and religious institutions.

Indeed, academic communication existed long before universities were founded. The first 'Western' European universities are only a thousand years old and even they were late-comers to the world's academic scene, appearing as they did after those in Africa: Al-Qarawwiyyin, in Fez, Morocco, 859 AD, which is still a university; the University of Timbuktu (West Africa) founded in 982 AD 'and attended, throughout the 12th century, by about 25,000 students' (de Sousa Santos, 2017, p. ix) and Al-Azhar University, Cairo, 970 AD. Earlier still, there were universities in China, where the *Dà xué*, the *Great Academy*, was founded in 200 BC by Emperor Wu Di of the Han Dynasty; in India, where ancient centres of learning existed in 300 AD; in Korea, where the Gukhak was founded in 682 AD, and in Japan, where the Daigaku-no kami of the Japanese Imperial Court existed before 794 AD (Peters, 2017). Today, it is the European academies that dominate the global stage, alongside their American and Australian progenies, which are younger still. In Europe, Bologna and Paris are said to be the oldest, founded in 1088 and 1150, respectively, although these dates are contested (Rüegg & Ridder-Symoens, 1992–2011), followed by Oxford 1150 (where teaching occurred earlier, in 1096) and Cambridge in 1209 (Collini, 2012).

These early mediaeval European universities did not require students to write. Teaching and learning were informal arrangements and their official establishment as universities grew out of a need to ensure the financial security of their students and teachers, to promote rationality in the belief of God and to cultivate *la vita contemplativa*, which involved reading, rehearsing and interpreting scriptures. These universities provided practical social solutions to trade and commerce, especially at Bologna University, which built its reputation around the study of Làw. The lecture, where a professor read from books for several hours and the oral *disputatio*, not writing, where students discussed and displayed their knowledge mnemonically rather than interpretatively, were the main forms of academic communication (Clark, 2006; Friesen, 2017; Leedham-Green, 1996).

The emergence of writing as a way to communicate academic knowledge can be traced to the Early Modern/Renaissance university (1500–1800) and specifically, to the advent of the printing press (1450–1700), which allowed the knowledge, languages and vernaculars of pre-print society to become visible and widespread. It became easier to classify information and collect data; to create index pages and multiple maps; and to circulate portraits of leading cultural figures, such as Erasmus and Luther (Eisenstein, 1983, p. 130). The Gutenberg Bible – which lent its name to the 'Gutenberg Revolution', aka 'The Printing

Revolution' – was the first Bible to be printed between 1450 and 1460 using a system of *incunabula* (movable print), allowing for several reprints which facilitated the dissemination of religion and individual, unmediated reading practices. A new, smaller pocket-sized format for books, called the *octavo*, also emerged during this time, making books more portable. This format became known as the 'Aldine' edition named after its Venetian printer-inventor, Aldus Manutius. It was smaller than the previous Gothic formats because it used the *italic* typeface which reduced the space taken on the page allowing more books to be printed more cheaply, thus contributing to the dissemination of knowledge.

Eisenstein (1983) has cautioned, however, that, contrary to default and prevailing historical classifications, what is commonly referred to as the 'Renaissance' took place before the advent of printing,[6] indicating that print simply allowed existing knowledge to circulate rather than to be created *ex novo*. Eisenstein's warning is important because, once again, it guards against unquestioning dispositions towards historical events: the printing press did not take Europe out of the 'dark ages' and into a 're-birth' (Renaissance), as many history books have had us believe. Rather, according to Eisenstein, print simply made visible what was already there. The surreptitious conflation between print and the emergence of knowledge, between the 'dark ages' and the absence of reason, has echoes of the conflation between writing and reason, discussed earlier.

At this time, writing and reading became firmly established in European cultures because of print and this triggered significant social and cultural consequences. For example, between 1500 and 1600, the Reformation movement of Martin Luther, a German Friar and Professor of Theology at Wittenberg University in Saxony, toppled the dominance of the Catholic Church. This was made possible because Luther's Protestant message spread via 'academic' writings called 'theses' famously pinned to his door. Despite the fact that they were not intended to be read by 'the people', Luther's writings became a powerful revolutionary tool that allowed his Reformation to gather momentum (Postman, 1993, p. 65):

> What Luther overlooked was the sheer portability of printed books. Although his theses were written in academic Latin, they were easily transported throughout Germany and other countries by printers who just as easily had them translated into vernaculars.

---

[6] In fact, Francesco Petrarca (1304–74), commonly referred to as a Renaissance poet, died before printing was invented.

This period in history witnessed further transformations such as the rise of individualism and standardization: for those who could read, reading alone and in silence became possible because reading no longer needed to be performed exclusively in a public forum (such as the Church or Lecture); and the sheer volume of publications that print generated meant that writing began to standardize in new ways. Tensions arose between individuality and standardization, for example, in how subjects and landscapes were reproduced in print. Ironically, impersonal standardization also spawned a 'heightened appreciation of individuality' (Eisenstein, 1983, p. 133; Good, 1988), which explains the success of humanist philosopher and essayist Michel de Montaigne (1533–93). His *Essais* proposed a new informal essay style that reclaimed a sense of the personal, private self as a way of counteracting the increasingly standardized, public self that print enabled. Montaigne's personal, introspective and contemplative style became popular because it spoke to the needs of an ever wider, geographically scattered and impersonal readership (Eisenstein, 1983, p. 58):

> Traditional rhetorical conventions had allowed for the difference in tone between addressing a large assemblage in a public arena, where strong lungs and broad strokes were required and pleading a case in a courtroom, which called for careful attention to detail and a more soft-spoken, clearly argued, intimate approach. But no precedent existed for addressing a large crowd of people who were not gathered together in one place but were scattered in separate dwellings and who, as solitary individuals with divergent interests, were more receptive to intimate interchanges than to broad-gauged rhetorical effects. The informal essay which was devised by Montaigne was a most ingenious method for coping with this new situation. He thus established a new basis for achieving intimate contact with unknown readers ... provided a welcome assurance that the isolated sense of singularity which was felt by the solitary reader had been experienced by another human being and was ... capable of being shared.

Montaigne's essay format was to greatly influence the genre of the scientific experimental article (discussed below) because of the way it represented human experience as being both narcissistically personal and distantly objective (Eisenstein, 1983, p. 58):

> Its [the essai's] abbreviated structure reflects both a prescriptive world view, empirical in spirit and observational in method and a sceptical despair of achieving any unified cosmological view. The kind of discursive informalism

and ordinary subject matter epitomized by the French familiar essay had immense philosophical appeal for growing scientific interests in seventeen-century England, which, Bacon had cautioned, would not succeed without a profound literary reform.

(Paradis, 1987, p. 60)

At the same time as Montaigne was challenging standardization and reclaiming individual expression, standards were being imposed by religious and political authorities in attempts to reclaim, stabilize and sanitize language: Latin, the language of authority and Catholicism, had been increasingly co-existing with local 'vulgar' vernaculars, as evidenced by Dante Alighieri's *Divine Comedy* written in Florentine vernacular in 1320 as an attack on and parody of the corruption and double-standards of the Church. The quest for linguistic standards culminated in the establishment, in 1584, of the Italian *Accademia della Crusca*. Some forty years later, in 1635, the French *Académie Française* boasted a similar language-preserving and tradition-entrenching mission (Rüegg & Ridder-Symoens, 1992–2011, p. 11, Vol. 2):

> For the French humanist the correct cultivation of language was the heart of the new educational movement …, in the mediaeval universities, language was raw and barbarous; scholastic textbooks darkened the intellect. It was through reading the ancient and biblical writings in the original languages that light was brought into university education.

The English language has never been able to police its language in this way, despite several attempts (see, for example, Crystal (2003)). As a consequence of this lack of language policing, it has evolved into a porous and flexible system able to accommodate new lexis (Yun & Standish, 2018). Oddly, despite its porousness, or possibly because of it, the English language to this day lends itself to heated controversies about standards and correct usage.

Unlike the Ancient university, the Renaissance university was projected towards action and novelty. It nurtured *la vita activa*, pushing the boundaries of knowledge through human discovery and technology rather than divine intervention. Famously, Columbus's explorations of the Americas in 1492 sparked a wave of 'humanism', understood as the waning of mediaeval and divine reverence and as the waxing of human reason and capacity to understand, explore, conquer and colonize the world (Rüegg & Ridder-Symoens, 1992–2011, Vol. 2).

The emergence of new genres to communicate this knowledge marks the humanist era.

Several important academic literary and scientific genres re-emerged during this period, including the Chronicle, the Dialogue and the Letters (Bazerman, 1988; Eisenstein, 1983; Taub, 2017). Chronicles were used to record the travels of explorers because this format lent itself to being written on the move and to recording un-analysed geographic, anthropologic and botanical observations. The dialogue afforded opportunities to engage in conversation and discussion *with* the classics rather than showing uncritical deference to them by reporting or transcribing them *verbatim*. This genre was revived by Galileo's well-known literary outputs. Crucially, Galileo broke away from the established scientific writing conventions of his time, including his own, to re-propose the discredited Copernican heliocentric theory both in dialogue form and in Tuscan, the local vernacular of Pisa (where he taught). In doing so, like Dante (and in an act of what might be considered by modern standards as 'public engagement' or 'open access'), he broke away from the use of Latin and was able to reach non-academic and non-scientific audiences who proved to be more open to persuasion than his recalcitrant and sceptical scientific colleagues (Eisenstein, 1983, pp. 251–3):

> Galileo's Dialogue on Two World Systems was such a provocative and polemical treatise, however, it almost seemed to court censorship in a way that is quite typical of most serious scientific work. The same thing cannot be said of his later treatise which helped to found classical physics: the Discourses on Two New Sciences. ... No great cosmic or philosophical questions intrude into this unimpassioned treatise ... it is about as controversial and stirring as some freshman lecture on mechanics, of which indeed, it is the ultimate source. ... The crowing irony of Galileo's career is that the failure of the great Dialogues should be so much more interesting than the success of the unobjectionable Discourses.

Other sixteenth-century scientists, such as philosopher Francis Bacon and mathematician Johannes Kepler, also broke with the tradition of using Latin, preferring instead to use vernaculars which lent themselves to greater dissemination via the printed word 'in an effort to convey the new spirit and methods of scientific philosophy' (Postman, 1993, p. 64).

And finally, the epistolary genre also thrived during these centuries as academics and natural philosophers (later to be called scientists[7]) began to publish work in and correspond via the two most influential academic journals

---

[7] The term 'scientist' wasn't coined until 1833 by William Whewell Ross, S. (1962). Scientist: The story of a word. *Annals of Science*, 18(2), 65–85. https://doi.org/http://dx.doi.org/10.1080/00033796200202722

of the time, the *Journal des Savan(t)s* and the *Philosophical Transactions*, both established in 1665. In particular, Henry Oldenburg, the first editor of the *Philosophical Transactions*, was keen to encourage correspondence and debate. He became known for being a 'present' editor who enthusiastically mediated between the readers and the article writers, publishing letters that became scientific documents in their own right and gradually allowing contributors to have more voice (Bazerman, 1988). Significantly, he published the work of international scientists, such as biologist Marcello Malpighi (Eisenstein, 1983), who were being ignored or censored in their native countries and published the correspondence with Isaac Newton in both English and Latin (Bazerman, 1988, p. 84), reflecting the widespread multilingualism of the scientific community.

Having briefly tended to the re-emergence of the chronicle, the dialogue and the letters as examples of ancient genres that were re-purposed to better communicate the knowledge of their time, I now turn to the specific relevance of the *Philosophical Transactions* to current academic writing practices. It is in fact the scientific genre of the experimental article that has survived and become the model for the ubiquitous academic essay. The genealogy of the experimental article has been meticulously traced by Charles Bazerman (1988) in *Shaping Written Knowledge*. Bazerman tracks its evolution from its early reports and descriptions of unusual events using the language of 'curiosity and wonder', whereby science was reported as uncontested and devoid of theory or methodology, to the increasingly careful illustration and precise reporting of methods and experiments. Attention to how methods were reported signalled the need to dispel controversies that were beginning to emerge as scientists were no longer individuals working alone to report what they saw in nature. Instead, they were increasingly being held to account publicly via the journals they corresponded in and in their presentations to learned societies. The function of drawings and illustrations also changed. Hitherto, they had been deployed to *represent* nature. By the 1700s, they became the methods and instruments for *understanding* it, as explained below with reference to Robert Boyle and his physico-mechanical experiments with pneumatics in the 1600s (Shapin, 1984, p. 492):

> The sort of naturalistic images that Boyle favoured provided a greater density of circumstantial detail than would have been proffered by more schematic representations. The images served to announce that 'this was really done' and that it was done in the way stipulated; they allayed distrust and facilitated virtual witnessing. Therefore, understanding the role of pictorial

representations offers a way of appreciating what Boyle was trying to achieve with his literary technology.

Along with images, language also developed to reflect greater attention to how methods were reported. In 1672, Newton writes with the intention of eliminating uncertainty towards his optical findings. He develops a new rhetorical style to deal with criticisms, a form of compelling argument which becomes a closed system in which opposing arguments are reduced to errors. He writes with the intention of making his writing appear as fact, not controversy and finds ways of shaping it to avoid ambiguity by artfully guiding the reader step-by-step through an experiment expressed in self-referential language – recalling the meandering, explorative and tentative style of Montaigne – all the while intending to report what he believes to be an objectively observable phenomenon: the style evoked is that of a neutral observer 'stumbling across a fact'. Bazerman analyses a section of the carefully crafted rhetorical style of Newton's 'A New Theory of Light and Colours', an article published in the *Transactions* in 1672, highlighting the prominence of first person pronouns to reflect that it is the author-narrator-scientist who is making the discoveries (Bazerman, 1988, p. 91):

> This earlier part of the article relies heavily on the language of personal thought and agency as it unfolds the attempts of a baffled investigator to come to terms with a robustly visible phenomenon. The first person followed by an active verb forms the armature of most sentences: 'I suspected', 'I thought', 'I took another Prisme', 'I then proceeded to examine more critically', 'Having made these observations, I first computed from them'. At key moments he offers quantitative descriptions of his experiments, switching to third person existential statements: 'Its distance from the hole or Prisme was 22 feet; its utmost length 13¼ inches.' But even experimental quantities are framed by his limited agency: "The refractions were as near as I could make them, equal and consequently about 54 deg. 4'" (93). The orderliness with which he pursues and isolates the phenomenon gives rhetorical warrant to the degree of facticity of language Newton allows himself in this section. That is, the credibility of the investigation helps establish the credibility of the fact and the credibility of the investigator.

Rather than a representation of speech (and its alphabet), the scientific language of seventeenth-century Europe is now a conduit for channelling mental thoughts from the mind of the truth-knowing writer/observer to the mind of the sceptical reader (Russell, 2002; Turner, 2010). Language becomes invested with the responsibility to not simply *report* what the scientist sees as an objective natural reality, but to also *persuade* a sceptical reader. Contrast this style of writing with the mnemonic verses of Homer, Pindar and Aeschylus which required no reporting verbs, suggesting that for the pre-Socratics, reality did not need to be interpreted, it simply needed to be told (Olson, 1994, p. 193). The term 'verbatim' had been coined by the 1400s, suggesting that already by then, a new linguistic awareness was dawning relating to how a text could fix and stabilize meaning. English began to borrow reporting verbs from Latin, such as *imply,* to signal mental state verbs which indicated that an interpretation was taking place as opposed to an unhedged factual description of nature (Daston & Galison, 2010; Olson, 1994). With the 1700s came the development of theories of interpretation to understand what was 'in' the text, not what could be 'read' into it (hermeneutics). Because knowledge was becoming increasingly contested, the following authority-conveying features began to emerge in scientific writing: the use of nominalizations as grammatical metaphors to reify and de-personalize activities, presenting them as facts rather than processes; acknowledgements (in the form of references) to build allegiances but also to comply with the new 1710 intellectual property copyright encoded into British law (Pennycook, 1996); hedging language such as *probably* and *might be* to indicate speculation before a bold conclusion; and introductions to conflicts between theories began appearing in Volume 40 of the *Transactions* (1737) to signal that a hypothesis preceded the account of the experiment, even when there was no contention. The need to report accurately and clearly meant that language became 'invested with the role of "mapping" knowledge, without drawing attention to itself as part of the map. In other words, it has to be transparent' (Turner, 2010, p. 63).

Fast forwarding to more recent times, a period of great university expansion occurred during the 1900s following their decline during the French Revolution and the Napoleonic wars. Of immense significance was the influence of Wilhelm von Humboldt, a German scholar and statesman credited with founding, in 1810, the modern 'Western' concept of the research university, which has particularly left its imprint on US universities and on Oxbridge in Britain (Rüegg & Ridder-Symoens, 1992–2011, Vols. 3 and 4; Russell, 2002). The Humboldtian university fully embraced the growing faith in science, reason, discovery and empiricism of the previous centuries making 'research' its core, essential nuclear foundation. According to Friedrich Schleiermacher, the liberal theologian and philosopher who inspired Humboldt (Vol. 3, p. 5):

> the function of the university was not to pass on recognised and directly usable knowledge such as the schools and colleges did, but rather to demonstrate how this knowledge is discovered, to stimulate the idea of science in the minds of the students, to encourage them to take into account the fundamental laws of science in all their thinking.

At the same time, the increased professionalization of research and of salaried university staff, coupled with an increase in standardization processes and widening participation – compared with the 1700s, when no academic qualifications were needed to study at university and no written exams existed before 1820 (Leedham-Green, 1996, p. 125)[8] – led to a steep rise in assessment procedures with written assignments becoming the main means through which to assess students, replacing the oral seminars or the more traditional *disputatio*. This, according to Kruse (2006, p. 348), 'turned writing into a constraint that threatened to exclude [students] if they did not master the writing assignments'.

In terms of content and the structure of language, the written research paper began to stabilize and increasingly emphasize methods, a phenomenon that had begun in the early 1700s. Findings and conclusions, especially in Medicine, discussed consequences of hypotheses and experiments at the end of a paper in terms of logical deductions of the facts. These were presented using impersonal language such as nominalizations and making explicit reference to methods; citations began to develop into codified networks of acknowledgements and sentence structure became increasingly complex: noun and subordinate clauses increased (signalling intellectual complexity), even though sentence length and syntactical complexity remained stable at around 70 per cent simple and 30 per cent complex (Bazerman, 1988). All this suggests that scientific discourse was fairly homogenous during this time. That it continues to remain relatively stable to this day can be explained by the fact that these fixed, somewhat formulaic, forms have become 'encapsulated' by a dependency on the way knowledge is produced whereby findings and bold claims are foregrounded to serve the interests of (Bazerman, 2015, p. 267)

> university departments and professional societies (with their structures of rewards and advancements), government and business interests and funding (based on perceived needs for scientific and technological knowledge), knowledge-based professions that pervade contemporary society (with their reliance on systems of authority and credentials), expanding educated populations who look toward science for knowledge and evolving technologies and systems for the production and distribution of texts (including cheap printing, commercial publishing companies, university and professional libraries, national mail systems and international agreements), despite advances in digital technology.[9]

---

[8] The grading of papers had been introduced for the first time in 1792 at Cambridge University. Postman, N. (1993). *Technopoly: The surrender of culture to technology.* Vintage Books.

[9] Despite the stability of genres described by Bazerman, Hyland, K., & Feng (Kevin), J. (2017). Is academic writing becoming more informal? *English for Specific Purposes*, 45, 40–51. https://doi.org/http://dx.doi.org/10.1016/j.esp.2016.09.001 have begun to detect some linguistic informality in academic writing in what they call 'illicit initials', i.e. starting a sentence with 'and', 'but' or 'so'.

But just as the humanist University was characterized by the contradictory dualisms of expressive individualism (epitomized by Montaigne) and technological standardization (triggered by print), so too was the university of the twentieth century caught between competing ways of thinking: on the one hand, a staunch faith in the precision and exactitude of science meant that hitherto 'unscientific' disciplines such as philology and (applied) linguistics became scientized (Orman, 2016), systematized (Harris & Taylor, 1989) and unified into an object of study that assumes language lies outside of us and can be a conduit for thought that is independent of its users (Yun & Standish, 2018). On the other, the emphasis on clarity, transparency of language and logic triggered a literary 'relativist turn' (Turner, 2010). This encouraged the reader to bring their own understanding to the text and to question the authority of both the author and the written word (Olson, 1994). Writers, historians, social critics and philosophers such as Richard Rorty, Michel Foucault, Jacques Derrida, Jacques Lacan, Roland Barthes, Thomas Kuhn and Paul Feyerabend, even the Ludwig Wittgenstein of *The Philosophical Investigations* (Sigmund, 2017), became controversially known as the post-modernists who 'relativized' knowledge, reified 'discourse' and generally questioned the power of language to 'refer' to reality. In so doing, they developed an influential rhetorical style of their own which, unlike the grammar of the research article, privileged sentence length and syntactical subordination[10] as a way of displaying *through form* the complex interconnectedness of reality, particularly social, psychological and philosophical reality.

Writing and Its Ideologies

As Bazerman has shown, writing has the power to shape knowledge. Because of this power, several scholars have been concerned with how writing also enacts political and social 'ideologies'. For the sake of brevity, I simply take ideology to mean 'worldviews', although I acknowledge the nuance and contention that such a loaded word warrants because of its connotations (see, for example, Hannah Arendt (1953), who defines ideology literally as 'the logic of an idea' and follows this through with an account of how following the logic of an idea can result in 'terror').

---

[10] Wittgenstein's aphoristic style is clearly an exception to this.

This section, therefore, limits itself to signposting rather than developing the link between academic writing practices and ideology because similar ideas have either already been hinted at or will re-merge in subsequent chapters. For now, it is sufficient to note that literacy practices, which include academic writing, are ideological in the sense that they enact worldviews. This has already transpired from the above discussion where I argued that 'Western' views of literacy have invested alphabetical writing with the power to 'raise consciousness' and improve thinking in ways that other writing systems do not. This worldview contrasts with other worldviews whereby literacies do not need to be alphabetic to develop and display 'good thinking' (Arnheim, 1969; Kara, 2015; Kuttner et al., 2017).

In his history of the American university curriculum, Russell (2002) documents how academic writings enact what he calls 'ideal' social practices. When these are dictated by the needs of industry, writing becomes specialized and technical. When they are motivated by a research ideal, such as the Humboldtian faith in the fundamental laws of science, not only do they prevent any other genre from taking root, but they impose a straightjacket on the genres of all disciplines (Russell, 2002, pp. 71, 79, 85):

> To understand why certain forms of student writing endured and others faded, or why certain pedagogies included writing and others did not, one must look to the character of the research ideal and the ways it interacted with writing in the new mass education system .... German scholarship rapidly set a new standard for academic writing, not only in the sciences but also in the emerging humanities and social sciences because disciplines viewed student writing through the narrow lens of their own research writing, they rarely explored other possibilities.

Russell further posits that these 'ideals' can morph into 'ideologies' (2002, p. 269). He exemplifies this with reference to two progressive US writing programmes in the 1950s and 1960s which were abolished because they prioritized the developmental and learning potential of writing over its specialized, skills-based technical nature. These programmes drew significantly on the progressive ideas of Arthur N. Applebee, an educationalist who regarded writing as integral to the learning process and was associated with progressive left-wing political ideals of equality and inclusion. Given the right-wing conservative political tendencies of the United States at the time, according to Russell, the association with a left-wing progressive thinker might explain why such programmes were not maintained. Several other writing scholars have similarly claimed that writing 'reproduces the ideologies and inequities of the institution and society' (Archer & Breuer, 2016, p. 42); that academic writing as it is practised and taught in today's academy is 'ideological, transparent, objective and autonomous' (Bennett, 2015; Lea & Street, 1998; Street, 1984); that it embodies 'exclusionary ideologies' (Lillis, 2001; Scott, 2013; Thesen & Cooper, 2013; Turner, 2018) and that by focusing on accuracy and standards, it privileges conservative, elitist and undemocratic 'ideologies' (Rose, 1985).

As also shown by Fairclough (2001) and Bourdieu and Thompson (1991), language wields great power in enacting political ideologies. The 1900s witnessed the emergence of English as the *lingua franca* of academic research, replacing French and German (and Latin). This signalled a shift in economic and political power from mainland Europe (once the heart of academia) to the UK and the United States (now setting higher education agendas). The key events that cemented the shift to English include: the establishment of the American university based on the German research model (Russell, 2002); the two world wars, which intensified and prioritized scientific research to serve the war industry (Russell, 2002); the consequences of nineteenth-century colonialism (Mbembe, 2008; Morris, 2010; Said, 1978), then of de-colonialism (such as India gaining its independence in 1947) and then again of post-colonialism, which meant that European countries, including the UK, had obligations to educate those it had colonized but also to maintain a form of 'soft power' to ensure allegiances (Peters, 2017). Indeed, the English language can be described as what Blommaert (2010) calls a 'language regime', namely a complex sociolinguistic 'multiplex item' that is mobilized to create dynamics of exclusion and marginalization. In this sense, language becomes ideological because it compounds what counts as 'good' and 'bad' English, even in multilingual contexts, where different kinds of English have evolved for a range of purposes that no longer warrant reference to a 'correct' standard.

Since English is the language of academia, it retains the soft power to enact the ideology of the dominant 'West'. However, and somewhat more insidiously, the dominance of English (and of a certain variety of English, the one that conflates objectivity with an epistemic virtue) as the language of academia enacts linguistic injustices that exclude many from global academic conversations. This has been documented in Turner (2010), Politzer-Ahles et al. (2020), Politzer-Ahles et al. (2016), Lillis and Curry (2010b, 2015) and Hanauer et al. (2019). This is why Turner, in discussing EAP, claims (2010, p. 78) that

Academic writing should not be seen as autonomous or given. It is not an autonomous set of skills or a discrete set of rhetorical values that have been arrived independently, or been designated as such by some kind of decree. It is rather a cultural practice that has been invested in rhetorical values that are themselves the effects of wider cultural processes.

Moreover, ideologies are gendered because worldviews reflect the values of all individuals. Feminist writings enact ideologies that are 'situated' (Haraway, 1988), meaning that they acknowledge, through language, the bodies that produce them, the emotions that accompany them and the processes, constraints and locations that engendered them. They are typically contrasted with the confident certitude of male-authored objective, rational, impersonal texts. For feminist scholar Haraway, like Laurel Richardson referred to in Chapter 1, discourses of 'objectivity' are 'enshrined in elementary textbooks and technoscience booster literature' (Haraway, 1988, p. 576); yet, even scientists know that this is not how science is 'actually made', because the history of science also tells us that science is achieved through trial, error and incertitude (Kuhn, 1962). Instead, Haraway argues her stance in a style that academic writing textbooks do not showcase, presumably because her writing does not display the features of academicness that the standardized academic writing industry privileges. This omission is ideological, too, because it denies students the opportunity to be exposed to forms of academic writing that embody different worldviews by subscribing to other epistemic virtues, such as situated knowledge and feminist epistemologies, and that communicate knowledge through the use other kinds of prose, such as creative non-fiction (Gutkind, 1997), to narrate factually accurate stories that draw on a range of literary styles, such as personal memoirs and lyric essays (which combine prose and poetry).

Ideologies are also technological. Postman describes these in terms of a 'competition' whereby one technology vies to dominate another in order to gain advantage (1993, p. 16):

> New technologies compete with old ones—for time, for attention, for money, for prestige, but mostly for dominance of their world-view. This competition is implicit once we acknowledge that a medium contains an ideological bias. And it is a fierce competition, as only ideological competitions can be. It is not merely a matter of tool against tool—the alphabet attacking ideographic writing, the printing press attacking the illuminated manuscript, the photograph attacking the art of painting, television attacking the printed word. When media make war against each other, it is a case of world-views in collision.

The idea that technologies embody a worldview is also captured in McLuhan (1964), who argued that technologies are 'extensions of man [sic]' because they embody the values of who creates them and deploys them. In his oft-quoted *dictum*, the 'medium is the message' (1964, p. 13), he was referring to the fact that language divorced from the context through which it communicates, its medium, becomes meaningless. For McLuhan, the 'context' of language includes the media (e.g. the words, visuals, sounds) through which language is carried. To understand a message one therefore needs to account for the medium through which that message is conveyed. Since that medium includes language, the affordances of language – its opportunities and potentials as well as its constraints – need to be acknowledged because as Bezemer and Kress (2008, p. 190) remind us in their multimodal and socio-semiotic analysis of scientific textbooks, there is always 'something lost and something gained' when we move between media (a process known as 'transduction', i.e. translating meanings from one medium to another such as from word to image) and that even in our choice of fonts and how we organize space on the page, we are communicating our ideologies to our readers:

> [The] use of layout realizes an ideology of simplicity of display that is comparable to what is often said about sans serif fonts: That is, providing less 'information' is seen as apt for those regarded to have a lesser capacity to process information.

A further way in which ideology can be enacted through writing relates to epistemic injustice. By measuring academic competence almost exclusively through writing assessments that require standards of literacy that are exclusionary, we restrict which knowledge and whose knowledge is allowed to emerge. This point has been made by Flores and Rosa (2015), who have called out the raciolinguistic ideologies that underpin the monolingual literacy standards to which bilingual Spanish speakers are expected to conform, standards which discourage multilingualism from the American classroom. In this sense, excluding knowledge and ways of thinking not traditionally communicated in writing amounts to a form of 'epistemic injustice' (Carel & Kidd, 2014), namely an unfairness towards the way somebody communicates their knowledge because their background, upbringing, education, interests and abilities differ from the standard and because *we* (the readers/receivers) don't understand why somebody is communicating the way they are. The phrase 'epistemic injustice' was coined by moral philosopher Miranda Fricker (2007) to refer to the ways in which the words of a speaker (in our case, a writer) are ignored, derided or simply misunderstood because the hearer (or the reader) is negatively or ignorantly pre-disposed towards the speaker (writer). This negative predisposition could involve racist, sexist or educational biases, such as those implied by Rose (1989) when discussing Lucia's exclusion from the psychology class (see Chapter 1): Lucia was excluded on the grounds that she didn't have the language of academic psychology; yet, she was knowledgeable because of her situated experience of mental illness. Instances of epistemic injustice also resonate throughout Sperlinger et al. (2018), who argue that higher education should be made accessible to a far greater range of people and throughout life, not only at the age of eighteen. And finally, since translanguaging and codeswitching form part of a complex ecology of literacies whereby multilingualism is the norm for many students and academics, not the exception, preventing writers from making meaning and communicating their knowledge by drawing on a range of resources (i.e. polysemiosis) amounts to an ideology of discrimination (Canagarajah, 2011, 2013b, 2013c, 2018).

Conclusions

History as a method for understanding the phenomena we care about has two main functions: it allows us to trace the genealogies of phenomena so that we can identify key junctures at which things might have turned out differently; it lends itself to being selected to advance a particular worldview. In this chapter, I have challenged the histories that conflate writing with the alphabet and with higher-order thinking, arguing instead that writing did not have to be conflated with the alphabet and that although it has been, this does not mean that alphabetic cultures are better at thinking than oral or visual cultures. I have also highlighted that within academic writing cultures there is a thriving diversity of genres; yet, modern-day standards of academic writing seem to have evolved from and reified only one, the experimental article. Selecting the histories that have colluded with the idea that writing raises consciousness and that academic writing is 'objective' amounts to an ideological stance that leads to unjust practices, such as the exclusion of knowledge that is not presented 'objectively' in written form.

3

What Makes Writing Academic: Learning from Writings 'in the Wild'

Introduction

> what is academic writing? What is an academic community? Wide-ranging change will occur only if the academy redefines writing for itself, changes the terms of the argument, (and) sees instruction in writing as one of its central concerns.
>
> (Rose, 1985, p. 359)

At this pivotal point in the story about what makes writing academic, I showcase the diversity of academic texts by drawing attention to writings that roam naturally, 'in the wild', so to speak. Like Rose, I call for a re-definition of academic writing, one that is more inclusive and diverse, less standardized and prescriptive, less wedded to the ideologies associated with alphabetic literacies and more open to diverse ways of communicating knowledge. With reference to multimodal and multilingual doctoral theses and other modes that do not rely on the linearity of the alphabet and of prose to be 'academic', I highlight the role that writer agency can play in shaping written knowledge. In this and the remaining chapters, I will argue that what makes writing academic are the emergent varied, current and future practices of the academy, including its values.

Chapter 3 posits that what makes writing academic, namely its 'academicness', cannot be reduced to any particular feature. Secondly, it explains the naturally occurring diversity of academic writings with reference to Adler-Kassner and Wardle (2015)'s threshold concepts in writing studies. And, thirdly, it shows that 'argument', commonly assumed to be *the* defining characteristic of academic writing, is one of the features that can make it academic, but it is not the only one.

Academicness

I use the term 'academicness' to refer to a holistic property of a text, i.e. the totality of what makes it academic rather than, for example, legal or poetic. A property is a quality that can be predicated of *whole* objects, like colour, shape, sound, or taste. It is a quality that does not pick out any single or uniquely identifying *part* of the whole object (Sellars, 1963). In this sense, academicness is like 'meaning': it emerges from a context and cannot be reduced to a 'single element that stands alone' because it is 'relational' and 'holistic' in structure (Malpas, 2002, p. 407).

Since it emerges, 'academicness' is not dependent on the presence or absence of specific features relating to language, genre moves or argument. If what made writing academic could be reduced to these specific features, then hoax academic papers such as those by Alan Sokal (Cuthbert, 2018; Franca & Lloyd, 2000; Sokal, 1996, 2008) and Ike Antkare (Labbé, 2010; Labbé & Labbé, 2012; Van Noorden, 2014) would count as academic in virtue of the fact that they display the features that standard academic writing programmes readily teach as 'academic' (such as the passive voice): despite displaying conventional academic *forms*, hoaxes promulgate 'nonsense' (Alvesson et al., 2017) and, in so doing, they fail to adhere to the standards of excellence (MacIntyre, 1985) inherent to socio-academic practices (SAPs). These SAPs include epistemic virtues such as a commitment to the truth (Connell, 2013), to academic integrity (Zgaga, 2009), to social justice (Case, 2013) and to innovation and research (Warnock, 1989). Such commitments require an ethical orientation towards honesty, an orientation that must be intentional and originate from an agent, in this case the writer. Neither an automated generator of academic jargon (C. Labbé, personal communication March 25, 2014; Labbé & Labbé, 2012) nor the deliberate human intention to mislead and distort disciplinary knowledge (Sokal, 2008) is commensurate with these standards of socio-academic excellence. It is in this sense that academic hoaxes do not count as academic because academicness cannot be reduced to its forms and because there are no inherent standards of excellence from which academicness can emerge. Clearly, however, those who published these articles, the editor-readers of *Social Text* and *Springer* (for Sokal and Antkare, respectively) believed them to be genuinely academic, probably because they based their judgements of academicness on the form of the texts (i.e. they looked and sounded academic). Sokal (2008) has documented these reasons. They include the editors' appreciation of post-modern academic jargon and relativist conclusions which suggested to them that the text was *bona fide*.

Similarly, Van Noorden (2014) has indicated that the fake papers published by *Springer* had 'characteristic vocabulary', meaning the kind of recognizable academic jargon that a fake text generator, in this case SCIgen, had been programmed to produce.

If the text itself, i.e. its form, has the power to generate this level of confidence in the reader, then this might suggest that the academicness of a text resides in the text itself and/or in the reader's perception of it. Accordingly, hoaxes might indeed count as academic in virtue of the reader's *perception* of their academicness. However, this is an uncomfortable position to hold because readers can be wrong, in the sense of being misled. Alternatively, rather than relying on the reader's perception, the academicness of a text might reside in the author's intent (Fish, 2017). The writings of twentieth-century analytic philosopher Ludwig Wittgenstein's are a case in point. Wittgenstein famously wrote his philosophy of logic and language using aphorisms, namely short, sequenced statements that express a definition or truth in a literary style that is terse and that can seem brusque (Wittgenstein & Russell, 1922). Do his aphorisms count as 'academic' writing? Would an undergraduate or postgraduate or doctoral student be allowed to write like this? Why? This remains contentious, yet the debate surrounding whether they count as academic hasn't prevented them from remaining established and cited, in the disciplinary (academic) discourses of analytic philosophy (Sigmund, 2017, p. 128):

> Wittgenstein confided to Russell [one of his PhD supervisors (the other was G. E. Moore)] that no one would ever understand the book, although it was, as he put it, 'crystal clear.' Elsewhere, however, he noted: 'I am aware that all these sentences are unclear.' As he seemed to realize at least to some extent, his style struck an odd balance between moments of dazzling lucidity and moments of total opacity, reflecting the tension between his yearning for clear expression and his awareness that some things simply cannot be expressed ... Wittgenstein's style was at once cryptic and crystalline.

How could a text that was both 'clear' and 'unclear' become such a classic of analytical philosophy? One possible reason is that Wittgenstein was well known and sufficiently well regarded in his intellectual circles, namely Cambridge University, for his ideas to be trusted and his writing respected. This suggests that it is the ideas, the extent to which a person is known and accepted in their academic community and the academic standards of excellence of an academic community, that determine what makes a text academic, not the form of the text itself. Compare this to the treatment of philosopher Jacques Derrida, deemed to be a 'charlatan' and unworthy of an honorary degree in Philosophy by philosophers trained in the analytic tradition of Cambridge University, like Wittgenstein and Russell: Derrida, unlike Wittgenstein, apparently, did not meet the 'accepted standards of clarity and rigour' of 'normal and universal' writing (Peters, 2009). Yet, Wittgenstein's *Tractatus Logicus Philosophicus* (which was also his PhD thesis) was rejected by several publishers because of its cryptic style, indicating that a judgement about the text was concurrently being made on the basis of the text itself and/or the reader's perception of it. Eventually, the *Tractatus* was accepted for publication thanks to Bertrand Russell's introduction and endorsement, which further signals that 'knowing who the author is and endorsing their intentions' may have more bearing on what is considered 'academic' than the form of the text itself.

This complex relationship between authorial intent, reader perception and text meaning lies at the heart of what makes writing academic. It matters because it has implications for who gets published and what grade an essay receives. Debates about this relationship have an established literary history that highlights the messy complexity of how and whether it is the text that represents knowledge or the author. This complexity can be described in terms of the tension between textual authority and authorship (linked to a foundational conceptualization of the author as the ultimate source of knowledge), on the one hand and interpretations and reader meaning-making (referred to as hermeneutics, whereby it is the reader who brings meaning to the text through interpretation), on the other. That the author's intended meaning is irrelevant to the interpretation of a text is referred to in literary theory as the 'intentional fallacy'. Proponents of this fallacy are Barthes (1967); Wimsatt and Beardsley (1946) and Foucault (1969). Strictly speaking, on their account, it would not matter that Sokal and Antkare are hoaxes because if the academicness (or meaning) resides in the text, not the author, then nothing more than the text is needed to judge its academicness. Conversely, proponents of the thesis that authorial intent *does* matter include Knapp and Michaels (1982) and Fish (2017). Knapp and Michaels collapse 'the author's intended meaning' with 'the text meaning' arguing that we cannot 'derive one term from the other, since to have one is already to have both' (1982, p. 724). For them, only authorial intent establishes text meaning in the sense that the intent *is* the text (i.e. the text is an expression of the author's intent). Stanley Fish also points to the culture of plagiarism as further evidence that authorial intent and originality *are* measures of academicness: if intent didn't matter, he argues, then why would the 'West' be so concerned with plagiarism and originality (Jones, 2014; Moynihan, 2015; Pennycook, 1996)?

The Sokal and Antkare texts complicate matters further. Despite both being hoaxes, they differ in at least one crucial way: one was written by a human and the other by a computer. If we appeal to author intent, following Knapp and Michaels (1982) and Fish (2017), then the Antkare texts are clearly not academic because they cannot enact any SAP (further outlined later in this chapter) since they were generated by a computer and, typically, computers do not have intent. But, following Barthes and other proponents of the 'intentionalist fallacy', Sokal's article could count as 'academic' because it displays 'predictable and recognisable patterns' that readers would normally expect in an academic text: it is researched in the traditional sense of 'referring to relevant literature'; it made sense to its intended audience; and, worryingly, it remains (as I write this) in circulation and available in *Social Text* via an established academic publisher, JSTOR (Sokal, 1996). The fact the text is published in an academic journal further confers institutional legitimacy to the text, giving it academic credibility. Moreover, at the time, the article generated genuine academic debate around what counts as knowledge (see, for example, Dawkins [1998]). What makes us reluctant to call it 'academic', however, is not its content but the *intention* with which it was produced and perhaps more importantly, the dishonesty of this intention: Sokal intended to parody and discredit critical theory and did not believe his own arguments.

In the Sokal case, intent becomes a contributing factor in whether a text is deemed to be academic, whereby his *dishonest* intent detracts from the academic credibility of his text. But this, too, is an uncomfortable conclusion to reach because it suggests that intent matters: if the intent were *honest*, would this change our perception of whether the text is academic? For example, despite being 'unclear', was Wittgenstein 'sufficiently honest' to warrant being published? Moreover, how do we establish authorial intent, when the author may not be available to confirm what their intent was? A further problem with appealing to the author's intention to determine whether a text is *bona fide* academic or not is that, to the joy of many students and academics, this would confer to the writer ultimate jurisdiction as to whether their writing counts as academic or not because only the writer can know what they intended.

Both the hoax and Sokal's subsequent justification for it raise further unsettling prospects for determining what makes a text academic: on the one hand, the hoax was read as an 'academic' text; on the other, none of it was 'true'. If we accept, as I do, that a necessary value of higher education is a commitment to 'truth' or to 'realness' (understood broadly from a critical realist perspective as the recognition that external ontologies exist [Bengtsen & Barnett, 2017]), then the hoax was not academic. But if we accept this, then we also have to accept that the commercial tests relied upon by universities to predict the writing abilities of students, such as the IELTS and Pearson Tests of Academic English, are not academic either. This is because they are written to display language and mimic academic essay forms, not to advance truthful, or real, accounts of the world.

To sum up, what I am claiming so far is that when we invoke the formal markers of academicness as standards by which to judge whether a text is academic or not, hoaxes would count as academic but the unconventional texts I refer to next would not. This is because unconventional texts – academic writings that don't conform to the imaginary of what an academic text should look like – display the 'wrong' sort of language and moves and certainly not the kind of academic language that EAP writing programmes and textbooks are likely to engage with because they do not meet putative standards of academicness. Yet, such texts circulate in 'the wild' and are imbricated in the structures of academic knowledge communication. They include, alongside many others, the graphic doctoral dissertation of Nick Sousanis (2015), the musical PhD exegesis of A. D. Carson (2017), the playful and feminist PhD thesis of Harron (2016), the aphorisms of Ludwig Wittgenstein and earlier still, the scientific dialogues of Galileo Galilei's *Two Chief World Systems*.[1]

Crucially, the need for these academic texts to break with convention was not driven by the arbitrary whim, or intention, of their authors. These academic writers broke the rules on epistemic grounds: their textual forms afford knowledge representation that conventional forms, arguably, do not. Theoretical physicist Daniel Shanahan (2015), for example, holds the form of the scientific article to account by calling for it to become a 'living document' that allows more space to report methods rather than results. Since what matters most in scientific research is the appropriateness of the methods used and the extent to which these can be replicated to yield sound findings, methods need to become more prominent in scientific writing. Instead, findings rather than methods tend to be given more prominence in abstracts and in the way journals 'market' key findings. By not giving due prominence to methods and by granting more visibility to the findings of scientific research, the 'form' of the academic paper amounts to a scientific 'fraud'. This fraud is further compounded when superlative language is

---

[1] Clearly, Galilei's dialogues were written before modern academic conventions existed. My point here, however, is that Galilei chose the dialogue genre to propose his heliocentric thesis as opposed to the more conventional prose and less controversial thesis of his other work on classical physics (cf. Chapter 2).

used to inflate the significance of the findings (Vinkers et al., 2015). By allowing more published space for methods, scientists would curb the *unscientific* drive that publishers have towards prioritizing controversial or trending results which are more likely to capture the attention of a superficial audience than satisfy the needs of the scientific community. Shanahan, therefore, advocates that we re-configure the scientific article so that we can move beyond the now-obsolete print model and truly embrace the freedom that online publication gives us, moving towards living documents that can be updated, amended, extended and indeed directly linked to other articles and data.

Shanahan's living physics document, Sousanis's visual interdisciplinary argument, Carson's aural anti-racist activism and Harron's black feminist mathematics can all be classified as examples of what Bazerman (1988) means by 'shaping' knowledge or of what literacy scholar Lunsford means when she claims that writing is 'epistemic', namely that it doesn't 'simply record thought or knowledge but ... has the capacity to actually produce thought and knowledge' (2015).[2] In drawing attention to these academic writers-authors, I am highlighting that the academicness of a text can be explained in terms of an *interaction* between the structural elements available in the textual environment (such as form, grammar, genre and reader expectations) and the disciplinary knowledge, values and intentions of the writer who has agency in shaping the text. What makes these four authors 'academic' thus becomes an interaction between, on the one hand, the writer's disciplinary values and their intention to 'shape knowledge' by giving more space to methods, visuals, rap and voice, respectively, thus upholding the epistemic integrity of the scientific, interdisciplinary, socially just and feminist endeavour and, on the other, what the textual environment affords in terms of structures that enable this to happen, such as the possibilities afforded by the online medium in the case of Shanahan's living document or the fact that there are other ways of writing non-fiction that still fulfil the academic standards of excellence required for the award of a PhD in mathematics.

What makes the text academic is thus irreducible to either the writer's intentions or to the structural form of the text.

---

[2] N. B.: As argued in Chapter 2 with reference to Ong and others, this is not tantamount to claiming that the thought and knowledge produced by writing is *better* than thought and knowledge produced by other media. My claim here is simply that since writing has the power to shape and produce thought and knowledge (as do many other modes of communication), the forms that writing takes matter to the kind of knowledge that is created. For example, Carson's anti-racist thesis would have been different – less persuasive? Less impactful? – had he written in conventional academic prose instead of performance poetry, rap and rhythm.

Socio-academic Practices (SAPs)

Despite breaking the rules, these 'wild' texts are academic. What makes them so are their SAPs. SAPs are the specific practices of the academy, what MacIntyre (1985) might have described as their inherent 'standards of excellence', standards that cannot be reduced to any finite set of external skills. This is because they are what philosopher of mind, complexity and emergence Fodor (1974, 1997) might have described as 'multiply-realisable', meaning that they are complex phenomena that have been caused by a range of interacting variables. The standards of excellence which are inherent to academic practices include acknowledging the work of others, establishing warrants (Toulmin, 1958), arguing, providing evidence, generating and crossing threshold concepts (Meyer et al., 2010) and creating new knowledge. Crucially, what makes these practices academic are their underlying epistemic virtues, such as scientific, social and human values and knowledge (Fricker, 2007; Harding, 1995; Wylie, 2003); qualified commitments to subjectivity, objectivity and trained judgement (Daston & Galison, 2007), to the truth or truthfulness (Connell, 2013), to academic integrity (Zgaga, 2009), to social justice (Case, 2013; McArthur, 2020), to innovation and research (Warnock, 1989) and to creativity (Besley & Peters, 2013; Robinson, 2001). SAPs can include problem-solving and problem-generating research; understanding, imagination and interpretation; care, wisdom and thinking; activism (Spivak, 1987); ideologies and identities; creativity and reflection; inclusion and diversity, *phronesis* (deliberation) and *eudamonia* (human flourishing); risk-taking and public engagement; and intellectual love (Rowland, 2008). References to these practices and epistemic virtues resonate throughout the literatures on higher education and the nature of academic study, yet they are rarely mentioned as conditions for what makes writing academic (Barnett, 2012; Bengtsen & Barnett, 2018; Besley & Peters, 2013; Biesta et al., 2019; de Sousa Santos, 2017; Nixon, 2012; Sperlinger et al., 2018; Thesen & Cooper, 2013; Warnock, 1989b).

When writers (and, by extension, their texts) are committed to SAPs and epistemic virtues (EVs) rather than to a display of form, they are more likely to mobilize a wider range of semiotic resources. This is because when academicness is conceived as a non-reductive property of texts, as I showcase below, there is no *a priori* semiotic resource to enact it. What this means is that an image, sound or movement (Roque, 2015) can confer academicness to a text.

SAPs emerge from an interaction between the writer (their agency, knowledge, intentions, values and abilities) and knowledge of the *textual environments* they operate in. This textual environment includes the readers and the institutional, social and linguistic structures which determine conventions and which writers need to be knowledgeable about so that they can make informed decisions about shaping their academic texts. In claiming that writers have agency in shaping their texts, I am not downplaying the role of the reader or of institutional expectations in establishing the academicness of texts. I recognize with Tardy (2016, p. 76), for example, that:

> In the traditional academic classroom, clearly defined roles of the teacher (as expert and assessor) and the student (as novice and learner) shape how student texts are both written and read and they limit the likelihood that a student will depart from genre expectations.

However, innovation, even at a relatively novice level, does occur, as the doctoral writings referred to earlier exemplify. It occurs through interaction, dialogue and negotiation with the 'experts', who belong to and have some agency in shaping the structures of the institutions that establish academic conventions. This innovation needs to be given a space in which it can be nurtured because it is what allows novel SAPs to emerge. For example, Harron (2016), in her mathematics PhD, uses language to disrupt her readers' expectations and to enact a socio-academic practice of inclusion: this is signalled by the claim in her Preface that 'Respected research math is dominated by men of a certain attitude'. Harron is using her academic writing to foreground her identity as a female mathematician in a male-dominated discipline and to advance her ideology of social inclusion (Adler-Kassner & Wardle, 2015). This is further compounded by writing her thesis for three different audiences, or readers: the lay person, the initiated person and the expert. Harron is knowingly and knowledgeably both anticipating and orienting her readers' expectations by disrupting the traditional genre of the PhD thesis that assumes one type of reader (the expert). She does this because she wants to write a thesis that is 'as mathematically complete as I could honestly make it' and for a community of mathematicians that includes those who 'do not feel that they are encouraged to be themselves'. By interacting with her textual environment and by choosing the forms and genres that allow her to express her identity and ideology, she is enacting a socio-academic practice of inclusion and social justice. Had she chosen to write a conventional mathematics thesis, she is unlikely to have shaped knowledge of mathematics in this way.

Threshold Concepts (TCs)

Having argued that academicness refers to holistic and relational SAPs that cannot be reduced to any single element in the text or to a writer's intent, the following section examines threshold concepts in writing studies (Adler-Kassner & Wardle, 2015) to further argue that what makes writing academic emerges from an interaction between the ways in which writers, i.e. agents, conceptualize their written texts and their textual environments, understood as the structures that both constrain and enable writer choice.

Threshold concepts designate a powerful heuristic for describing knowledge and how we come to understand it. Threshold concepts can be understood as 'portals' that open 'a new and previously inaccessible way of thinking about something' (Meyer & Land, 2006, p. 4). This new way of thinking has a 'transformative function' because 'once students have understood a key disciplinary concept, they are taken into a new intellectual and emotional space'. For example, Reimann and Jackson (2006, p. 166) discuss the threshold concept of 'opportunity cost' in economics. This is explained as 'the sacrifice made, when resources are scarce, to seek opportunities between competing uses of finite resources'. An 'opportunity cost' is therefore not actually a cost. It is a ratio that measures 'the best alternative' in the range of resources available. Understanding this, for an economics student, is part of a 'liminal' state in their learning whereby they may feel confused, stuck and challenged (Kiley & Wisker, 2009, p. 432) as they try to 'integrate' their previous understandings with the new 'troublesome' understandings that seem 'conceptually difficult, counter-intuitive or even "alien"' (Meyer & Land, 2006, p. 39).

Similarly, understanding that what makes writing academic cannot be reduced to a set of prescribed conventions requires entering a liminal state where the familiar comfort of previous knowledge (e.g. prescriptive paragraph patterns or impersonal grammar) becomes troublesome. Although threshold concepts are referred to as 'troublesome' because they disrupt previously held understandings, this does not presuppose that there is a 'correct way' to understand a concept: the point is that *any* shift in conceptual understandings is likely to be troublesome. This point is implied by Cousin (2006) when she reminds us that threshold concepts are 'bounded', meaning that concepts border with other concepts that index new conceptual areas. Their boundedness requires us to resist 'essentialist readings' by remaining open to questioning the concepts themselves. This is because of the 'provisional explanatory capacity' of disciplinary concepts rather than because of any 'congealed property' that might be defining them. For example, understanding that in economics an 'opportunity cost' is not actually a 'cost' but a 'ratio' does not mean that understanding it as a 'ratio' is correct: this, too, may be a 'provisional explanation'. It is the conceptual shift in crossing the threshold that matters because this shift will be required again for new and evolving disciplinary understandings. In what follows, I am proposing that a similar conceptual shift is needed to understand that what makes writing academic are its practices and not its forms. The shift consists in the troublesome recognition that when writing is reduced to a relatively finite and closed set of skills, it may fail to 'encapsulate' new SAPs, but that when it opens up to new skills it can shape knowledge in new and creative ways.

In *Naming What We Know: Threshold Concepts in Writing Studies*, Adler-Kassner and Wardle (2015) articulate thirty-seven threshold concepts of academic writing. These threshold concepts foreground the diversity, the affordances, the social practices and the mobility of both writing and writers in ways that a standard EAP writing class, for example, typically, does not. An example of a threshold concept in writing includes what Lunsford (2015) calls 'performativity',[3] meaning that written texts can make things happen 'beyond their own terms of reference' (Back, 2016), such as a policy change. Another example is the power of texts to build *identities* (Villanueva, 2015), such as feminist writings (Haraway, 1988; Harding, 1995) and ecologies of knowledge (de Sousa Santos, 2009), which allow non-dominant epistemologies and ontologies to become visible. Policy changes and new epistemologies and ontologies are examples of SAPs that emerge from the performativity of a text and from the identities it foregrounds. They are irreducible to prescribed language forms. When a writer is knowledgeable about the range of options that the textual environment affords, they can then make informed choices about the shape, form, genre, language, modality of their written text. Below, I list and illustrate what two of these threshold concepts look like when applied to academic writing.

Threshold Concept 1.5 refers to the fact 'writing mediates activity': 'The concept that writing mediates activity [e.g. a STOP sign or a performative] is troublesome because it goes against the usual concepts of writing as "just" transcribing ... thought or speech' (Adler-Kassner & Wardle, 2015, p. 27). What makes writing *academic* with regard to this threshold concept is its capacity to make things *happen*. An example of such a text might be O'Dwyer et al. (2018), who invite us to resist the pressures of academia by *performing* a manifesto. By choosing to write a manifesto, the authors are perceiving their writing as a 'Mediating Activity'. The academicness of their text (published in a journal of reflective practice) emerges from the authors' intention to perform a manifesto and their knowledge of the textual possibilities available to them,

---

[3] This is not the same meaning of 'performativity' found in Macfarlane (2021b).

in this case a poem that represents the self-care they wish to perform (taken from pages 245–7):

> An invitation: to our reader
> The poem that follows is both a representation of our self-care and reflective practice and an invitation to others to engage in dialogue with us. We invite you to read, to reflect and to resist.
> Self care: a manifesto
> Eat apple pancakes smothered in Nutella.
> Practice yoga
> Watch The English Patient
> Turn off email notifications
> Walk
> Drink wine
> Have a massage
> Eat fish and chips
> Swim.

Threshold concept 3.0 refers to the fact that writing enacts and creates Identities and Ideologies: 'When we seek to "apprentice" students into academic writing, what ideological imperatives are being asserted in the ways we choose to conceive of academic writers and writing?' (Adler-Kassner & Wardle, 2015, p. 50). Here, what can make writing *academic* is the recognition that writers are different and as such, not only do they bring different kinds of knowledge to their texts, they also shape their texts differently. Examples of such writing include Harron (2016), Carson (2017) and Kunju (2017), the latter having chosen to write his thesis in isiXhosa, one of South Africa's eleven languages. In doing this, not only does he obtain his doctorate, but he also asserts his humanity through an ideological imperative that consisted in reclaiming as academic an indigenous language and in resisting the dominant geopolitics of academic English (Lillis & Curry, 2010a). By choosing to write in isiXhosa, the academicness of Kunju's text emerges from the interaction between his intention to challenge a dominant ideology and the textual possibilities available to him (namely writing in isiXhosa instead of English).

When read cumulatively, these and many other threshold concepts afford creative possibilities for re-thinking academicness. These possibilities include de-centring language to embrace multimodality and dethroning English as the lingua franca of academia.

Argument, Logic and Why Language Isn't Enough

I have so far indicated that academicness, a holistic non-reductive property that makes a text academic, resides neither in the text nor in the intention of the writer for their text to count as academic. Instead, academicness can be said to emerge from a space that facilitates the interplay of writer agencies and their textual environments. These environments include reader expectations and the range of threshold concepts that define writing. I articulate this position more explicitly in Chapter 4, but before then, reference must be made to the role that argument plays in determining the academicness of a text. This is because argument is often associated with what makes a text academic.

My contention will be that argument can make a text academic but that it is only one of several non-defining features. It, too, emerges from the interaction of a writer's purpose (their agency) and their perception of what the textual environment (the structure) affords. I begin this section by assuming a shared and generic understanding of argument as the means through which we persuade others (Fish, 2017), but as the section draws to a close, I will offer more specific definitions with the intention of showing that an argument does not need to be linguistic. This is intended to further foreground and disrupt the historical contingency, introduced in Chapter 2, of the 'Western' logo-centric legacy that conflates logical thinking with alphabetic literacy and, ultimately, language.

Although there are times when academic communication doesn't need to be about argumentation (Allen, 2015; Bammer & Joeres, 2015), generally, we think of argument as being a marker of academicness (as discussed throughout Andrews, 2010; Archer, 2016; Björkvall, 2016; Fish, 2017; Gourlay, 2016; Wingate, 2012). In this section, therefore, I assume argument to be one of the properties that emerge from the interaction between the writer and their textual environment, but I also take it to be just one of the many non-essential SAPs that arise from this interaction. I further demonstrate that there is no univocal understanding of argument and because of this, academic arguments can take many forms. I focus on the ways in which 'argument' has been conflated with language to show that this conflation has led to marginalizing multimodal affordances of argument. I conclude by claiming that an over-reliance on language limits our ability to argue and that a multimodal approach to argument affords greater academicness.

How Language Came to Define Argument

As shown in Chapter 2, academic writing instruction has inherited a legacy which considers language, and language alone, to be the primary enabler of complex, higher-order thinking that 'raises consciousness'. This 'higher order thinking' is further associated with 'argumentation', understood simply, but by no means simplistically, as the 'art of persuasion' (Fish, 2017, p. 6): what Fish refers to as the 'art of persuasion' is shorthand for the Aristotelian legacy of *ethos*, *pathos* and *logos* which underscores much current literature on what argumentation consists of (Ramage et al., 2009). Because of its persuasive powers, argument has come to define academic communication (Andrews, 2010; Wingate, 2012). However, we are now faced with yet another conflation, that between alphabetic language and argumentation.

This conflation is a problem because we know from the histories of literacy and of philosophy that language is both limited and fallible in capturing and, therefore, doing justice to the ontologies we seek to represent and cognitively engage with. Philosopher Miranda Fricker (2007) has not only re-iterated the limits of language in representing the world, she has also shown that epistemic injustices emerge from these limits. She describes several social situations in which knowers who do not have the linguistic resources to interpret and then describe a social event can become victims of a 'hermeneutical injustice'. This is when somebody (a knower) becomes disempowered and then disadvantaged by social realities that have not developed the linguistic repertoires to describe an event. Some of her examples relate to instances of sexual harassment whereby women must develop the language needed to describe situations that may not be adequately captured by previously established words, such as sexual 'coercion', 'intimidation' or 'exploitation': in the contexts that Fricker describes, 'harassment' helps women describe behaviours that were not adequately captured by the other terms. She shows that language can create conceptual spaces to frame thoughts and experiences in new ways, but, in doing so, she equally indexes how readily language fails to describe what is happening.[4] It is this failure that I wish to foreground.

For our present purposes, the limits of language signal the possibility that human cognition might develop through a range of representations whereby

---

[4] Interestingly, the word 'harassment' does not exist in Italian. It is generally translated as *molestia* (as in 'being molested'). However, since the 2019 #MeToo scandal, whereby several women took to social media to call out male harassment, the English word has increasingly been used in Italian media, often untranslated.

(academic) reality is not dependent on being represented by a single mode, namely language. When argument is allowed to draw on the *most fitting* modes rather than the *most conventional,* the richness and fullness of SAPs are more likely to emerge. As artist and psychologist Rudolf Arnheim reminds us (1974, p. 2):

> The scientist builds conceptual models he [sic] wants to understand about a given phenomenon. But he [sic] knows that there is no such thing as the full representation of an individual instance.

That language is the most fitting modality to be the transparent carrier of our thoughts has had many critics. Literacy and EAP scholar Karen Bennett, for example, has described this conceptualization of language as a 'transparency trope', claiming that rather than a conduit for reality, language is constitutive of it. This view challenges the widely deferred to Orwellian metaphor whereby language is seen as a 'window pane' that is detached from, but through which we represent, the outside world: this view of language as a window onto reality assumes that language is 'clear' and 'transparent'. A more robust challenge has come from socio-semiotic integrationist linguists, such as Harris (2011), who claims that the 'window pane' view of language falls into the 'fallacy of telementation'. The fallacy assumes that words are adequate carriers of our thoughts and that our listeners and hearers are able to intend our words as we intended them to be understood, as though the meaning of these words were transparent and complete, needing no further integration with the context in which they were uttered or with the receiver's own understanding of those words. In this sense, traditional linguistics (in the tradition of De Saussure and Chomsky) is *segregationist* and has failed to recognize that 'languages must be conceived as systems that are entirely *dependent* on their use in communication' (Harris, 2011). Meaning emerges from the *integration* of the word and the social context it is uttered in by the speaker or writer. It does not emerge from its segregation, as the 'window pane' metaphor suggests. This explains why writers need knowledge of their readers by interacting with their textual environments and integrating meanings accordingly to allow academicness to emerge, but it also explains why readers need knowledge of their writers: how else can we explain why Wittgenstein and Derrida were understood by some but not by others?

In his later writings, Wittgenstein himself adeptly captures the problem of signification when he wonders what it means to 'point to something', in the sense of trying to give an ostensive definition. He asks (1953, #33):

> [W]hat does 'pointing to the shape', 'pointing to the colour' consist in? Point to a piece of paper. – And now point to its shape – now to its colour – now to its number (that sounds queer) – How did you do it? You will say that you 'meant' a different thing each time you pointed. And if I ask you how that is done, you will say you concentrated your attention on the colour, the shape, etc.

Instead, Wittgenstein proposes that we think of meanings in terms of 'language in use'. This frames language as a social practice and not as the mental representation of what it refers to (Wittgenstein & Russell, 1922). Thinking of language in this way, as integrated with its uses, has important implications for how we think about academic writings. Integrating meanings and fixing referents to ensure we all understand what we mean is a troubled process, as painstakingly demonstrated by philosopher Saul Kripke (1972). What is meant by 'academic' is not fixed because, in Kripkean terms, 'academic' is not the 'rigid designator' of a fixed external referent in the same way as the word 'bachelor' is in designating an 'unmarried man' (or even a university degree). Since the meaning of 'academic' cannot be fixed, what makes writing academic remains open to how we integrate its meaning with its uses. From a linguistic perspective, Harris (2011) claims that the 'semiological value' of using any linguistic structure 'depends on the circumstances and activities in which they fulfil an integrational function' rather than on external referents. Harris gives the example of how the seemingly unequivocal word 'tree' can refer both to a plant and to a landmark that signals 'the need to turn left': to understand 'tree' as 'landmark', we need to integrate a wide range of signs, circumstances and activities.

On an integrationist reading, then, the visual literacies of Sousanis (2015), the aural thesis of Carson (2017), the messy social scientific methods of Law (2003) and the call by English (2015) to conceive of academic writing as a creative venture can be said to have an 'academic semiological value' because they depend on the academic 'circumstances and activities', namely the *practices*, and their inherent standards of excellence, that generated them.

Yet, despite the ways in which writers translanguage and integrate signs and meanings to advance their polysemiotic arguments, the burden of a 'full representation' of our thoughts and meanings has historically been on (a mono) language (Blair, 2008, p. 44):

> Arguments are traditionally associated with speech, either written or oral, for a couple of linked reasons. First, because the reasons they use are propositions. Second, because propositions are standardly expressed by propositions in language.

Like language, what is meant by 'argument' is contested and varies according to its purpose (Fish, 2017), its disciplinary norms[5] (Andrews, 2010; Toulmin, 1958) and its cultural forms (Galtung, 1981; Kaplan, 1980 [1966]). Once we start to investigate the structural diversity of propositional arguments and how this might affect representations of reality, deeper questions arise about how form and content relate to each other. Philosopher Martha Nussbaum has a long-standing interest in this area and has focused on how form and content influence each other in the field of philosophy (Nussbaum, 1990, p. 3):

> How should one write, what words should one select, what forms and structures and organisation, if one is pursuing understanding? ... Style itself makes its claims, expresses its own sense of what matters. Literary form is not separable from philosophical content, but is, itself, a part of content – an integral part, then, of the search for and the statement of truth.

An example of how 'style itself makes its claims, expresses its own sense of what matters' is the Manifesto of Care (O'Dwyer et al., 2018) article referred to earlier, which invites us to reflect on and resist the pressures of academic life by affording us the opportunity to read an academic text written as poetry.

I now highlight how the meaning of argument has changed over time and how it becomes conflated with language. This opens up the possibility for argument in academic writing to go beyond language, making it inclusive of a range of 'ecologies of knowledges' (de Sousa Santos, 2017), 'textual ecologies' (Canagarajah, 2018), 'intellectual styles' (Galtung, 1981) and 'creativity' (Besley & Peters, 2013).

The Limits of Language

Stephen Toulmin (1958)'s *The Uses of Argument* was a turning point in the way argumentation can be understood. This is because Toulmin repudiated the logical positivist reduction of argument to a series of symbols that divorced argument from natural, or ordinary, language. Instead, he proposed that we re-think what we mean by logic. His response consisted in recognizing that argumentation shares some of the features of psychology, understood as the study of 'healthy laws of thought' and of sociology, namely the study of 'habits and practices developed in the course of social evolution and passed on by parents and teachers from one generation to another' (1958, p. 3). He argued that language is

---

[5] For example, a deductive mathematical argument is different to an inductive historical argument.

only one of the modalities that allow us to be 'logical' in both the psychological and the sociological sense but he also posited that framing argument in terms of psychology and sociology imbued the thinking process with a subjective and relative quality, such as a reliance on induction that 'proper' deductive logic did not (Toulmin, 1958, p. 5):

> [I]t cannot be custom alone that gives validity and authority to a form of argument, or the logician would have to wait upon the results of the anthropologist's researches.

His discomfort with subjectivity and relativity was not, however, resolved by turning to the kind of logic that posits formal relations between propositions and that reduces the validity of an argument to its deductive form. This is because logic is concerned with statements about logic itself and not with the thinking process per se. The mistake of equating logic with correct and rational thinking is known as 'qualified psychologism'[6] and assumes that logic, rather than psychology, is the study of thought. Toulmin invokes logical positivist Rudolf Carnap to refute the way in which logic has arrogated the thinking to itself (Toulmin, pp. 86–7):

> The characterisation of logic in terms of correct or rational or justified beliefs is as right but not more enlightening than to say that mineralogy tells us how to think correctly about minerals. The reference to thinking may just as well be dropped in both cases. Then we say simply: mineralogy makes statements about minerals and logic makes statements about logical relations. The activity in any field of knowledge involves, of course, thinking. But this does not mean that thinking belongs to the subject matter of all fields. It belongs to the subject matter of psychology but not to that of logic any more than to that of mineralogy.

By the same token, it can be argued that when it comes to the practice of academic writing – *pace* Ong (1982, 1986), Emig (1977), Kaplan (1980 [1966]) and other literacy scholars who have in various ways subscribed to the view that writing raises consciousness in ways that are qualitatively superior to other forms of communication – the reference to 'good thinking' may as well be dropped. This is because it amounts to an instance of 'qualified psychologism', whereby writing has arrogated to itself the process of correct thinking, a process that more properly belongs to the enquiries of the field of psychology. Since the activity of any field requires 'good thinking', it is not clear why it should belong to the practice of writing any more that it does to that of drawing.

---

[6] For an overview and explanation of qualified psychologism, see https://plato.stanford.edu/entries/psychologism/ [accessed 14 December 2018].

Rather, Toulmin proposes that we shift our conflation of logic with correct and rational thinking to thinking of logic as a way of making sound claims that give prominence to warrants instead of prominence to form and truth (Toulmin, 1958, p. 7):

> Logic is concerned with the soundness of the claims we make – with the solidity of the grounds we produce to support them, the firmness of the backing we provide for them – or, to change the metaphor, with the sort of case we present in defence of our claims. The legal analogy implied in this last way of putting the point can for once be a real help. So let us forget about psychology, sociology, technology and mathematics, ignore the echoes of structural engineering and collage in the words 'grounds' and 'backing' and take as our model the discipline of jurisprudence. Logic (we may say) is generalised jurisprudence.

In re-framing logic as jurisprudence, where what persuades is a convincing and reasonable case, not the truth, Toulmin discards much of the language associated with logic, such as 'premise' or 'proposition' and replaces it with legal terminology, such as 'data', 'warrants' and 'qualifiers': data are the situations we wish to make a claim about; warrants are legitimate 'steps' that act as 'bridges' which 'authorise' further 'steps' culminating in further 'claims'; and 'qualifiers' provide conditions under which a claim can be considered *reasonable* (as opposed to 'true'). By introducing this terminology, he shows that what constitutes an argument is not its reliance on logic and language (propositions) but its reliance on the legitimacy of the warrant. As will be revealed, the 'legitimacy of a warrant' can also be established in several non-linguistic ways.

Toulmin further cautions against the mis-use of the term 'logic'. He does this by reminding us that non-mathematical and non-logical arguments are substantial. This makes their truth and validity contingent on external conditions, not on the internal, logico-deductive conditions of formal logic. Since the majority of meaningful academic arguments, ones that extend our knowledge – in the sciences, social sciences and humanities – are substantial and inductive, they require warrants and qualifiers as well as linguistic modalities for expressing attitudes of probability, possibility and necessity, rather than formal logic (Toulmin, p. 154):

> The only arguments we can fairly judge by 'deductive' standards are those held out as and intended to be analytic, necessary and formally valid. All arguments which are confessedly substantial will be 'non-deductive' and by implication not formally valid. But for the analytic syllogism validity can be identified with formal validity and this is just what the logician wants to be possible universally.

It follows at once that for substantial arguments, whose cogency cannot be displayed in a purely formal way, even validity is something entirely out of reach and unobtainable.

Reaching similar conclusions in response to those who objected to her use of poetry to represent sociological data, Laurel Richardson has cautioned against the mis-use of 'rational' to describe the academic endeavour (Richardson, 1997, p. 41):

> [T]he fact that social science research does not meet the logic of enquiry model of research does not mean that the research is irrational. The problem is not with social science, but with the inappropriate narrowing of the meaning of 'rational'.

Drawing on philosopher Richard Rorty (who is unfortunately also associated with problematic relativist ontologies), Richardson rightly calls for the meaning of rational to include a set of 'moral virtues' such as tolerance, respect, a willingness to listen and persuasion. This is quite different to reducing rationality to a set of logical linguistic propositions.

Language Is Field-Dependent Rather than Clear, Precise or Transparent

A further key move in Toulmin's critique of classical logic and its arrogation of argument is that substantive arguments require more than a reliance on the univocal meaning of language. He develops this thesis by drawing attention to the *field-dependency* of arguments (1958, p. 15):

> How far, for instance, can one compare the standards of argument relevant in a court of law with those relevant when judging a paper in the Proceedings of the Royal Society, or those relevant to a mathematical proof or a prediction about the composition of a tennis team?

A specific example of 'standards of argument' might be that what counts as evidence for a warrant or qualifier in each discipline will differ. In a court of law, a *blood-stained garment*, rather than a linguistic proposition about how the victim had blood on their clothes, may provide a warrant for claiming that the victim had been injured; in a scientific paper, *references* to previous studies can serve to qualify a new theory; in mathematics, an *axiom* such as $A = \Pi r^2$ to calculate the surface area of a generic circle can provide the warrant for establishing the surface area of a specific circle; in tennis, the use of past *performance statistics* can establish which players are the most competent for the formation of a new team. The point being that by narrowing and reducing the meaning of argument to propositional logic, we fail to capture the wider-ranging uses of argument that occur in other fields of human enquiry, uses which may or may not include language itself. This is why the frequent designation and juxtaposition, in EAP and other general academic writing courses, of academic writing as 'logical' and 'linear' is misleading: both terms are highly field-dependent and it is not clear what they designate when they are used to describe the arguments in generic student essays.

Toulmin's focus on warrants and qualifiers now creates a space within which to think of arguments as non-linguistic, since neither warrants nor qualifiers need be expressed in language.

The Case for Non-linguistic Argumentation

Richard Andrews (2010), whose scholarship on academic literacies has been influential in studies on higher education and EAP, draws significantly on the seminal work of Toulmin. The claim that 'arguments may be of different kinds' (Toulmin, 1958, pp. 158–9) is of specific relevance to this section. Arguments can and do include, but need not be reduced to, the logical characterizations favoured by EAP (Chapter 1) and the Enlightenment research genres (Chapter 2) but they can further be conceptualized in terms of composition, as dialogic, as (inter)disciplinary and as multimodal. Specifically, by drawing attention to the interdisciplinary nature of argumentation, Andrews is highlighting that the form and the aim of an argument are not paradigmatic, meaning that there isn't a standard to which all arguments conform. In the absence of a paradigm, arguments are not universally transferable across disciplines: a mathematical argument is substantially different to a historical argument, for example. Because arguments are not paradigmatic, Andrews leaves open the possibility for arguments to be non-linguistic and multimodal, showing that these 'can operate inductively, not just as evidence for a verbally conceived set of propositions but as a set of propositions in [their] own right' (Andrews, 2010, p. 52). The existence of a range of academic arguments signals that what makes writing academic goes far beyond the narrow requirement to be 'logical' and 'linear' and includes requirements that are usually ascribed to creative writing, such as the need to be 'refreshing', 'modest' and 'curious' (Andrews, 2010, pp. 99–101); to be open to interpretation (Marin et al., 2018); and to develop authorial identities (Ivanič, 1998; Kamler & Thomson, 2006).

To achieve such wide-ranging qualities, propositional arguments themselves frequently rely on non-propositional forms, such as implicit or unstated premises. Enthymemes are an example of this. These are the 'missing parts' of an argument, such as a premise or conclusion (Hurley, 2000), that require readers' knowledge or interpretation to 'fill in the gaps'. They rely, that is, on the reader's 'cooperation' (Turner, 2018). According to Andrews, visual argumentation creates opportunities for this kind of inference, which matters in education: it is what Dewey calls a 'forecast', a 'leap from the unknown', a 'creative incursion' (cited in d'Agnese, 2017, p. 451). Similarly, Tarnay (2002) argues that moving images can argue without being reduced to propositional content. This can be illustrated with reference to *Fuocoammare* (2016), Gianfranco Rosi's 2016 documentary about the plight of refugees arriving on the small island of Lampedusa in Sicily. In one scene, we are shown that ordinary life continues on the island despite the tragic loss of life: two young boys play together throughout the documentary while rescue boats, helicopters and other medical services concurrently deal with migrant emergencies. It is a mostly silent documentary, yet, as viewers, we become aware that Lampedusa's children are being affected by what they see and hear around them. Despite this never being stated linguistically (i.e. propositionally), the inference that their lives are being affected is clear and the viewer cannot help but make that inference because their knowledge of life, or maybe even shared experiences, allows them to fill in the gaps. This documentary film, narrated visually, meets the conditions for what Toulmin (1958) calls substantive arguments and as such, can be said to meet the criteria for being 'academic' in the sense of enacting the socio-academic practice of advancing an evidence-based claim (or thesis): it provides data (D) of migrants arriving on a small island and claims (C) that this affects the local children. The steps the director takes in moving from D to C are realized by the editing and juxtaposition of images and overlay of sounds to provide warrants (W), or bridges, between the data and the claim, a form of arguing that relies on recursive composition rather than linearity (Palmeri, 2012). A full analysis of this documentary might further show that backing and qualifications are also present in the film when considered as a whole. The reason we can make inductive inferences, rather than formal deductions, from the data to the claims is because images and motion are being arranged according to what Tarnay (2002, p. 4) calls intentional 'compositional' features (in the sense of *intended by* the director) that cannot be reduced to propositions that merely guide the eye in a linear and sequential way or that are left open to unqualified interpretation. Such features include 'depth', 'motion', 'distance' and, following Groarke (2015), 'non-verbal sounds', which are 'perceived' by the viewer through the senses rather than directly processed as propositions (Tarnay, p. 5):

> [T]he operation of our sense organs (or whatever it is that computes and processes sense data) can be described as an inferential activity under the level of phenomenal consciousness (The strongest version that our eyes 'argue' can be found in Bonfantini, 1987). .... The retrieval of arguments should not be confined to higher – semantic and pragmatic – level of processing, but it should be grounded on certain 'automatic' processes.

Some may object that a documentary such as *Fuocoammare* does not count as an academic argument on the following grounds. Firstly, as discussed above, argument is traditionally understood as a propositional, not visual, endeavour. In the case of *Fuocoammare*, the scope for interpretation is, arguably, far wider than it might be in a traditional academic format. A film or an image allows the viewer to see much more in a single frame or panel than does a sentence containing a proposition or a paragraph containing several sentences. Secondly, whilst acknowledging that language is 'unstable', some writing scholars such as Gourlay (2016, p. 88), for example, remain of the view that 'written text is still more suited than visual images' to the complex requirements of argumentation and critique, especially within the context of a literature review (Gourlay, 2016, p. 87):

> The dense, precise and closely-argued nature of much academic argumentation in reference to other academic texts seems to demand a system which delivers nuance and can be readily and unambiguously shared with a readership beyond the immediate context of text production – the complexity of language still appears better suited to the task than images alone.

A third objection is that films and images tell stories which rely on narrative rather than argument. This third contention relies on the common acceptance that argument and narrative are mutually exclusive methods for communicating knowledge. The implication of this contention seems to be that by doing the former one is not doing the latter and vice-versa. The contention indexes that since narrative is not traditionally valued as a method of inquiry, the documentary genre which relies on narrative to advance a thesis is less likely to be accepted by academic writing programmes, such as those taught in EAP. The assumption that narrative is not deemed to academic is made explicit by

Ingraham (2005, p. 49) in discussing whether the BBC documentary entitled *Walking with Beasts* can be considered 'academic':

> [A]n obvious way in which documentary often differs from conventional scholarly discourse is in the use of narrative. Documentary programmes are much more likely to use narrative as a strategy to maintain and direct an audience's attention than are scholarly articles or books. There is nothing intrinsically wrong with using narrative within the context of scholarly discourse. Many historical and biographical studies almost inevitably involve narrative.

The extent to which the documentary being analysed by Ingraham can be considered as a 'carrier of academic argument' has been deliberated by Gourlay (2012, p. 95) who concludes that it cannot be classified as academic. This is because academic argument should be explicit, something that narrative is not seen to be and unambiguous, something only words can be (Gourlay, 2012, p. 97).

It is, however, possible to challenge the above three objections to the thesis that a documentary and its non-verbal forms of argumentation can be academic. Firstly, we need to remind ourselves that even traditional argument and its investment in language is fallible and requires constant refining clarifications. If linguistic argument were as precise and as clear as Gourlay and others claim, then why is so much academic time spent on revisiting and surmising over the ambiguous meanings expressed through the language of academic writers? As Fish (2017, p. 19) notes:

> [I]f we could confine ourselves to a language that did not admit [uncertainties], there would be no need for argument; for argument is required when there are competing accounts of what is the case. If everyone agreed on how a set of facts should be characterised, there would be no competing accounts and there would be nothing to argue about. And such agreement would be assured if there were prior agreement about the correct vocabulary for stating things.

Secondly, Toulmin has shown that traditional propositional logic fails to capture the substantive nature of human argumentation which includes understanding argument as an 'invitation to inference' and not merely as a logical deduction to establish the truth of a premise (Pinto, 2001 cited in Groarke (2015, p. 135)). Since inferences and interpretation are very much part of the academic endeavour, it seems unwise to defer so extensively to the power of propositional arguments to convey unambiguous meaning. Similarly, Tseronis (22 May 2013) shows that argumentation is a social and discursive activity in which images, in addition to playing a role in conveying premises and conclusions, communicate something about the argumentative process that goes beyond mere representation to include the ways in which images contribute to the context in which they are being used. The scene where the two Sicilian boys in *Fuocoammare* are pretending to shoot down targets in an imaginary war is therefore not to be viewed for its representational value, namely two boys shooting, but as contributing to the overall narrative argument, namely that migration is affecting life on the island. Crucially, Tseronis also reminds us that meaning and truth are distinct concepts and that 'the meaning of a proposition cannot be reduced to its truth-evaluable propositional content'. In other words, meaning, rather than truth, can equally be the aim of an argument. To quote Fish again (2017, p. 8):

> Argument is protean – ever changing, mutable, kaleidoscopic, voracious – and almost anything can be its vehicle, swinging a big stick, putting on a badge, intoning a holy phrase, making the sign of a cross, wearing a uniform, speaking in a stentorian tone.

Thirdly, and contrary to Ingraham's and Gourlay's claims, narrative methods *are* used in academic research (see, for example, Chanock [2014]; Richardson [1990a]), including the use of ethnographic methods in anthropology, sociology, education and science. As evidenced in Chapter 2, Isaac Newton himself deploys the narrative of 'stumbling across a fact' to persuade the reader of an epistemic virtue, that of the 'objectivity' of his findings. Despite the ubiquity of narrative in academic communication, academic writing programmes such as EAP, with their underlying positivistic ideologies, rarely foreground multimodal narrative as a valid form of argumentation.

And finally, since academia is, or ought to be, moving on from the discredited logical-positivist endeavour of seeking to establish a strict correspondence between word and object, what counts as an academic argument also needs to move on (Paré, 2017). One way of moving on is to recognize that privileging monomodal practices narrows what can and cannot be said (Bezemer & Kress, 2008; Laurillard et al., 2000 [2]), making it more likely that by mobilizing a wider range of semiotic resources to communicate meaning, academic arguments will become more persuasive. This likelihood stems from the fact that our meaning-making capacities and ability to think in abstract conceptual ways extend beyond language (Arnheim, 1969, p. 228):

> [L]anguage is widely assumed to be a much better vehicle of thought than other shapes or sounds …. Nobody denies that language helps thinking. What needs to be questioned is whether it performs this service substantially by means of properties inherent in the verbal medium itself or whether it functions indirectly,

namely by pointing to the referents of words and propositions, that is to facts given in an entirely different medium. Also, we need to know whether language is indispensable to thought. The answer ... is 'no'.

Arnheim's point is that if the sole function of language is to describe, or point to, a reality that is beyond it – such as a thought or an object – then art and other modalities can do this, too. But since words, images, sounds and other media are ontologically distinct from what they are describing, none can be said to provide a 'full representation' of that reality. From the perspective of what makes writing academic, this entails that words are not inherently superior to any other forms of representing reality because something is always lost and gained through semiotic choices.

Conclusions

This chapter has argued that what makes writing academic cannot be reduced to formal features of language and grammar because doing so would allow hoaxes and IELTS essays to count as academic. These are not academic because they transgress values of academic integrity (such as a commitment to the truth), which are emergent SAPs. Rather, what makes writing academic are the ways in which writers knowledgeably interact with their textual environments to allow these SAPs to emerge. These environments include the threshold concepts that trouble and re-configure what we think makes writing academic. In considering the role that argument also plays, I claimed that whilst arguments can make writing academic, there is no requirement for them to be propositional (i.e. linguistic) or logical because most academic arguments are substantive and inductive rather than logical in any formal sense. Because of this, they are possibly better described as reasonable. Given this non-reductive nature (non-reductive to logic), argument, too, can be considered as a socio-academic practice that emerges from the interaction of the writer's warrants and claims with the range of socio-semiotic resources available to them in their textual environment.

4

Critical Realism: Re-claiming Theory for Practice

Introduction

> Critical realists do not deny the reality of events and discourses; on the contrary, they insist upon them. But they hold that we will only be able to understand – and so change – the social world if we identify the structures at work that generate those events and discourses.
>
> (Bhaskar, 1989, p. 2)

In what follows, I propose to move beyond the skills *versus* practice binaries presented in Chapter 1, because, as we have seen, neither fully captures the complexity of what makes a text academic: skills and their associated mechanistic approaches are unsatisfactory because they reduce the academicness of texts to its forms, namely formal features of grammar, lexis and genre. This foments a culture of performativity (Macfarlane, 2021b) that can encourage academic writers to display language at the expense of deep knowledge engagement and creativity. This kind of performativity would allow hoaxes and IELTS essays to count as 'academic', further compounding the 'Western' imaginary of what and whose standards of literacy are acceptable. They also make copying and plagiarizing easier because formulaic templates lend themselves to being transferred across contexts. Conversely, practice approaches to academic literacies and their associated critiques of standards and conventions risk being equally unsatisfactory because they potentially allow anything to count as 'academic'. This, in turn, can result in relativizing and 'romanticising' all forms of writing, something which anthropologist and academic literacies scholar Brian Street, for example, has cautioned against in his response to McCabe, 1995, in Prinsloo and Breier (1996). Donald Judd (2003), too, has stood against relativism in his critique of the American expressivist literacy tradition of the 1960s because by focusing on the originality, creativity and subjectivity of the author, expressivist rhetoric reifies the 'authentic self' at the expense of objective and socially just knowledge (more on this later). Moreover, as Boughey remarks in her Foreword, whilst academic literacies approaches acknowledge multiplicity and diversity – showing a deep understanding of why academic writing is difficult for some but not others – they do not as readily identify the agencies and mechanisms needed to challenge the powers that impose a one-size-fits-all literacy. To escape the fractious reductionist and relativist entanglements of the skills-practice aporia, I now mobilize the philosophical and sociological theory of critical realism. The appeal of critical realism is that it necessitates both relativism (or subjectivity) and foundationalism (or objectivity) to account for the social reality of phenomena, of which academic writing is an instance. But rather than looking for academicness in either the subjective will of the writer or the objective, i.e. standard(ized), rules and conventions of what counts and does not count as an appropriate academic text, critical realism allows us to anchor and reclaim academicness as a property that emerges from the critical judicious and reflexive *interaction* between the writer's agency (their subjectivity) and their textual environments, or structures, which are objectively real. For example, on a critical realist account, to produce his multimodal thesis, Carson (2017) enacted his agency and subjectivity by interacting with his supervisors and with the full range of modalities available to him in his textual environment. The academicness of his thesis emerged from this interaction rather than from his personal whim or from adhering to a particular set of academic writing conventions. Critical realism puts interactions at centre-stage, what Donati and Archer (2015) call 'relations' between phenomena. Interactions are ontologically real and have effects that transcend the effects of the individual phenomena involved in the interaction. For example, when individual people are part of a crowd, their individual behaviours interact in such a way as to have effects that the individual alone could not have: a crowd can attract attention, be threatening or inspire action in ways that the single individuals cannot. Similarly, an academic text can make us think and learn in ways that the individual words, sentences and references cannot. Thinking about academic writing in this way affords a conceptual space within which to understand academicness in a way that is non-reductive, i.e. irreducible to either the writer (their intentions, literacies, etc.) or the features of the text (namely grammar or style). Within such a conceptualisation, changes and innovations in writing practices require informed structural responses to the full range of skills and conventions needed to uphold the totality of standards of excellence that make writing academic. This range transcends both the writer and the text because it is historical and potential as well as beyond our contingent empirical experience. The totality of standards may include new or unacknowledged standards that the writer (and their instructors) may be unaware of and that conventional academic texts may not possess. An 'informed structural response' presupposes that agents are able to knowledgeably interact with the total potential range of standards of excellence. It is this interaction that allows academicness to emerge. In the case of A. D. Carson, these standards of excellence included his values of social justice and his literacies, namely his ability to communicate through poems and music. Because he wanted his thesis to be understood by the communities he was researching, he chose to rap his thesis 'chapters' as five-minute podcasts of performance poetry to ensure they reached his intended audience. In doing so, he democratized his knowledge. But he similarly wanted his PhD examiners to acknowledge his intellectual contribution and to confer his doctorate in compliance with institutional requirements. His thesis, therefore, duly referenced social theories, histories and literacies in order to satisfy his institutional committees. The interaction of his individual intentions and values with his knowledge of the deeper structures that lead to the award of a PhD allowed an academic text to emerge. Moreover, it is unlikely that this kind of thesis could ever be commissioned to an essay mill to be ghostwritten or that its author would even be motivated to plagiarize. If academia were a culture where writers had the space to explore the most fitting ways of communicating their knowledge, their values and their research, they would be far more likely to treat their 'writing' as acts of love, recalling Cocteau, and as an instance of what Spinoza calls 'intellectual love' (Rowland, 2008).

Now, surely love of knowledge, of thinking, of being just is a standard of academic excellence worth nurturing!

To appreciate the relevance of critical realism to what makes writing academic, I begin with an introduction to the theory, enough to then make sense of the extant literature on writing that adopts critical realism as a theoretical lens. I extend this theorization to further propose that academic writing be conceived as a complex open system in which writers interact with their textual environments to shape written knowledge. The chapter concludes with a reminder that the standards of excellence of higher education practices are wide-ranging and evolving and because of this, what makes writing academic must necessarily broaden its scope and evolve accordingly. This prepares the terrain for articulating the foundations for a future pedagogy of academic writing, outlined in Chapter 5.

Mobilizing Critical Realism to Explain What Makes Writing Academic

Critical realism is a philosophy of science and social science oriented towards change and social justice. It addresses the complex 'structure and agency' discourses that have characterized social theory since Max Weber and Emile Durkheim, through to Pierre Bourdieu, Basil Bernstein and Anthony Giddens by asking, for example, what powers do we, as agents with free will, have to enact social change or what must the world be like for our theories and practices to be correct (Archer, 2000; Bhaskar, 1989). At the same time, critical realists acknowledge that we are bound and constrained by history and its social structures and that this makes it difficult for individuals to enact change. Critical realism distinguishes itself within this sociological tradition by disambiguating the structure-agency binary and by introducing an explicit analytical construct referred to as 'analytical dualism'. The reason critical realism opts for this disambiguation is to counter the tendency of previous sociological theories to explain social phenomena by either reducing the ontology of society to the level of individuals, thus denying the existence and influence of 'society' all together (as in Margaret Thatcher's infamous claim,[1] which can be understood with reference to a sociological position known as 'methodological individualism'[2]) or by reifying society to such an extent that it denies the agency and powers of individuals to enact change because their choices are entirely determined by society (a position known as 'methodological collectivism'). Instead, critical realists attempt to give structure and agency their own independent realities so that they can be studied separately and so that claims about each can be made without being reduced to the other. Their relationship is then established via a 'stratified ontology' that links them via reflexive and emergent relations rather than via relative, deterministic or reductive claims. This allows critical realists to 'reclaim' the reality of agents who have 'powers' to intervene and change social structures which are equally real and which exist independently of individuals (i.e. the structures are there even if we are not). It is for this reason that the theory is generative for reconfiguring written knowledge as a socio-academic

---

[1] Former Conservative UK prime minister made the following claim in an interview on 23 September 1987 for *Woman's Own*: 'there is no such thing as society........ There are individual men and women and there are families' (https://www.margaretthatcher.org/document/106689).

[2] See Sawyer, R. K. (2001). Emergence in sociology: Contemporary philosophy of mind and some implications for sociological theory. *American Journal of Sociology*, 107(3), 551-85. http://iscte.pt/~jmal/mcc/Keith_Sawyer_Emergence_in_Sociology.pdf for a nuanced and comprehensive account of the philosophical and sociological tensions, contradictions and implications of methodological individualism and collectivism.

practice that can be changed by writers (namely agents) in relation to their values, abilities, capabilities and the affordances of their textual environments (i.e. their social structures). This re-configuration can then pave the way for laying a foundation for future practices that can transcend (or emerge from) standard rules and conventions (which are real social constructs) and for explaining why some writings 'in the wild' are academic and can be taught as such. As we shall see, critical realism seems to have had relatively little uptake in academic writing studies for reasons that are not yet clear to me but that may have to do with its associated ideology, namely Marxism. Interestingly, educationalists working in contexts where inequality of access and social injustice are prevalent, such as Jennifer Wright (2011), Jennifer Case (2013), Chrissie Boughey (2013) and Boughey and McKenna (2021), have turned their attention to critical realist theory. This suggests that it affords a generative heuristic for mobilizing change in educational practices and policies, especially those that are unjust.

Critical realist philosophy is associated with Roy Bhaskar (1989, 1998) and further developed by sociologist Margaret Archer (1995, 1998, 2000, 2003), amongst several others, including Keith Sawyer (2001) and Andrew Collier (1994), who has helped to introduce the theory to a wider audience. It is underpinned by three fundamental notions of reality which are referred to as 'stratified': the first is that there is an objective reality that exists beyond our human perception. This reality is made up of causal mechanisms, such as the physical laws of nature and the structures that constitute the social world. It is not a relative or subjective reality, it is a reality made up of facts that have effects, it is ontologically real and intransitive and is referred to as REAL.[3] So, for example, in the case of the laws of nature, gravity is real and exists regardless of whether we perceive it or not. Similarly, social phenomena are also real. For example, poverty is real: it exists regardless of whether we perceive it or experience it because its effects are real: people are objectively homeless, hungry, ill and uneducated. In this sense, reality is intransitive and objective because it is independent of human enquiry (e.g. the sciences, social sciences, humanities and other methods of enquiry, such as writing). The second fundamental notion is that there is an actual reality where specific events emerge, or don't emerge, from the intransitive mechanisms and structures. For example, trees may or may not fall because of gravity and people may or may not die because of poverty. This is what is referred to as the ACTUAL. It is the visible and potential manifestation of underlying powers and structures, whether the event

---

[3] I am capitalizing the terms that Bhaskar uses. For the original systematic and nuanced articulation of his theory see Bhaskar, R. (1989). *Reclaiming reality: A critical introduction to contemporary philosophy*. London: Verso.

takes place or not. The final level of Bhaskar's triumvirate classification of reality is the EMPIRICAL. This stratum describes how we investigate and understand the ACTUAL and the REAL through experience, measurement, observation and dissemination at the individual level. This investigation takes place via our methods of enquiry, such as disciplinary research and writing. It, too, is real but not in the ontological sense. It is real in the epistemological sense of being relative and transitive because it varies according to an agent's disciplinary orientation, to their knowledge, their standpoint, their abilities, their values, their resources, their intentions and so on. In other words, agency exists at the level of the EMPIRICAL because methods of enquiry are relative to humans. As such they are contingent, they can change and they are fallible, but what they all have in common is their teleological nature, namely their shared goal of understanding the mechanisms and structures at the intransitive level of the REAL.

The three levels are related by a complex stratified ontology, a full explanation of which exceeds the scope of this book so I will limit myself to asking: how might the REAL, the ACTUAL and the EMPIRICAL map on to an understanding of what makes writing academic? I offer this initial proposal: the REAL refers to the total textual environment available to a writer, including all possible texts, genres, modalities (or, in philosophical-speak, the REAL refers to all possible worlds). This includes the full range of past, present and future semiotic and semantic resources (such as grammar, vocabulary, genres, visuals and all other textual and technological features, as well as rules, conventions and institutional requirements and standards) but it also includes all of history's contingencies and the present and future threshold concepts that account for academic writing reality as a social and academic practice. The ACTUAL refers to any given instance (or event) of an academic text: a traditional written essay, a monograph, a graphic dissertation, a dialogue, a poem, a visual essay (Thomas, 2018) or an audio/dialogic essay (see, for example, the pre-digital pioneering work of Shor and Freire [1987]). These are all potential or actual manifestations of the real and they include texts that have yet to become manifest (such as haptic essays or 3D virtual essays). These ACTUAL texts don't have to happen, but there is real potential for them to happen because of the opportunities afforded at the level of the REAL. The EMPIRICAL refers to how writers go about investigating what is available at the level of the REAL, how they experience the level of the ACTUAL (via institutional practices of assessment, for example) and how they then choose to represent what they notice at the manifest 'actual' level: the methods of enquiry at the EMPIRICAL level are multiple and transitive, allowing writers (agents) to notice a very wide range of academic texts which further triggers their agency to investigate the level of the REAL in order to uncover what else the textual environment might afford. The 'empirical' allows writers to notice writings 'in the wild' and to then enact their agency by knowingly and reflexively making choices about how to write. Academicness emerges from the critical interactions that take place across the EMPIRICAL, the ACTUAL and the REAL. These critical interactions require reflexive judgements, referred to in critical realism as 'judgemental rationality' (Mirzaei Rafe et al., 2020). Figure 1 offers a diagrammatic summary of this. I also refer the reader to the work of Boughey and McKenna (2021) and Mirzaei Rafe et al. (2020), who, respectively, mobilize critical realist ontology to explain how changes can be enacted at the level of educational policy and of curriculum design.

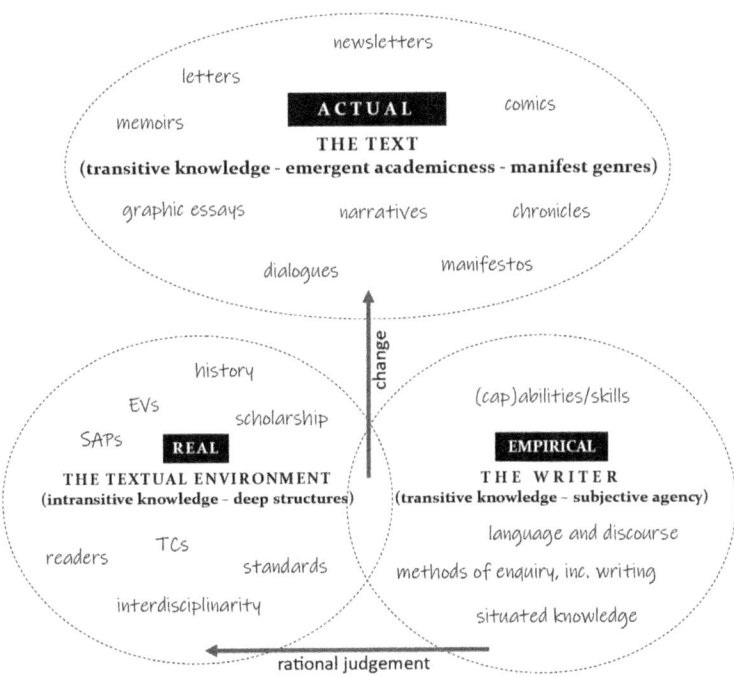

Figure 1 A critical realist conception of academic writing.

The analytical dualism of structure (intransitive) and agency (transitive) is part of critical realism's overarching ambition to transcend deterministic and positivist accounts of social reality, on the one hand, and relativist constructivist ontologies, on the other. This is because, critical realists argue, both these theoretical frameworks have been unable to explain social phenomena: positivism fails because it reifies the epistemic virtue (or vice) of 'objectivity' as a 'value-free' judgement about the nature of reality; it also tends towards deterministic and mechanistic explanations that undermine agency. Constructivism is inadequate because it tends to relativize judgements about what counts as 'real' (Collier, 1994), potentially denying the existence of social reality by over-emphasizing the role that agents play in constructing it. Instead, critical realists argue that ontological claims about the reality of social phenomena (such as social structures) are justified because social reality is not a construct, it is 'real' and 'objective', but not in the positivist sense of being value-free: it is real and objective in the sense that humans have created social realities that embody their values – we might say that for critical realists social reality is objectively ideological. This makes the reality of the natural and the social worlds *ontologically real*. Whilst ontological reality is harder to change, the reality of the social world at the level of the ACTUAL can be changed by individuals (agents) operating at the level of the EMPIRICAL through their judgements and understandings of how social structures work at the level of the REAL: critical realists argue that individuals do not engage in neutral, objective and value-free descriptions of the world, they judge it and act upon it through their values, which include epistemic virtues and vices, namely how they value knowledge (Daston & Galison, 2010). These value claims, which are relative to the EMPIRICAL (where we experience the REAL through the manifestations at the level of the ACTUAL), are what enable individuals to intervene *critically* in changing epistemological reality. The reality of individual value judgements is thus *epistemologically real*, albeit relative to our EMPIRICAL and ACTUAL experience of the world. What this entails for academic writers is that knowledge of what is available in the textual environment can inform their choices about what kinds of texts they value and therefore wish to write. This knowledge can be accessed by learning *about* writing (as opposed *to* learning to write [Downs & Wardle, 2007; Mays, 2017]) through scholarship, whereby academics and writing instructors can become knowledgeable of the textual environment at the level of the REAL and make this knowledge available to their students so that they, students and their writing instructors, can make informed choices at the level of the ACTUAL, where their writing becomes manifest.

As introduced in Chapter 1 and developed here, transitive knowledge is epistemological, i.e. it is knowledge of *how* we come to know things, not knowledge of what things are. It is what I have also referred to as procedural knowledge, for example, *how* a doctor comes to establish that a patient is ill or *how* a researcher comes to write about something they wish to understand better. Intransitive knowledge, on the other hand, is ontological and declarative knowledge, namely knowledge *that* something is the case. It is knowledge that something is real (e.g. poverty is real, regardless of how – what methods we use – we come to know about it). Ontological (intransitive) and epistemological (transitive) reality includes both the social and the natural world. For example, social structures, such as capitalism, are ontologically real, until they are epistemologically shown to be otherwise. Natural phenomena, such as gravity, are ontologically real, until they are epistemologically shown to be otherwise. However, the 'how' (epistemology) should never be collapsed into the 'is' (ontology) because knowing how to do something (e.g. to detect an illness) does not entail knowing everything about what that something is: I may know how to measure my temperature, but I don't know what caused it or even what is happening to me physiologically. Equally, I may know how to teach a student to write an EAP or IELTS essay, but I may not know all that there is to know about academic writing or the student's future writing requirements. This is why it is misleading for academic service providers such as EAP units to claim that they teach 'academic writing', as if academic writing were a homogeneous and static genre.

Moreover, when we collapse the 'how' into the 'is', there is a danger of misunderstanding the world at the level of the REAL. For example, a patient may not actually be ill (REAL) despite my methods of enquiry (EMPIRICAL and ACTUAL) indicating or representing them in a way that suggests that they are: think of the many cases of false positives in science (e.g. positive pregnancy tests that turn out to be negative or misdiagnoses of cancer). When writing is understood as a method of EMPIRICAL enquiry to represent reality at the level of the REAL, then when I erroneously claim that my use of the passive voice, for example, with its putative connotations of impartiality and objectivity, makes *my writing* objective, I am collapsing the 'how' (how I am representing reality) into the 'is' (what that reality is). My use of the passive does not make my writing objective any more than my use of a thermometer makes me have a temperature: the passive is simply a rhetorical device, an instrument, so to speak, that allows me, the writer/enquirer, to tell my reader that I *believe* an event to be objective at the level of the REAL, even though that event might turn out to not be objective (just as a thermometer allows a nurse to tell his patient that he believes they may have a temperature). Like other rhetorical devices and methods of enquiry to represent reality, the passive is epistemological and transitive, it does not establish the intransitive reality at the level of the REAL of the event I am describing: that event would exist regardless of whether or how I represent it, whether in the active or passive voice, via statistical analysis, ethnographic enquiry, a sculpture, a thermometer or a tune on a piano.

To illustrate the danger of collapsing the 'how' with the 'is', let's consider the computer-generated hoaxes referred to in Chapter 3: these were written in such a way that they persuaded the editors at Springer to publish them (Van Noorden, 2014). A tentative explanation as to how this could have happened is that the texts displayed all the surface features of *how* an academic text should look (e.g. academic jargon, passives, paragraphs, to suggest the text was 'objective' and 'rigorous'). Yet, there was nothing objective or rigorous about any of the nonsense generated in these hoaxes: how this nonsense was written, supposedly 'objectively', did not represent any objective reality whatsoever.

The ontological reification by socio-constructivists of what is in fact transitive (i. e. relative) knowledge amounts to what critical realists refer to as an 'epistemic fallacy', namely the reduction of intransitive knowledge, which is ontological, to its transitive method of discovery, which is epistemological. For critical realists, therefore, our knowledge of reality and our experience of reality are not the same because the mechanisms underlying each are different. To conflate reality with our experience of reality amounts to committing an 'epistemic fallacy' (Archer, 2002, p. 12):

> Realism can never endorse the 'epistemic fallacy' and, in this connection, it must necessarily insist that the world has a regulatory effect upon what we make of it and, in turn, what it makes of us. These effects are independent of our full discursive penetration, just as gravity influenced us and the projects we could entertain, long before we conceptualised it.

The relevance of the epistemic fallacy to conceptualizing academic writing is twofold. On the one hand, it alerts us to the fact that what I am calling the 'textual environment' at the level of the REAL has a 'regulatory effect' on writing, when writing is understood as a method of enquiry and representation at the level of the EMPIRCAL. This means that the shape and form of our methods of enquiry is to a great extent constrained by what already exists at the level of the REAL. For example, institutional practices, reader expectations or technologies exist prior to anybody entering academia and they will regulate what we can and cannot change. The level of the REAL represents what 'is' in the objective and intransitive sense of being outside of our power and agency to transform practices. For example, a student taking an IELTS test must display the standards of writing imposed by the IELTS genre. On the other, however, power and agency also exist in a transitive and subjective sense (recall that critical realism conceptualizes reality as a 'stratified ontology', meaning that there are several levels at which things are real). Power and agency exist at the level of the EMPIRICAL (where humans have values and skills) and they represent the potential we have to understand the mechanisms and structures at the level of the REAL so that we stand a chance to knowledgeably influence what then becomes manifest at the level of the ACTUAL. The level of the EMPIRICAL represents the 'how' we come to know about the 'is' at the level of the REAL. For example, that same student taking the IELTS test and who has knowledge of the expectations and requirements of the genre can, potentially, *also* exert their agency by demonstrating their knowledge of a topic and articulating an informed, thoughtful and sensitive judgement on it, rather than simply display language skills at the expense of saying anything truthful or meaningful or just. The implication of this for academic writing is that as a method of enquiry at the level of the EMPIRICAL, it can change to better reflect our values as humans and how we, as writers, interact (i.e. take into account) with what is possible at the level of the REAL. But as a standardized and de-personalized artefact at the level of the REAL, writing also limits (regulates) our powers to bring about change in how we write. It is in this sense that 'how' we (choose to) write is not the same as what writing 'is' because *how* we write could always *be* different.

According to Bhaskar, the epistemic fallacy is a legacy of Cartesian rationality which posits that our thinking can determine what there is. In this sense, Cartesianism is subjective and relative because what 'is' is determined by the human subject. It is also a relic of Kantian idealism whereby the categories of our mind (space and time) impose structures on a world that may not exist (or at least not exist outside of how our cognitive categories describe them). Critical realism dismisses Cartesianism by showing that it commits an epistemic fallacy. Critical realism flips the equally subjective Kantian ontology by asking 'what must the world be like for humans to have knowledge of it?' replacing the Kantian 'what must humans be like in order for the world to be as it is?' (Collier, 1994, pp. 137–68). This commits the critical realist to enquire about the world retroductively, namely from how the world 'must be' to the subjective knower rather than from the subjective knower to the world. Retroduction ensures that we all have something firm and REAL to investigate in the first place. If we apply retroductive reasoning to establish what makes writing academic, we are committed to asking: what must academic writing be like for writers to have knowledge of it? We must, therefore, begin our enquiries at the level of the REAL where we encounter all possible, past, present and future instances of academic texts (because history is also located at the level of the REAL). A retroductive enquiry of this sort would soon reveal that the number of exemplars of academic writing at the level of the REAL exceeds those at the level of the ACTUAL. The implication of this, from a critical realist perspective, is that there is potential for a great deal of variety at the level of the ACTUAL because not everything at the level of the REAL is manifest in the ACTUAL (but it could be).

Transitive methods of enquiry include language, discourse and the disciplines. They allow us to designate the existence of an objective phenomenon and to understand its nature (e.g. the patient's illness). A danger of reducing ontological knowledge to epistemological methods, namely to *how* knowledge is discovered, is that this knowledge risks being understood and potentially believed, only by the communities that share the same discourses and methods of enquiry. For example, to determine the level of a nation's inequality, I might either focus my investigations on income or on wealth. If I focus on income, I may reach the conclusion that a nation is unequal (because of the huge gap in individual incomes). On the other hand, if I focus on wealth (namely accumulated monies as an aggregate), then I may reach the conclusion that a nation does not have a problem with inequality. This epistemological relativism is dangerous because it leaves no scope for being wrong since methods of enquiry are incommensurable and, as such, are rarely measured against each other because their methodological paradigms are too disparate: for example, a deductive method of inquiry can be valid and true in formal logic in virtue of the conclusion following from its premise, even if the premise turns out to be substantially untrue or wrong when measured against an inductive or abductive method of enquiry. If left unchallenged, this kind of epistemological relativism becomes an epistemic fallacy which creates the space for intransitive knowledge to become 'weaponized' (Peters et al., 2020), in the sense that the knowledge that exists at the level of the REAL becomes relative rather than objective. The post-truth politics that emerged during the Donald Trump presidency of 2016–20, in the United States, are an example of how intransitive knowledge can be weaponized by being relativized: 'alternative facts' and 'fake news' were phrases used to discredit and prevent attempts to establish the truth, understood in its common sense and well-intentioned meaning of wanting to know what is happening so that action can be taken to either prevent or initiate change. If the objective intransitive reality of a truth such as climate change, a deadly virus or poverty, all of which are ontologically real, is conflated with its subjective transitive methods of enquiry, methods such as ethnography, logic, experimental and control groups, economic and statistical data, investigative journalism, political or dictionary definitions, writing, photography, video footage and so on, then it becomes possible to deny the existence of such truth because each method of enquiry can potentially show that no such truth exists. In this sense, a real phenomenon such as poverty or racism can be argued out of existence! This is clearly a very dangerous conclusion to reach, particularly if you are poor or belong to a discriminated group. To counter this relativist truth-denying tendency, Donald Judd, critical realist and writing scholar, reminds us that knowledge can be understood *dialectically*, rather than relatively, as an interaction between transitive knowledge and intransitive knowledge, which in critical realist theory is made possible by the 'judgmental rationality' of agents.

Judgemental rationality can be understood in critical realist terms as the ability of agents to reflexively learn from their environments and adjust their actions accordingly. This requires knowledge at the level of the REAL because it is at this level that agents can understand the structures and the mechanisms that lead to the manifestation of phenomena at the level of the ACTUAL. Judgemental rationality can be further understood scientifically as 'trained judgement', namely as an epistemic virtue that guides agents towards having knowledge of the world (Daston & Galison, 2010), or philosophically as 'practical wisdom', in the Socratic sense (Smith, 1999). The common denominator that underpins 'judgement', understood as a human rational, trained and practical disposition, is an ethical orientation towards knowledge, the truth and the common good. This explains why critical realism is a theory that is motivated by change that leads to social justice.

The dialectical interaction across the stratified ontology represented in Figure 1 is essentially an interaction between agency and structure, between a writer and their textual environment. It allows us to reclaim a realm of reality that can *potentially* be known by everybody, regardless of their methods of enquiry. With regard to writing, I have represented this dialectal dimension in Figure 1 as 'judgement' to signal that what makes writing academic is the writer's judgement about which SAP they wish to enact given their knowledge of what the textual environment affords them. This means that writers are required to acknowledge (and have as much knowledge as possible of) the existence of the vast historical and social textual environment at the level of the REAL, because by knowing what the textual environment affords, they are more likely to make rational, trained and ethical choices about how to write. They may, of course, not be able to act upon and make those choices because of a range of constraints (such as institutional practices or lack of access to technology), but the fact that they are knowledgeable about what is possible at the level of the REAL empowers them to investigate a far greater range of ways of enacting their choices so that they can become manifest at the level of the ACTUAL. Because judgement requires knowledge of the objective deep structures and mechanisms at the level of the REAL as well as knowledge of one's own subjective values, disciplinary orientations, capabilities and skills at the level of the EMPIRICAL, constraints on what can make a text academic do exist. For example, a hoax cannot be academic because it lacks the epistemic virtue of a commitment to the truth (REAL) and it contravenes reader expectations (REAL) about what an academic text should be. The more attuned, reflective and reflexive the writer's judgement becomes through knowledge of what is available and possible at each level, the greater the range of texts at the level of the ACTUAL that can count as academic. As I explain below, these three levels of stratified reality form an open system that allows new knowledge and new possibilities to move between the different strata.

Once we agree that some things are ontologically real (unless reasonably and knowledgeably judged to be otherwise) and that they are intransitive, we stand a better chance of ensuring that different communities are able to talk about the same reality. The fact that different communities (with different theoretical and disciplinary traditions) mobilize different methods and, ultimately, different values to investigate the world does not change the ontological reality of what they are talking about (e.g. poverty is always real, regardless of which methods are deployed to investigate it). Rather, what these differences allow for is an ongoing conversation about what is possible at the level of the ACTUAL based on the objective affordances at the level of the REAL.

The relevance of all this to academic writing is that there can be far greater variation of what makes writing academic at the manifest level of the ACTUAL when we understand and know what is possible at the level of the deep structural and potential level of the REAL.

Critical Realism and Academic Writing

Not much has been written about the relevance of critical realism to academic writing, but what has been written provides generative insights to potentials that warrant further investigation. Three theorists, all of whom are also teachers of academic writing, stand out in this regard. These are US scholars Michael Bernard-Donals (1998) and Donald Judd (2003) and South African scholar Deirdre Pratt (2011). I will review them briefly in chronological order.

The Practice of Theory: Rhetoric, Pedagogy and Knowledge in the Academy

Bernard-Donals (1998) writes from within the literary tradition of American rhetoric and composition which is rooted in the classics (Plato and Aristotle). His book is a reminder of how varied, ideological and contested writing traditions are. For Bernard-Donals, rhetoric is a method for knowing the world. This chimes with Richardson and St. Pierre (2005)'s portrayal of writing as a method of enquiry and it assumes that the world is real and composed of both social and natural structures and mechanisms that are measurable, observable and objective. Because of the foundational (i.e. objective) ontology of the world, writing (and the language it is composed of) is not *constitutive* of reality but *descriptive* of it. By being descriptive of reality, it remains ontologically distinct from it. In advancing this thesis, Bernard-Donals is positioning himself against the post-modernism of philosophers such as Richard Rorty and Michel Foucault, for whom it is the discourses of language and writing that seem to be intransitively real. However, on a critical realist reading, they cannot be intransitively real because writing is always *about* something that is external to it. This makes it an epistemologically transitive method of enquiry and not an ontologically intransitive constituent of reality. If writing were intransitively constitutive of reality, this would potentially commit us to claiming that reality can only be accessed or realized through language and writing, which further suggests that only written (or linguistic) reality exists. But this would deny other modes of representation (the visual arts, for example) the right to claim their legitimacy as constitutive of reality, or it would at least make them incommensurable with writing. Moreover, if writing were constitutive of reality, rather than its *proxy*, as I argued in Chapter 1, it would make human communication unintelligible: if there is no external non-linguistic reality to refer to, because what is real is simply language (which further begs the question of 'whose' language?), what then becomes of our shared human endeavours to understand and interpret both the natural and the social world? I have located writing at the level of the EMPIRICAL in Figure 1 because it is ontologically distinct from the REAL. This matters because it allows us to think of writing as one of many methods for interpreting and describing the world, alongside music, the visual arts, statistics, mathematics and countless other methods deployed by disciplinary enquiry. At best, writing remains a partial representation of reality. Although Bernard-Donals makes no such normative claim, I would argue, along with Olson (1977, 1994) and Harris (2000) that because it is an empirical and transitive method of enquiry created to describe the intransitive world, writing is not inherently superior to other methods of enquiry. Indeed, writing is as fallible as other methods for interpreting the world and regularly fails to represent reality, as we saw in Chapters 2 and 3 with reference to the epistemic injustices inflicted when words fail to describe discrimination.

Crucially, what a critical realist theory of writing entails is that it is not the writing, *qua* method of enquiry, that is 'objective', it is the ontological reality at the level of the REAL that is objective in the sense that it is independent of how the observer-writer describes it. This is why I challenge the characterization of writing as 'objective' (see Chapter 1): writing choices are always at the level of the empirical and, as such, are always relative and subjective. What is objective is the intransitive reality a writer wishes to describe using their text as a proxy *for* reality, not as a substitute of this reality. For this reason, academic writing can never be 'objective'.

Having established that the social and natural worlds exist independently of their knowers (and writers) by appealing to Bhaskar's critical realism, Bernard-Donals argues that writing can then intervene critically in how it describes reality because writers make rhetorical choices. It is in virtue of their rhetorical choices (which include linguistic and non-linguistic choices) that the writer *qua* agent also becomes an agent of change and transformation whereby their text describes reality as the writer wishes to describe it from a position of knowledge. In other words, it is through informed choice about how to write about the world that writers can have an influence on and therefore change reality. For example, Piper Harron's PhD thesis (referred to in Chapter 3) was written from a position of knowledge: transitive knowledge of her agency at the level of the EMPIRICAL and intransitive knowledge of what was textually possible at the level of the REAL. This allowed a novel mathematical PhD genre to emerge by becoming manifest at the level of the ACTUAL.

Critical Realism and Composition Theory

Judd (2003) is a teacher of English and Composition Studies, what the Americans call 'Academic Writing' and which continues in the tradition of the

United States' established field of rhetoric and composition. His book is inspired by his predecessor Bernard-Donals, whom he credits for having helped him make the link between academic writing and critical realism. Judd takes to task three cornerstones of American composition studies. To varying degrees, these writing traditions have influenced the UK tradition of EAP (Russell et al., 2009), particularly the cognitivist tradition which underscores several textbooks that foreground process approaches to academic writing. The theories of writing that Judd challenges are:

- Expressivist theory and voluntarism
- Cognitive rhetoric and empirical positivism
- Socio-constructivist rhetoric and super-idealism

According to Judd, none of these three mainstream pedagogies recognize the distinction between transitive and intransitive knowledge and, for this reason, all are inappropriate academic writing pedagogies. After subjecting each to an immanent critique by identifying their theoretical inconsistencies with regard to their practical classroom implications and applications, he provides a radical transcendental critique by proposing the social philosophy of critical realism. Unlike Bernard-Donals, who recognizes that each approach has considerable merits at different stages of writing instruction and that each tradition has evolved and continues to evolve in response to very specific contexts, Judd is less forgiving. Rather, Judd seems intent on simplifying in order to magnify the undesirable consequences that each approach potentially commits its writer to and on exposing their inherent theoretical inconstancies via an immanent critique.

Judd berates expressivist theory for being individualistic and having the (un)intended consequence of becoming wholly subjective, whereby all writing counts as 'good writing'; he accuses cognitive rhetoric of falling foul to the linear, mechanistic determinism of input–output computer analogies, whereby each step in the writing process sequentially leads to a predictable outcome that takes no account of context or human agency; and he takes serious issue with socio-constructivist and post-modern theories of writing because, he argues, they lead to the kind of relativism that makes knowledge wholly transitive and incommensurable rather than intransitive and shared. His main contention is that each writing approach runs the unintended risk of thwarting the educative and epistemically transformative purpose of writing. Expressivist pedagogy is uneducative because it encourages students to dwell on individualistic, relative and transitive knowledge (i.e. what I think, how I got there, etc.) at the expense of intransitive knowledge; cognitive pedagogy encourages students to think that knowledge is sequential, logical, linear, predictable and value-free and that academic writing is meaningful and good as long as it is well planned and well written: IELTS essays or other skills, genre and template-based approaches to academic writing might be examples of the cognitive approach, as might hoaxes, in the sense that they can be well-written but meaningless. Because this kind of writing is ultimately devoid of content, its knowledge is neither transitive nor intransitive; socio-constructivist pedagogies deny expert positions (such as the expertise of the teacher) by suggesting that knowledge is co-constructed and sanctioned by the community (e.g. the teacher and the students). This, like the expressivist tradition, reifies epistemic relativity at the expense of intransitive objective knowledge: academic literacies approaches might be an example of socio-constructivist approaches because it is not clear where or how they might draw the line between what counts and does not count as an academic text.

By not recognizing that knowledge is both epistemological (transitive) and ontological (intransitive), the three pedagogies fail to fulfil their ultimate function, which is to be educational. To be educational is to be transformative, as already highlighted in Chapter 1 with reference to Bereiter and Scardamalia (1987), who, although cognitivists in their approach to learning the process of writing, recognize the socially transformative role of building a kind of knowledge that changes beliefs, skills and attitudes. If education is to be transformative it needs to be able to change our knowledge of reality, re-configure the *status quo* and advance social justice, an epistemic virtue that underpins the mission of some modern-day higher education. To do this, writing instruction needs to foreground the development of students' knowledge of the topics they are expected to write about (rather than disproportionately focus on the myriad surface features that will allow them to write about this knowledge). The implications of a critical realist writing pedagogy are that writers must work retroductively from knowledge of the world (i.e. knowledge of the topics they are interested in) to making decisions about how best to represent that knowledge in their texts. This approach turns much current general academic writing instruction on its head because it starts with knowledge of content and then decides on the most fitting genres, modalities, languages and technologies for representing that knowledge.

Judd's more positive transcendental critique consists in proposing critical realism as an alternative theoretical foundation for academic writing. His reasons are fourfold:

1. From a critical realist perspective, the reason we need knowledge is to further human emancipation. This means that writing instruction, if it is to have educational value in the academy, must create the conditions for writers to emancipate themselves. On this reading, what makes writing academic is knowledge. Since a hoax or an IELTS essay or any other kind of writing that displays conventional or performative forms of academicness (such as plagiarized texts) does not need knowledge to be deemed worthy of publication or a grade, it cannot be considered academic. As such, symbolic citation and other forms of plagiarism would place the necessary constraints on what counts as academic. However, the use of personal pronouns or contracted forms would not constitute such a constraint because they do not prevent knowledge from emerging;

2. Knowledge is neither individualistic (expressivist), cognitive, nor relative (socio-constructivist), but always *about the social* in the sense that a writer must be knowledgeable about the objective reality of the social and institutional structures that generate the social phenomena they are writing about (e.g. poverty; capitalism; climate change, injustice). On this account, for a text to be academic, it needs to engage with deep knowledge and research. Judd proposes, in keeping with critical realist philosophy, that this deep knowledge is best approached in an interdisciplinary way. His suggestion aligns with sociologies of knowledge that require multidisciplinary approaches to understanding reality (see, for example, Michael Gibbons (1994) in Baber (1995) on the differentiation between Mode 1 (disciplinary) and Mode 2 (interdisciplinary) knowledge) and with decolonizing ecologies of knowledge so that we become better attuned to what counts as knowledge and to whose knowledge counts (Collyer et al., 2019; de Sousa Santos, 2009);

3. Knowledge is corrigible. Through self-reflexivity and an ongoing quest to understand and to know things, we can correct mistaken beliefs. Writing pedagogy should be educative in this respect, i.e. it should lead students away from mistaken beliefs and provide them with authentic and meaningful tasks to ensure they are always writing from a position of knowledge. This would imply that for writing to be academic, it must always be research-informed and truth-oriented. An implication of such a condition would be that any writing instruction that is not research-informed and truth-oriented would result in writing that is not academic; truth and consistency are epistemic virtues that involve value judgements about social and natural reality. This means that writing tasks which require

students to communicate their positions on social (and natural) phenomena need to allow students to learn content, do research and read up about the phenomena they are being asked to write about. This ensures that writing pedagogy honours its educational mission to be emancipatory and transformative. The implication of this for what makes writing academic is that writing instruction needs to engage meaningfully with content. When content becomes a pre-condition for meaningful writing, the 'myth of transience' lamented by Rose (1985) and Russell (2002) is exposed for what it is: a myth. Writing choices that depend on writing content having a meaningful purpose are rarely universally transferable, as Sam, from Chapter 1, found out in the transition from writing at secondary school level to writing in tertiary education.

To sum up, both Judd and Bernard-Donals think of writing as 'epistemological', as a method of enquiry that allows us to make value-laden claims about a world that is external to us. In this sense, all academic writing is subjective. They argue that by 'reclaiming reality' (which is Roy Bhaskar's socio-scientific project), a realist ontology does away with the reification of relativistic and anti-foundationalist ontologies and replaces these with the concept of the dialectic, namely a relational and stratified ontology whereby human agents interact with their environments by shaping them and being shaped by them. This assumes that there is an objective reality to shape and to be shaped by and that social change is possible when agents intervene critically, rationally and using their judgement. Realist philosophy acknowledges that there are material structures, mechanisms and tendencies that exist independently of language and of how we name and classify reality. Once reality has been reclaimed, language and its written forms, via the intentional agency of the author, can do the methodological and dialectical work of intervening critically on these material structures but only through research and working with content rather than by changing discourses: simply changing how we name phenomena does not change the structural nature of those phenomena (e.g. re-naming 'climate change' to 'climate emergency' does not substantially alter the phenomenon we are describing, it simply provides an indication as to how the observer views that phenomenon). Only a deep knowledge of the structures of reality at the level of the REAL can lead to change at the level of the ACTUAL, which is where writing is manifest. Re-describing these structures by, for example, changing how we name something, e. g. replacing 'writer' with 'author' to signal authority; or 'customer' with 'student' to signal resistance towards a lexicon of neoliberalism;

or 'writing' with 'composing' or 'academic literacies' to signal an ever-increasing range of nuance, goes some way towards re-configuring imaginaries, but it does little to fundamentally modify what happens at the level of the ACTUAL. Indeed, critical realists tend to be sceptical of what they see as *sui generis* language games whereby we claim to have enacted change simply through changes in discourse: 'Re-description does not change the material [real] constraints by which you are bound' (Bernard-Donals, 1998, p. 228). In saying this, Bernard-Donals is explicitly criticizing the post-modernist and socio-constructivist tendency to locate change at the level of the EMPIRICAL, which is where I have located language and discourse, rather than at the level of the ACTUAL. Instead, a critical realist framing of academic writing posits writing as a socially transforming self-reflexive and transitive methodological practice that recognizes the agency of the writer whilst acknowledging that there are material constraints to writing as one would like. However, through a process of dialectical judgement that requires knowledge of the REAL, writers can harness the opportunities that exist at the structural level. What this dialectic nature further entails is that although academic writing is *subject to* established conventions, it is not *reducible to* or *determined by* these conventions. Because of this non-reduction, change in writing forms can occur.

Modelling Written Communication: A New Systems Approach to Modelling in the Social Sciences

Writing in the South African context, Pratt (2011), too, has mobilized critical realism to provide an alternative to relativistic post-modern approaches. Her work is aimed at proposing a theoretical model for creating what she calls a 'computerized writing tutor'. I refer the curious reader directly to her book for the finer details of her technical analysis and limit myself here to quoting her at length because her words provide an apt conclusion to what has been said so far. They also afford a natural segue into thinking about writing as a 'complex' open system, which can provide students like Sam, from Chapter 1, with a sense of 'empowerment' rather than confusion (Pratt, 2011, pp. 27–8):

> Critical realism offers an appropriate perspective from which to view the complex processes involved in composing [writing]. The critical realist philosophy represents reality as complex and dynamic and inquires into the way things work – particularly the deep-structure causes of events and social processes …. The participant focus is also favoured by critical realism, which views human

action not as governed by behaviouristic laws, nor as a conditioned response to pre-determined social structures, but as individual agency (M. Archer, 2002) with a fair amount of free will within any given social order. Human agency is both enabled and limited by the opportunities and constraints afforded by social structures, at the same time maintaining the fabric of these social structures, which are fairly stable, but capable of gradual change, usually by one or more of the complex social mechanisms which maintain these structures rather than as the result of individual human agency (or specific interest groups) per se. This means that, while learner writers often find themselves operating in a 'given' (but not fixed or static) context, where academic writing is an undisputed fact of academic life, they are able to make efforts to empower themselves by gaining insight into and expertise in academic composing, in spite of the constraints set by academic requirements and other factors (e. g. lack of experience and/or background knowledge).

To better understand the critical realist project, I now turn my attention to explaining the role that complexity theory plays in this endeavour.

Academic Writing as a Complex and Emergent Open System

In Molinari (2019), I articulated a systematic account of how complexity theory has been understood in the domains of philosophy, sociology, science and linguistics and of how its related concept of emergence can be further harnessed to conceptualize academic writing as an 'open system' in which change and novelty become possible. For my present purposes and readers, I offer the following definition of complexity by social philosopher Dan Little (Little, 2018), whose fascinating blog on *Understanding Society* provides several analyses of social phenomena that draw on critical realism:

> A complex system is one in which there is a multiplicity of causal factors contributing to the dynamics of the system, in which there are causal interactions among the underlying causal factors and in which causal interactions are often non-linear. Non-linearity is important here, because it implies that a small change in one or more factors may lead to very large changes in the outcome.

Little refers to two fundamental concepts in complexity theory: change and non-linearity. These are essential to understanding critical realist philosophy and its relevance to re-conceptualizing academic writing as a complex open system.

Complexity Affords Change and Non-linearity

Several writing scholars in the sociolinguistic tradition of Academic Literacies seek to explain how writers can push back against the conventions that constrain them in order to change them by invoking the metaphor of a 'crack' in the system, which is presumably 'how the light gets in' (echoing singer-song writer Leonard Cohen's famous 'Anthem' refrain). Brian Street, for example, in conversation with Theresa Lillis and Mary Scott, claims (Lillis et al., 2015, p. 389):

> One metaphor I'd use comes from the person in Algeria who was appointed to follow Kofi Annan as the UN representative in Syria. He said: 'all I can see in front of me is a wall but I know that walls have cracks in them and that's what I'm going to work on.' So that's what we're doing. Universities look like walls but there are some cracks.

Writing scholar Catalina Neculai similarly refers to how she has resisted neoliberal terminology in dissertation descriptors in a 'subcutaneous' way. What she means by this is that she defied the institutional requirements to give prominence to certain information by deliberately choosing to foreground the disciplinary contributions of her students rather than focus on the neoliberal jargon of student 'employability', which she nevertheless had to refer to 'obliquely' and 'indifferently' (Neculai, 2015, p. 405).

Complexity theorists (e.g. Kuhn, 2008; Parnell, 2012) and critical realists deploy similar metaphors but they possibly conjure up a more prominent role for the agent, particularly in signalling the need for the agent to more actively 'seek' the cracks and force them open or to create the opportunities for those cracks to form in the first place. What sociolinguistics in the academic literacies tradition call 'cracks' and 'subcutaneous' acts of resistance (which conjures up a more serendipitous, happenstance image, as though you happen to be walking past the crack or you chance upon a document with neoliberal jargon), complexity theorists call 'levers' that need switching to re-direct the course of history and shift the deep structures of power (Mason, 2008, p. 38):

> Complexity theory seeks the levers of history, the sources and reasons for change, in the dynamic complexity of interactions among elements or agents that constitute a particular environment. It is in this sense that seemingly trivial accidents of history may increase dramatically in significance when their interactions with other apparently minute events combine to produce significant redirections in the course of history, significant shifts in the prevailing balance of power.

It is because of the need to enact change that some applied linguists have also turned to complexity theory to explain and to justify diversity and change in linguistic practices, particularly in response to deterministic, building-block approaches to language learning. With regard to the dynamism of language and the unpredictable non-linearity of language development, they argue that when language is conceived of as a complex system, changes in language development can occur in interactive, dynamic an non-linear ways because language is an open system (Cameron & Larsen-Freeman, 2007, p. 227, emphasis added):

> Complex systems are composed of elements or agents that interact in different ways. Their interactions lead to self-organization and the emergence of new patterns at different levels and timescales. Such systems are also adaptive and dynamic. The elements and agents change over time, but crucially so also do the ways in which they influence each other, the relations among them. Complex systems are open rather than closed; energy and matter can come into the system. The dynamic nature of element interactions and the openness of a system to the outside lead to non-linearity, *which in complex systems theory signifies that the effect is disproportionate to the cause.*

Here the emphasis is explicitly on the language learner as agent and how they interact with their environments to develop language competence. This competence emerges from a series of interactions, the effects of which on learning a language are non-linear and unpredictable.

What complexity theory signals, in contrast to the seemingly similar concerns of academic literacies, is a recognition that there is a 'multiplicity' of factors that contribute to phenomena (such as language development or, in our case, particular conventions in academic writing practices). For deep structural change to occur in any social practice, it may not be enough to notice a crack and presumably pick away at it until it gets bigger and the system eventually collapses, or engage in serendipitous acts of linguistic resistance, because this approach may not reveal or may even remain silent on the underlying causal factors that led to the structures that allowed a crack to form in the first place. Rather, in order for an agent, in our case, an academic writer, to stand a chance of writing in diverse ways, they need knowledge of the nature of the complex structures they belong to in virtue of being a student, an academic, or a teacher, so that they might become empowered to identify what caused these structures and where the *levers of change* might be located. The complex stratified ontology that critical realism reveals indicates that change is simply not possible at all levels of reality: the structural level of the REAL, for example, remains largely beyond the reach of any single individual. Whilst it is easy to see that there are 'cracks' in the system that can be picked at – signalled, for example, by a rise in cases of plagiarism, which indicates dysfunctionality in academic writing practices that might warrant more creative pedagogies – it is much harder to know what to do about and with those cracks. Crucially, it is hard to know *who* has the power and agency to do something about them. A critical realist response involves going beyond noticing that something is wrong to knowing where to put pressure on the system through a deep knowledge of the system. A student writer alone cannot pick at a crack and resist. Nor can a writing teacher employed on a casual and fixed-term contract, for example, because they will more likely teach to the default standard of templates and conventions. But a student writer equipped with agency and a knowledgeable teacher with a secure and permanent contract that allows them the time and the resources to engage with writing scholarship and connect with writing communities might be able to action the pressure needed for change.

To begin appreciating the significance of complexity theory and its relevance to what makes writing academic, we must also distinguish between a 'complex' system and one that is 'complicated'. This distinction is important because it affects how events are analysed and understood. A complicated system can be explained in terms of its constituent parts whereas a complex one cannot. For example, a bicycle is complicated, but it is not complex. A sailor's knot is complicated, but it is not complex. This is because although both a bicycle and a knot are intricate and are made of many inter-connected mechanical parts, a full understanding of what these parts are and how they connect to each other is sufficient to explain how the bicycle and the knot, as *whole* systems, will work. This allows us to predict what will happen when we turn the pedal or move the handlebars on the bike or when we pull at the loose end of the knot. Complex systems, on the other hand, do not allow for such predictions because their 'whole is greater than the sum of their parts' (Beckett & Hager, 2018). Complex systems include social phenomena, such as education and economics, whose constituent parts inter-relate to such an extent that they cannot be explained in isolation and without a full account of how they relate and interact to other parts: the reasons for rising inflation rest as much on human purchasing behaviour and psychology as they do on the mechanics of price increases and the value of national currencies. This means that in a complex system, changes in the constituent causal parts are not directly proportional to changes in the whole i.e. changes in individual spending habits (one of several causes of inflation) do not provide a full explanatory account of why inflation occurs. This now explains what is meant when complex systems are described as *non-linear*: cause and effect are disproportionate in the sense that the whole effect cannot be explained by an isolated cause.

Here is another illustration of what is meant by *non-linearity* in complex systems. The seemingly simple act of dropping a single coin in a fairground coin pusher can lead to a disproportionate effect whereby the entire mass of accumulated coins suddenly drops. What caused the drop, though, was also the cumulative pressure of the mass of coins that were already in the system, the time it took for this pressure to accumulate, the timing of dropping the coin in the first place, the amount of pressure and precision exerted by the machine and the position of the new coin in relation to the other coins. From a complexity perspective, that single coin played a relatively small part in causing the whole mass to drop. Moreover, the effect of this huge drop results in the player winning a prize that by far exceeds the value or investment in time and energy of dropping the initial coin. It is in this sense that cause and effect are disproportionate and *non-linear*. By contrast, a complicated system is said to be *linear* because a change in a constituent part can more straightforwardly explain a change in the whole. For example, by taking the pedal off the bike, the crankshaft can't properly turn.

Rather than an aggregate composed of concatenated parts that add up to a whole, as skills-based, cookie-cutter and template approaches to writing encourage, academic writing is a complex social system of dynamic inter-relations whose multiple causes cannot be reduced to its constituent parts in a linear, i.e. mechanistic, manner. On a complexity account, academic writing becomes *non-linear* because what makes it academic as a whole (its effect) cannot be reduced to any specific part (the cause). This can be illustrated with reference to the effect that conventional academic forms can have on representations of knowledge. For instance, the use of personal or non-personal language (discussed in Chapter 1), such as the active or passive voice, can have a disproportionate effect on how knowledge is re-presented. The personal, active voice in ethnography, realized by the use of 'I', for example, indexes that the researcher, not the 'reality', influences what counts and does not count as 'data'. 'I' thus becomes more than a grammatical item (a personal pronoun). It becomes an epistemological rhetorical device to signal the positionality of the researcher, a statement about the researcher's orientation towards their area of research: it signals that the data aren't 'out there' and that it is the researcher who confers upon their samples the status of 'data'. As Thomson (2013) reminds us, '[t]hey aren't data until we make them data' and it is our choice of personal or impersonal language that signals where we stand, i.e. how we position ourselves with regard to whether we deem something to count as data or not. Even when I claim 'these are samples of x, y, z' without rhetorical recourse to personal pronouns, my choice of language, in the guise of the impersonal demonstrative deictic (*these*) and the present simple (a tense that allows you to describe an event as an established fact), signals my objective stance towards the data. It does not signal that the data are objectively 'out there', but that I think and am saying that they are. By not using personal pronouns, a particular ontological stance also emerges, namely that 'data are out there', they exist. Similarly, if I claim: 'here is how I have established that samples x, y, z can be part of my data set', a more epistemological stance emerges, namely 'this is how I know they are data'. From a complexity perspective, the use or non-use if 'I' causes a disproportionate effect in terms of how knowledge is represented. The simple, almost-imperceptible and seemingly innocuous grapheme – I – generates enormous ontological and epistemological effects! Moreover, these effects cannot be reduced to the single use of the pronoun 'I' because there are far greater causes that determine whether writing, as a complex whole, is perceived as having a subjective or objective orientation towards its object of enquiry. These causes include the disciplinary paradigms that establish methods and methodologies for how research is conducted, the assumptions about the role of the researcher in the research process and the language of the text as a whole (Hyland, 2002).

Crucially, in a complex social practice such as writing and what makes it academic, the effects cannot be reduced to their causes. This explains why popular skills-based textbook descriptions of academic writing as 'linear' make no sense: they make no sense because what makes writing academic cannot be reduced to any single factor, such as structure, vocabulary, syntax or language itself. There is multiplicity of factors which explain an effect, what philosopher of mind Jerry Fodor (1974, 1997) refers to as 'multiple realisability'. This signals that a 'heterogeneity of realisers' is involved in explaining how something as complex as life itself is possible. This multiple realizability, however, does not commit us to a relativistic 'anything goes' approach to what makes writing academic, as practice-based approaches might suggest because, as argued throughout Chapter 3 and above with reference to Judd, although there are multiple ways to represent knowledge, a critical realist writing pedagogy requires that writers be committed to the truth of their claims rather than wedded to any particular form to make those claims.

It is at this point that the concept of 'emergence' becomes a useful heuristic to explain how complex phenomena can be explained non-reductively and why insisting that any particular feature of language that forms part of a dynamic complex system is more academic than any other is confusing and misleading.

Emergence Affords Novelty

Emergence is a widely debated philosophical and scientific concept and, like complexity theory, it is key to understanding critical realism. For our present purposes, emergence can be simply understood in the terms outlined by philosopher Jaegwon Kim (2006, p. 548):

> [A] purely physical system, composed exclusively of bits of matter, when it reaches a certain degree of complexity in its structural organisation, can begin to exhibit genuinely novel properties not possessed by its simpler constituents.

Examples of emergent properties include water, pain and consciousness (Chalmers, 1996, 2006). Much philosophical debate centres on whether these properties are weakly or strongly emergent (which I explain below), but at the core of the debate is the extent to which an emergent property (a whole) can be reduced to its parts, or constituents. For example, to what extent can a complex property like human consciousness be reduced to and explained by the chemical composition of the brain? This is referred to by philosopher David Chalmers as the 'hard problem' of science. It is also referred to in the literatures on emergence in terms of what constitutes the 'supervenient base' from which complex phenomena emerge (Eaton, 1994; Hohwy & Kallestrup, 2008). For example, what makes a work of art 'beautiful' emerges from a complex set of interactions between variables (such as the materials used to create, the symmetry, aesthetic theories, cultural background of the viewer and so on). These variables and their interactions are referred to as the supervenient base, namely the physical and social properties that give rise to a complex phenomenon, such as beauty. This debate extends to critical realist understandings of the nature of social phenomena and can be understood in the context of methodological and collective individualism referred to earlier in this chapter (Kaidesoja, 2009), namely the extent to which social phenomena such as poverty emerge from individual or collective behaviours.

Arguably, water is an example of a weakly emergent complex phenomenon: it is emergent because it is a liquid that comes into existence from two gases, hydrogen and oxygen. Its psycho-physical property of liquidity is novel because it is not contained in the property of a gas and, as such, it cannot be reduced to its constituents (Wongsriruksa et al., 2012). Liquidity, therefore, is an example of a complex (rather than complicated) novel property because its characteristics are not possessed by its simpler gaseous constituents: in fact, it is the term 'water', rather than the chemical designation of H_2O, that is the emergent property. Emergent properties are further characterized by the fact that claims can be made about them that cannot be made of their constituents: we can describe water as thirst-quenching but cannot say the same about hydrogen or oxygen. Water is arguably 'weakly' emergent because the science of chemistry can provide stratified, finely grained explanations, or 'bridges' (Fodor, 1974), that can account for why two gases can result in a liquid. In other words, the science of chemistry allows us to predict that when two atoms of hydrogen combine with one atom of oxygen, water results. A complex phenomenon such as consciousness, on the other hand, can be considered as 'strongly' emergent because it is not possible to explain or predict its manifestation from the parts of its constituent supervenient base (there is heated debate in philosophical circles about whether there are any strongly emergent phenomena at all. See, for example, debates between physicalist philosophers of science and mind, such as Patricia Churchland, and philosophers of consciousness, such as Philip Goff and David Chalmers).

My contention is that academicness, namely what makes writing academic, be understood in a similar way: it is a weakly emergent property that is novel because it does not share the properties of its constituent, or supervenient, base. This base coincides with the three layers of stratified reality represented in Figure 1 from which academicness can be traced and explained. The SAPs that can make writing academic, referred to in Chapter 3, such as a commitment to the truth, knowledge and to social justice, can be understood as novel properties that are multiply realized by the range of constituents that exist within the complex and stratified interactions at the level of the REAL, the ACTUAL and the EMPIRICAL. This allows me to claim that the graphic dissertation of Sousanis (2015) is academic on a weakly emergent account: although few of its academic characteristics, as a whole, can be traced back to its constituent parts (he has no topic sentences or paragraphs and very few in-text references), its parts do explain why it is academic. It is academic because Sousanis complied with the fundamental requirements of research practice, such as being evidence-based, theory-led, (visually) argumentative and making an original contribution to knowledge. These requirements make his dissertation academic at the emergent level rather than at the supervenient level of its parts. This has significant implications for teaching, assessment and academic misconduct practices. Since these requirements belong to the deep structural level of the

REAL and are therefore less likely to be changed than what can be changed at the level of the ACTUAL, they are sufficient to anchor and constrain what makes a text academic. They do not entail an 'anything goes approach to academic writing'. Quite the opposite. They show that when writing, or any other method of enquiry, is understood as transitive, it simply acts as an EMPIRICAL proxy for representing the REAL, in this case knowledge of visual thinking and of interdisciplinary philosophies. This commits me to claiming that any method of enquiry that enacts a genuinely socio-academic practice can lead to an academic text.

For example, what makes Harron (2016)'s PhD thesis academic (as a whole) cannot be traced back in a linear way to any specific words or arrangement of her text (the parts), as might be done in an IELTS essay or academic hoax. Instead, what makes it academic are the SAPs that emerge from the interaction of her agency as a writer (particularly her values and her academic need to meet the requirements of a doctorate in Mathematics) and the range of opportunities available to her in the intransitive textual environment, such as threshold concept 3.0 (Villanueva, 2015). What emerges from this interaction is a novel entity, a thesis that is unique but that can be explained by its constituent parts and interactions thereof because it met the knowledge requirements of Princeton University. But it is also a thesis that *re-sets* the 'requirements of a doctorate in mathematics' by transforming this knowledge: Harron's thesis re-configures the *standards of excellence* of a doctorate to include social justice in the field of mathematics because she has introduced a new standard of excellence: being accessible to an audience that transcends her examining committee.

Open Systems Afford both Change and Novelty

Complexity is further related to the notion of permeable open systems and what emerges from them. Thinking of academic writings as open systems allows us to see that they are permeable (Molinari, 2021b). As such, they are subject to change whilst also remaining recognizable and stable because they remain systems. A human body is an open system because it emerges from countless variables and their interactions none of which it shares its properties with, when considered as a whole. For example, a human body can be described as tall, slim, large, heavy and so on, but its constituent cells, limbs and degree of attractiveness cannot. This is because a human body emerges from an identifiable and relatively finite supervenient base of multiple realizers that interact physically, chemically and biologically in a permeable system that is nevertheless open to multiple mechanisms and variables that continue to enter the system: what makes a human being tall or short or having any other kind of physical characteristic can be explained by some of these variables and their interactions, but not all. Once a human body has emerged from its supervenient biological base, a distinct and relatively unpredictable phenomenon can be said to have emerged, i.e. a social, political, psychological human being, not just a biological body, whose specific characteristics, such as personality and looks, can be explained in a weakly emergent sense at the cellular level but whose overall essence is unlikely to have been 'written in the genes', so to speak. That human essence is an emergent property.

Academic writings (like human beings) are similarly open to variables which have causal relevance. These variables include the purposes, languages, values, agencies and literacies of researchers (the writers) as well as myriad environmental structures (e.g. SAPs, epistemic virtues, institutional conventions and constraints). In this sense, academic writings are not 'closed', meaning that their characteristics are not determined by finite criteria that are impermeable to the complexities and contingencies of academic social reality. On the other hand, an IELTS essay could be described as 'closed' because all it needs to be successful are isolated features, such as standardized paragraphs or linguistic devices, that do not reflect the naturally occurring influences that shape academic writing and affect language choice, such as disciplinary genres, citation practices and the writer's voice (Ivanič & Simpson, 1992).

Conclusions

Whilst there are several limitations to the critical realist project, or, at the very least, there are areas that require further theorization – such as the specific nature of the generative mechanisms that take place between the three stratified realms of reality (the REAL, the ACTUAL and the EMPIRICAL) and how writers might be further empowered to shape their academic texts according to their values and their knowledge – it nevertheless offers a fresh conceptual space within which to radically re-think academic writing practices so that they can become genuinely transformative and educative. This transformation is warranted by a human need to respect the agencies, knowledge, values, abilities, capabilities and literacies of diverse writers and to uphold standards of academic excellence, which include universities' missions to further knowledge through social justice. This chapter has argued that the social philosophy of critical realism affords these possibilities because it allows us to think of academic writing as a complex open system where both change and novelty become the norm and not the exception in the pursuit of epistemic justice.

5

Foundations for a Future Writing Pedagogy

Introduction

Figure 2 Sousanis (2015, p. 66 © Harvard University Press).

Often, when caught up in the day-to-dayness of my own teaching microcosm, I need to remind myself of why academic writing is troubled and why it needs changing. This is not because I ever doubt the problem or because there is a shortage of colleagues who also recognize that it is a problem, but because it isn't always seen as a problem at the macro structural level of institutional, disciplinary and higher educational decision-making. It has taken me a decade of teaching, assessing, course design, research and finding like-minded communities of writing scholars and practitioners to recognize it as a problem. Had I not researched, I would have believed everything I read in popular 'how to' textbooks and would never have scratched beneath the surface of feedback and advice that tells writers their writing is 'not academic' or that it is 'unclear', such as 'don't use personal pronouns or start a sentence with but': much of this feedback is either unwittingly misguided or wilfully fake because so much evidence has been published and is available on 'bad writing' advice (see, for example, Ball and Loewe (2017) or the zombification of academic writing (Sword, 2009)). Unfortunately (because I think my professional life would have been easier if I had gone along with the 'academic writing is logical, linear and objective' status quo), during this research process, I have become aware of trouble and fake news where many don't see it – the 'need-to-learn the rules' (i.e. 'my' rules) brigade has power, either through silent collusion or through institutionally sanctioned recognitions, such as awards and promotions; it has resources; and it can silence dissenting voices by mocking them as idealistic anarchists who have no standards, or by side-lining and ignoring them. It creates what Bourdieu calls 'censorship and the imposition of form' through symbolic power (Bourdieu & Thompson, 1991, pp. 138):

> The metaphor of censorship should not mislead: it is the structure of the field itself which governs expression by governing both access to expression and the form of expression and not some legal proceeding which has been specially adapted to designate and repress the transgression of a kind of linguistic code. This structural censorship is exercised through the medium of the sanctions of the field, functioning as a market on which the prices of different kinds of expression are formed; it is imposed on all producers of symbolic goods, including the authorised spokesperson, whose authoritative discourse is more subject to the norms of official propriety than any other and it condemns the occupants of dominated positions either to silence or to shocking outspokenness.

In the UK field of EAP, the field with which I am familiar through paid teaching practice and labour, this censorship manifests itself by ensuring that academic writing practitioners remain at the service of an outsourced commodity operating via what Ding and Bruce (2017) have called 'the edge of academia': even when EAP units are on the university payroll, they nevertheless remain marginalized as 'handmaidens to the proper disciplines' because of limited opportunities to conduct systematic research on academic writing. This is because EAP centres are bound by and committed to commercial imperatives that are more tangible and monetizable than the epistemic virtues of deliberation and reflection, virtues that underpin an educational praxis that is orientated towards nuance and is more likely to push back against the ideologies underpinning template-driven, performative, 'one-size-fits-all' cookie-cutter approaches to academic writing. These commercial units, therefore, see little need to invest in writing scholarship of teaching and learning (Braxton et al., 2002; Davis, 2019; Hutchings & Shulman, 1999), preferring instead to rely on popular textbooks and well-crafted ready-to-use internet resources as their main source of knowledge, despite the fact that even John Swales (1980) and others have shown many textbooks to be 'educational failures' because they compound popular knowledge to suit the commercial interests of publishers and not the academic literacy needs of writers. The failure to develop procedural knowledge through scholarship prevents the practice and theory of academic writing from having equal disciplinary status as a method for representing and creating academic knowledge because it maims from the outset the agency needed to transform practice. In the US field of writing studies, a field I have learned about through unpaid scholarship and intellectual labour, this censorship manifests itself through maintaining deficit models of literacy, such as the five-paragraph essay, which encourages writers to 'perform' academicness (Warner, 2018) and through de-contextualized, impersonal and universal approaches to writing instruction (Wardle, 2017; Williams, 2017), which frame writing as an autonomous, universal and transferable skill. Since academic writing is a method of enquiry and the main academic proxy for enacting SAPs, a lack of institutional investment and parity in its scholarship amounts to censorship.

In light on the above, this chapter is a reminder of why academic writing practices need changing in the first place, but it goes further. It identifies the 'levers of change' needed to do this. These levers include a material – not vocational or vicarious or voluntary – commitment to writing scholarship: a far greater range of pedagogies and assessments that include more than language, and deficit models thereof, needs to emerge. Tinkering around the edges won't make this happen: radical, systemic and macro-structural transformation is needed if higher education writing practices are to be socially just, educationally transformative and epistemically complete.

Why Change: Rationales for Re-thinking Writing Practices

The reasons why universities need to change their academic writing practices have been addressed throughout this book, but as we draw towards a close, now is the time to summarize them and distil their implications so that the alternatives can gain visibility and credence and hopefully earn their place at the academic writing table. In what follows, I list twelve key changes needed to lay the foundation of a future writing pedagogy that is open, non-linear, transformative and humane. I do this by extending previous arguments with new reflections and suggestions. At the end of each key change, I draw on my teaching experiences and on writing scholarship to suggest what kind of academic text might emerge if the change were implemented. Having listed all the changes, I offer three examples of how a future critical realist writing pedagogy might allow for a greater range of texts to count as academic.

Change 1. Towards Multimodal and Multilingual Textual Ecologies

First and foremost, 'academic writing' is a misnomer. As we have seen, it makes more sense to refer to this transitive method of enquiry in the plural, as academic *writings*. But I propose we go even further and remove the noun 'writing' all together: academic 'texts' would be by far more fitting because a 'text' can be understood as a 'communicative event' that nevertheless must satisfy certain criteria. These criteria include coherence, argumentation and intentionality (Titscher et al., 2002, pp. 20–30), all of which, as we saw in Chapter 3, are equally features of non-linguistic texts. Much of what academic writers do is multimodal: Carson's PhD included music, voice and rhythm, as well as a written exegesis; Sousanis's EdD was a visual argument with words to support it; in the arts, particularly, writing plays a minimal role (Ravelli et al., 2013); and in the sciences, applied sciences and social sciences writers are increasingly required to communicate their knowledge visually, interactively and creatively to a range of audiences via social and other digital media (Andrews et al., 2012). Moreover, as multimodal scholars remind us, *all* writing is multimodal (Ball & Charlton, 2015) so narrowing its meaning to a designator ('writing') that might suggest it is not is misleading, especially since language itself only partially defines what writing is (Canagarajah, 2013a, p. 1):

> Writing is multimodal, with multiple semiotic features (space, visuals), ecological resources (objects, people, texts) and modalities (oral, visual and

aural) contributing to its production and interpretation. Language is therefore only one of the resources that goes into writing. If text construction, circulation and reception involve diverse social, semiotic and ecological resources, we have to ask if we should continue to define writing according to language considerations alone.

Indeed, as evidenced in Chapter 2, the etymology of writing includes 'drawing'. The implication of what Canagarajah says is that by de-privileging the high status that language – including the English language – enjoys in academic writing practices, we can move towards an ecology of multimodal texts. This would have far-reaching ethical implications for English second or additional language writing instruction, too, because it would provide opportunities for writers whose main academic language is not English to communicate their knowledge by harnessing the skills they may already have, such as digital composition, art and multilingualism (understood here as a modality that de-centres the hegemony of English – see also Canagarajah [2018]). An ecology of multimodal and multilingual texts might go some way towards re-calibrating the imbalance of power and removing the barriers to epistemic access created by convergence towards English as the dominant language in academia. The multimodal pedagogies described in Archer and Breuer (2015) and Palmeri (2012) provide rich insights into how the linearity of traditional academic writing prose can be disrupted to become more recursive and open to creating meanings. The rich body of work on multilingualism and translanguaging referred to in Wei (2016), Canagarajah (2011, 2013b, 2013c), Ávila Reyes et al. (2020) and Zenger et al. (2014) further offers several insights into what multilingual classrooms might look like if they were given space to mobilize, or *mesh*, all the resources of communication available to writers in the joint endeavour to enhance meaning-making and equality of access in the process of composing texts.

Emergent academic text

Academic e-newsletter

Why? Because it would afford flexibility, creativity, collaboration, interdisciplinarity, and a fair amount of writer agency in creating, composing, editing, entertaining, informing, collaborating, communicating to a diverse and multilingual student community and bringing about change within/empowering the academic community it is aimed at (e.g. information about access to health services). See pedagogic example on page 149 for a fuller account.

Change 2. Academic Writing as Composition

Secondly, all texts are compositions and composing is a creative process. The resulting composition is equally creative because it could have been otherwise. Composing and composition, process and product, are also recursive rather than linear because they rely on the selection and ordering of elements that, like a musical symphony or work of visual art, overlap, repeat and intertwine in a process that recalls the creative methods of counter-mapping and creative non-fiction (see, for example, work by sociologist Patricia Leavy). In this sense, even the linearity of the most conventional academic essay or PhD thesis, with its five-paragraphs or default IMRAD (Introduction, Methods, Results, Analysis, Discussion) sequence is a form of composition, albeit one that has fossilized into a template. The US tradition of Rhetoric and Composition has long argued for thinking of writing as a form of 'composition' but Palmeri (2012) has taken it to the next level by arguing for *multimodal* composition that transcends the tyranny of the alphabet. There is much in this well-established field of writing studies that we can learn from. By drawing on (rather than fetishizing) the richness of the classics, writing scholars in this tradition have been able to harness the insights that history affords with regard to different ways of thinking about writing. US Composition Studies is more process and activity-oriented, it reveals the 'tangible ways in which learning to write within a discipline involves much more than learning particular forms or vocabularies but rather relates to socially preferred ways of knowing and acting' (Tardy & Jwa, 2016, p. 61). So much so, that recent trends in Composition Studies are increasingly focusing on teaching students *about* writing, the assumption being that teaching students *to* write academically is potentially self-defeating. This is because of 'the impossibility of teaching a universal academic discourse' (Downs & Wardle, 2007, p. 552) and of 'teaching genres out of context' given that writing is a disciplinary activity that requires a purpose, or 'exigence' (Wardle, 2009, p. 767).

Emergent academic text

Infographic/poster

Why? Because it would afford a range of multimodal compositional skills, both digital and paper-based; agentic skills and abilities, such as drawing and graphic design; opportunities to consider a wide range of semiotic features, such as colour, fonts and layouts to convey meaning.

Change 3. Academic Texts Must Afford Thinking

Performativity as Macfarlane has described it is anathema to thinking. It encourages the use of language for display purposes and relies on 'serviceable templates' to jump through the hoops of assessment, hollowing out and demeaning the act of authentic knowledge creation and communication in its wake. When mechanical skills are foregrounded at the expense of cultivating the more complex SAPs that make academic writings and text genuinely academic, thinking suffers, hoaxes get published and academic misconduct cases rise. This is unacceptable in a place of higher learning and it raises very uncomfortable questions about the purpose of university in relation to thinking and learning, especially given the internationalization of English-speaking universities and the EAP markets that they have created (Yun & Standish, 2018).

Emergent academic text

Blog/living document

Why? Because it would afford both the academic writer and the reader opportunities to think together in a public or other shared space; knowledge and expertise would grow through accountability and justification of viewpoints as interaction via comments grows.

Change 4. University Must Take Responsibility for Academic Misconduct and Proctoring

Anecdotally, in February 2021, I received a university email looking for 'expressions of interest to join the growing team of academic misconduct officers' and stating that this was 'an opportunity to get an insight into other parts of the School'. The wording and tone of this email struck me as odd, yet it was a reminder of how normalized and embedded misconduct has become in the business discourses of higher education: the university has 'officers', which at best connotes that an office clerk is in charge of judging student writing and at worst, it conjures up the image of a police constable, further connoting that the job of the university is to root out and punish, not educate and prevent; it is a 'growing' team seemed to echo the neoliberal enchantment with the imperative of growth. Why do I never receive emails offering an opportunity to 'understand' the economic, social and pedagogic conditions that have led to such a 'growing team' of plagiarism police in the first place or on the extent to which there may be links between cheating and assessment design and breakdowns in trust, including disenchantment, between students and the institution (Bretag, 2018; Harper et al., 2019; Peters, 2018)? The 'plagiarism declaration' forms students are required to sign after they have either self-declaredly admitted to reading university guidance on avoiding plagiarism or to having had sufficient 'training' on what is a highly complex issue amount to the same kind of performativity denounced by Macfarlane (2021b). Plagiarism software tools are far more likely to 'detect' (another policing metaphor) writing that exhibits mechanistic performativity which in turn leads to an ever-ending spiral in which savvy writers become increasingly adept at gaming the system in order to not be caught (e.g. by paying an essay mill to write a plagiarism-proof essay). The Covid-19 pandemic of 2020–22 has further seen a proliferation of private proctoring surveillance services (Mckenna, 2021; Weller, 2021) to monitor online behaviours in assessments being conducted online and from home. What all of this indicates is that traditional academic writing practices and the ways in which they are assessed are more likely to be the problem because they lend themselves to a culture where cheating is desirable and possible (Medway et al., 2018).

> Emergent academic text
>
> ## Reflective assignments
>
> Why? Because these would afford opportunities for writers and their readers to talk around the texts that are being written. Reflective assignments include portfolios of practice, exegeses to explain the how/why of an experiment or artefact and other holistic approaches that might combine written and oral accounts of research.

Change 5. Re-think Writing as a Fallible Proxy for Representing Knowledge

Writing is a method of enquiry that is transitive. This means that it is a proxy for knowledge. It is not knowledge understood as the intransitive reality that it seeks to investigate. As such, it can never provide a full representation of reality. Other research methods, such as laboratory experiments or statistical analyses, are equally transitive, functioning as proxies for the reality they are investigating. In virtue of being a proxy, writing must be held to account with regard to assumptions about what it can and cannot represent. The following account of epistemic virtues is taken from a book on the history of science written by Lorraine and Peter Galison (Daston & Galison, 2010) and I share it here to highlight the inherent subjectivity and fallibility of any epistemic proxy, including writing. I do so with the explicit intention of *de-centring* the privilege that writing has as a method of communicating knowledge: this does not amount to *eliminating* writing as method of enquiry but to re-positioning it within an ecology of methods that have parity to equally contribute in making knowledge visible.

Before the 1800s, artists and scientists worked together to depict idealized paradigms of reality. They were driven by a pedagogic imperative that reified the epistemic virtue of 'truth-to-nature' and worked together with 'four eyes' to capture what they considered to be the 'essence' of nature. This involved interfering in the representation of nature by airbrushing out anomalies in order to select those features which they deemed to be representative of a species. Art allowed them to do this because the artist could, as directed by the scientist, correct, embellish, give more prominence to or ignore one or other details of a plant or human anatomy. This was seen as the prerogative of the pedagogue and scientist (or natural philosopher) who was invested with the authority to embellish nature in this way in order to illustrate textbooks. The 1900s, on the other hand, reified the epistemic virtue of 'eliminating the self', believing that machine-mediation, such as the telescope, afforded the ability to see objects 'as they really were'. This coincides with the gradual elimination of the self in writing, as we saw in Chapter 2, but it also cultivates other epistemic virtues that indicate that the 'self', understood here as the researcher, is very much present in the research process: in order for reality to be represented as 'objective' and untainted by the pedagogic motives of the natural philosopher-cum-artist, the scientific self needed to be 'patient', 'persevering', 'slow', 'methodical', 'reasonable' and 'diligent' (recall Newton 'stumbling across a fact' because of these virtues). But this scientific self was still interfering in their representation of nature because their subjective methods still mediated between the self and the object: however patient, slow and diligent, the scientist was still viewing reality second-hand, through a proxy, i.e. the mechanics of a machine and relying on only two eyes now, meaning that any representations of reality remained even more partial. Although scientists were increasingly able to report their knowledge with high levels of accuracy, the level of detail that machine-mediation afforded also meant that it could no longer be straightforwardly communicated for pedagogic reasons (because textbooks needed to simplify reality for the purpose of teaching it) or for dissemination purposes across the scientific community (because a wider and more educated readership now meant a more discerning audience). Instead, this highly specialized knowledge needed to be 'ventriloquized', meaning it had to be separated from the self so that it could speak 'on behalf of nature' by making decisions about what aspects of this nature to communicate. This 'ventriloquizing' needed a self to be able to speak on behalf of nature, and so, yet again, the self could never be eliminated. This is why sociologists of science Latour and Woolgar (1986, p. 28) have claimed that scientific communication necessarily *mis*represents reality because it will always be a partial proxy for reality:

> [T]here has been a growing dissatisfaction with outside observers' reliance on scientists' own statements about the nature of their work. Some participants have themselves argued that printed scientific communications systematically misrepresent the activity that gives rise to published reports.

Ventriloquizing requires judgement, namely deciding what to ventriloquize and how much. The epistemic virtue of 'trained judgement' characterized the scientific virtues of the 1900s and beyond and was founded on the premise that there is always a self who judges and interprets reality. The intransitive objects of reality – the facts, so to speak – are represented through classifications, rankings and orderings that are determined by the values and judgements of a self. It is in this sense that science is fallible, social and subjective, making any method or proxy that is deployed to communicate it equally fallible, social and subjective. This includes the fallibility of the proxy of academic writing. It is this fallibility that provides a rationale for questioning its reliability as a method of representation.

Emergent academic text

An animation of writing as a method of enquiry

Why? Because it would afford the composer an opportunity to reflect on what is lost and what is gained in representing knowledge via the medium of language. It provides opportunities to justify choices in how knowledge is represented and opens up possibilities for learning new ways to represent that knowledge .

Change 6. Question the Politics, Ethics and Ideology of Writtenness

Writing is inherently ideological. It is one method for representing the world, of which there are many, the logic of which has been extended by universities to a 'totalitarian' conclusion, namely that it is the only way of measuring thinking and of representing and disseminating knowledge. Moreover, this logic has been extended to privileging one type of writing, the 'objective' and 'formal' type, at the expense of others. The conflation of writing with thinking amounts to what Turner (2018) calls an 'ontological complicity'. The fact that English, through political and economic expediency rather than any inherent superiority of its language and academic culture, has come to dominate the standards to which academic writing is held further indicates that its script can never be 'neutral' or 'objective' (Bennett, 2010; Lillis & Curry, 2010b) because bias and injustice ensue (Politzer-Ahles et al., 2016). In virtue of remaining the standard against which other epistemologies are measured, such as those of the Global South (Collyer et al., 2019), academic writing encapsulates and perpetuates the value of 'writtenness', a highly contentious and slippery property which, as implied in Chapter 3, can amount to a 'fraud' and can lead to the publication of hoaxes when left unchallenged. Writteness has been likened to Received Pronunciation (RP) and its discriminatory effects. Measuring the standards of English spoken by the diverse global majority against the putative superiority of RP, spoken by around 3 per cent of the British population, creates 'language regimes' and continues to fuel accent wars (Donnelly et al., 2019; Orelus, 2017) that are reminiscent of the literacy wars referred to in Richardson (1997). Exposure to the underlying assumptions of writtenness can, at the very least, create a space within which diverse forms of writing and textual expression can enter the arena as potential contenders for academic legitimacy. Pedagogic approaches to co-designing writing tasks (Bovill, 2020) could generate opportunities for the literacies of students to emerge as legitimate forms of communication.

Emergent academic text

Student-led peer reviews, assessments and criteria designs

Why? Because designing assignments, co-creating criteria, reading and commenting on the work of others as 'partners' provides opportunities to explain and justify ideas followed by feedback that is relevant to communities who are learning from each other. Feedback between peers affords the emergence of democratic syllabi that respect the literacies of the community.

Change 7. Remind Ourselves That Clarity Is Often in the Eye of the Beholder

Writtenness is further imbricated with the equally contested notion of 'clarity' in academic writing. This, too, like the notion of accent and standards, ignites controversy, often originating in the Anglo-American tradition of analytic philosophy (Law, 2014). 'Western' standards of clarity are rooted in formal logic, language, positivism and the British Enlightenment via the legacy of philosopher John Locke, for whom words could be chosen in the interests of 'precision and economy' (Turner 2018). However, as noted by Peters (2008, p. 828):

> '[C]larity' in philosophical discourse also has its history and ... 'normal forms of academic scholarship' have become 'normalised' or institutionalized and are in the process of changing again, especially in response to the rise of the electronic journal. The use of 'normal' here betrays a politics of philosophy writing and a deep history of the politics of writing in philosophy that still embraces the false dichotomy of Analytic and Continental philosophy in its material forms and perpetuates the myth of a universal form of writing and the dream of a universal form of language called philosophy.

However, notions of what counts as 'clear' are being revisited because of the affordances of new technologies, as the quotation above suggests and because of the epistemic injustices enacted through assessment practices that judge a diverse student body against the ideological literacy standards of writtenness (see, for example, McArthur [2020]). Researcher Carmichael-Murphy (2021) refers to ideologies that lead to the assumption that there is only one standard of clarity, that of the 'Western' gaze. In her higher education blog post on decolonizing the PhD, Carmichael-Murphy reflects on the barriers faced by racially minoritized students who are still expected to refer predominantly to a 'Western' canon of knowledge in their research even though it may seem wholly 'unclear' to them (simply because it is not a form of literacy they are familiar with). The requirement to reference 'Western' literatures potentially also risks stifling the emergence of new knowledge by requiring that non-'Western' researchers remain within the boundaries of traditional 'Western' thought:

> The stance taken here is not to discard Western philosophy, but to reject fixed hierarchies of knowledge which 'other' alternative ways of knowing. If the original contribution of the thesis is to add to the discipline, does this mean that a thesis should also cement what is already 'known'? By failing to identify the boundaries of our thought and expression we stifle the emergence of new and alternative knowledges.

Sperlinger et al. (2018) have similarly shown how literacy exclusion at university leads to epistemic injustice. They point out that literatures that are derided by the 'West' for being unclear and outright 'bad' (such as the writing of Gayatri Spivak [1987]) are, in fact, perfectly understood by those who may share the experiences or be familiar with the ideas these authors are discussing. The assumption that clarity is a universally recognizable and definable property of written texts raises troubling questions about who universities are actually for and what kinds of texts students should be reading and writing. Moreover, by insisting that 'Western' standards of what counts as 'clear' writing are the most desirable, writing instruction re-enforces the very mechanisms of exclusion and injustice that led to those standards becoming dominant in the first place.

Emergent academic text

A manifesto

Why? Because it would afford the opportunity to challenge and provoke assumptions by declaring a position, intention and ethical orientation towards a contested idea. It would develop the socio-academic practice of critical engagement with relevant scholarship and a chance to explore authorial voice. See pedagogic example on page 150 for a fuller account.

Change 8. Hold Writing as a Socio-academic Practice to Account

Socio-academic practices refer to the specifically academic social practices of higher education and to the *standards of excellence* to which they aspire. They concern what and whose purposes and values are served by a university education, as evidenced throughout Connell (2019), de Sousa Santos (2017) and Sperlinger et al. (2018). Their focus on what is valued in the pursuit of knowledge through a higher education closely aligns them with epistemic virtues and vices. As we head towards considering what levers of change are available to agents who wish to transform academic writing practices, the SAPs of the neo-liberal and capitalist university must be mentioned. The following remarks are brief and can be read as promissories for a future conversation. These are inspired by a thought-provoking and controversial reflection by educationalist Bruce Macfarlane (2021a) who argued that activism and social justice have been co-opted as SAPs by neoliberal universities. Traditionally, activism fell outside the remit of the SAPs of the university because it was the prerogative of grassroots movements which approached change from the bottom-up, from 'the street', so to speak (see, for example, Choudry [2020] on 'activist knowledge'). It certainly was not the mission of the traditional Humboldtian university, which was explicitly oriented towards the SAP of research excellence and methodological rigour in the pursuit of scientific knowledge (modern universities are, of course, also oriented towards research and scientific knowledge, but my point here is one of emphasis, namely that 'social justice' was not visible in the mission statements of past universities). The recent prominence of Black Lives Matter, LGBTQ+, Athena Swan (a measure to promote women in academia), decolonization, EDI (a measure to promote Equality Diversity and Inclusion in academia) and 'social justice' movements, as a whole, have traditionally not been part of the university's mission. Regardless of whether activism, understood as the pursuit of social justice and human rights, should or should not be 'what or who universities are for', it remains, in critical realist terms, one of the *de facto* realities of several university visions. This makes social justice a twenty-first-century socio-academic practice and, because of this, writing practices must be held to account by being given the space to be transformed so that they can become agents of change in virtue of their transitive status as methods of enquiry. Pedagogies that allow academic writings to be transformed so that they can function as levers of change are more likely to further the cause of justice because they would allow new and emergent ecologies of knowledge to break free from the chains of their current encapsulations: Carson (2017) ensured the oral culture and rhythms of the communities he was researching could be read/listened to by those communities. He did not want the accounts and the histories of these communities to be transcribed into the straightjacket of standard and impersonal academic writing prose. The knowledge that has emerged from his thesis may in turn become the knowledge that is needed to transform and dismantle the socially unjust imperatives of the university, which either exclude from the outset those whose literacies do not conform or impose a standard of 'Western' academic literacy as a pre-condition for accessing university in the first place. In her call to reclaim the PhD as an 'open dialogue', Carmichael-Murphy seems to share a similar sentiment:

> Knowledge should be accessible to stakeholders, not guarded by shareholders. Universities continue to accrue knowledge in the form of physical theses, only ever read by people who are also constructing theses. A prime example of knowledge being 'known' but not comprehended. This is where public engagement becomes

a vital source of agency for the prospective PhD; but public engagement should not be conflated with public good. Academic communication with the public thus far, has been didactic; accumulating shared knowledge which is simply formalized by the researcher and the university. So, perhaps, the PhD should be reclaimed as an open dialogue with the world.

If academic writings are to become 'open dialogues' (see, for example, Abdulrahman et al. [2021]) as part of a socially just pedagogy, their genres need to change so that what makes writing academic can include a far greater range of communicative practices.

Emergent academic text

Dialogues, tetralogues and metalogues

Why? Because these would afford opportunities for public engagement and dissemination across diverse interdisciplinary communities. Writers with different disciplinary and cultural perspectives in dialogue on shared concerns, clarifying as required, explaining, interjecting, suggesting synchronously on the page. See pedagogic example on page 151 for a fuller account.

Change 9. Re-thinking Writing Requires Threshold Concepts

Another reason to re-think writing practices is that research in writing studies has shown there are several ways of defining academic writing and that there are multiple exemplars of what academic writing looks like. An understanding of these threshold concepts significantly extends the narrow and flattened definitions favoured by deficit approaches to academic writing instruction. Understanding that academic writing is multimodal and that it mediates activity, for example, is a far cry from describing it as 'objective' and 'linear'. These studies index the richness of the academic writing landscape pointing to further evolutions in the ecology of academic texts.

Emergent academic text

The comic and the graphic essay

Why? Because these would afford opportunities for their authors to engage multimodally in communicating their meaning in ways that represent their histories, literacies and identities (e.g. threshold concepts 2.4 and 3.2).

Change 10. Change Academic Practices and Standards

Further reasons to change writing practices include the fact that what makes these practices academic in the first place is changing. Recall the discussion on practices from Chapter 1: if the practices change, then so must the skills needed to enact the practices. This is because the skills are external to the internal *standards of excellence* of a practice. Skills are the means to an end. Thinking of skills as means to an end also entails, for example, that if the skill of writing a six-sentence paragraph is no longer achieving the *standards of excellence* needed to give voice to the dialects of an indigenous community or to convey the urgency for environmental reform, then the skills of paragraph-writing may need to be replaced with the skills of digital composition, animation and social media engagement.

Several writing scholars, including Paré (2018), Paltridge and Starfield (2020), Badenhorst et al. (2021) and Mewburn (2020), are challenging academia to a radical re-think of its traditional genres, particularly with regard to dissertation writing and its relevance to the world of work. This is because the traditional paper-based thesis may no longer be fit-for-purpose since it rarely reflects the kinds of worlds that newly minted research graduates inhabit. Even if a graduate remains in academia, they will be expected to communicate through a range of literacies that are multimodal. Their audiences will be equally diverse and will transcend the narrow pool of specialists in their research fields. Moreover, research also shows that the majority of university graduates do not go on to have careers in academia (Hancock, 2020). What this entails is that university students (and their parents) measure the investment they make in higher education against their chances of securing employment. This socio-structural reality has become an intransitive one, to use critical realist terminology, and it amounts to a real socio-academic practice, one that is based as the epistemic virtue (or vice) of 'employability'. As such, students have limited power throughout the duration of their studies, at least, to dismantle the economic imperatives at the level of the REAL that position them as consumers (Naylor et al., 2020). And once they have been positioned as consumers, they are more likely to demand that a university education equip them with skills that are transferable to the job market. Whether or not this requirement should impact on the kind of writing they do at university has a bearing on whether the traditional 'big book' 400-page doctoral thesis (Eco, 2015), for example, is still relevant. Whatever changes emerge in academic writing practices, these should not come at the expense of the complexities of a 'thinking university' (Beckett & Hager, 2018; Bengtsen & Barnett, 2018): the challenge, rather, is to ensure that any changes to writing requirements, such as those of the PhD thesis, maintain the *standards of excellence* inherent in the SAP and epistemic virtues that a PhD or any other marker of academic excellence needs to meet (Andrews et al., 2012).

Emergent academic text

The digital thesis

Why? Because this would afford writers the agency and autonomy to shape their knowledge in ways that serve their futures. Writers would develop the skills needed to communicate complex knowledge in the interests of composition and creative recursiveness rather than the linearity of standard writing.

Change 11. Ecrire: Reclaiming the Art of Writing

A penultimate reason for the need to change academic writing practices is what I referred to in Chapter 1 as the aesthetic rationale. This should not be confused with vanity projects that pit spurious notions of 'good' writing against 'bad' writing nor does it mean that paying attention to the beauty of form diminishes the truth of the content. Rather, it needs to be understood within the broader and well-established tradition of how form and content are inextricably bound (Nussbaum, 1990). The history of writing, including scientific and academic writing, can be read as a chronicle of which forms best afford the communication of knowledge. As Taub (2017) evidences, prose is a relatively late comer (fifth century) to the art of communicating scientific knowledge and even once prose did establish itself as the most ubiquitous form of literacy in 'Western' academia, it still provided writers with choices: letters, encyclopaedia entries, commentaries, biographies, dialogues and chronicles are just some of the genres deployed throughout history to communicate knowledge. Charles Bazerman's influential and compelling body of work (Bazerman, 1988, 2007, 2015) chronicles the evolution of the eighteenth-century experimental journal article to highlight how changes in form affect content and how changes in content become 'encapsulated' in genres. This encapsulation can ossify and become performative. It therefore needs to be 'rattled' so that the information chain can be broken and knowledge can continue to be shaped, allowing new forms to emerge. Writers can and do reclaim the art of writing by drawing on the broad pool of genres that is available to them at the level of the REAL, as evidenced throughout, for example, Phillips and Kara (2021). The example of an emergent academic text that can reclaim the art of *écrire*, below, is inspired by stand-up academic and anthropologist Kate Fox (2021).

> Emergent academic text
>
> ## Humorous writing
>
> Why? Because this would afford writer-researchers to negotiate through humour the 'in-between spaces' that exist in inter-disciplinary and inter-methodological academic discourse. Humour allows writers to "interrupt the traditional hierarchy in which monologic, 'detached' academic discourse is the best way of showing that you are gathering and disseminating knowledge" (Fox, 2021, p. 160).

Change 12. Respect a Writer's Right to Flourish

Last but not least, writers, as agents in their own right, have a human right to express themselves in accordance with their abilities (what they are physically able to do) and with their capabilities, understood as the approach to human rights and ethics pioneered by Amartya Sen: this approach highlights the human right to material, emotional and educational resources that enable them to flourish (Nussbaum, 2011; Robeyns, 2016). As long as higher education remains dependent on (and reduced to) monolingual (English) and monomodal (language) proficiency and as long as we continue to measure academic success (almost) exclusively against language proficiency, then we will necessarily judge as 'deficient' students who come to university with diverse multilingual, multimodal, dyslexic, autistic, artistic, social, cultural and physical repertoires. Moreover, if language is an expression of socio-cultural identity (Evans, 2014; Holmes, 1992), then by insisting on linguistic homogeneity, we are asking for 'cultural and social' homogeneity. And by asking everybody to speak and write in the same way, just as was once the case with RP (Received Pronunciation), we are creating the conditions for a homogenized academy that communicates via a mono-literacy.

Emergent academic text

Code-meshed and translanguaged writing

Why? Because this would afford opportunities for writers' to harness a fuller range of meaning-making resources and ensure their linguistic repertoires and identities were visible in their writing. Readers would need to cooperate to make more effort to decode meaning and writers would need to ensure they were intelligible. Deviation from standard norms and expectations become justified in terms of "rhetorical and communicative functionality" (Canagarajah, 2011, p. 414).

The above provides a non-exhaustive list of reasons to consider change in our academic writing practices. In what follows, I offer three glimpses of what a future critical realist writing pedagogy might begin to look like. My intention is to provide a nascent rationale for making a far greater range of texts count as academic in virtue of the socio-academic practices (SAPs) and epistemic virtues (EVs) that motivate them and because of the positive (socially just) impact that they may bring about.

Example 1. The Newsletter

Authentic task* prompt: *form an editorial team to write, review, edit and publish an e-newsletter to help a student community and aimed at a student readership; draw on your collective socio-semiotic knowledge and skills to convey knowledge and information that is relevant to your readers in both content and form; design an interactive tool (e.g. a survey) to generate and collect feedback; reflect on your individual contribution and on the impact of the newsletter.*

*Task can be adapted to suit undergraduate, postgraduate and doctoral requirements and can be set as individual or collaborative.

Example assessment criteria

Learning Outcomes: communicate knowledge intelligibly, multimodally and multilingually		
Impact of text	Semiotic resources	Reflection
Did the text lead to change? What kind and for whom?	*Were the most fitting resources used for your readership?*	*What did you learn? What worked and why?*

| Who did it benefit, harm, include, exclude? | Was the communicative aim achieved? How? | What would you do differently? |
| How will you follow up/ build on this task? | What peer/readership feedback did you receive? | Did you enjoy this task? Why? |

Educational principle: to represent, create, innovate, transform knowledge collaboratively. **Critical realist principle:** to harness writer skills (EMPIRICAL) for the creation of text (ACTUAL) by mobilizing knowledge of which genres, threshold concepts and linguistic affordances are available in the textual environment (REAL) in order to bring about positive change in a community (EMERGENT ACADEMICNESS). See Figure 1 on page 105.

Pedagogic principle: multilingualism and multimodality as methods for representing knowledge.

Scholarship: task ideas and rationales inspired by Bezemer and Kress (2008), English (2011) and Canagarajah (2011).

What makes the text and task academic: it fulfils the socio-academic practice (SAP) of writing for an authentic audience and is motivated by the epistemic virtue (EV) of benefitting the community.

Example 2. The Manifesto

Authentic task* prompt: *identify what 'clarity' means to you, your knowledge area, your discipline and your audience. Refer to relevant literature and examples. Compose a manifesto using a range of socio-semiotic resources to create a list of tenets designed to provoke thinking about what clarity is. The aim is to challenge prevailing assumptions, persuade your readers of the alternative; indicate your ethical orientation and epistemic values, and use it as tool that can be re-visited to guide your own writing practices and understandings.*

*Task can be adapted to suit undergraduate, postgraduate and doctoral requirements and can be set as individual or collaborative.

Example assessment criteria

Learning Outcomes: to challenge assumptions knowledgeably and purposefully		
Impact of text	**Semiotic resources**	**Reflection**
Did the text lead to change? What kind and for whom?	Were the most fitting resources used for your readership?	What did you learn? What worked and why?

| Who did it benefit, harm, include, exclude? | Was the communicative aim achieved? How? | What would you do differently? |
| How will you follow up/ build on this task? | What peer/readership feedback did you receive? | Did you enjoy this task? Why? |

Educational principle: to critique received wisdom.

Critical realist principle: to develop an authorial voice (EMPIRICAL) for the creation of text (ACTUAL) that mobilizes knowledge of what genres are available in the textual environment (REAL) in order to stimulate deeper thinking (EMERGENT ACADEMICNESS). See Figure 1 on page 105.

Pedagogic principle: understanding genre, its purpose and its readership.

Scholarship: task ideas and rationales inspired by Hanna (2014) and Hodgson et al. (2018).

What makes the text and task academic: it fulfils the socio-academic practice (SAP) of critical engagement with relevant scholarship and is motivated by the epistemic virtue (EV) of questioning established knowledge.

Example 3. The Dialogue

Authentic task* prompt: *you are going to explain your disciplinary understandings** of a complex idea and/or threshold concept to someone who is not as familiar as you are with this knowledge. Record or imagine a conversation between you and them in which you explain, exemplify, re-cast, your understanding in response to your interlocutor's questions, objections, re-formulations and counter-examples. Write this conversation as a play, radio interview, children's story or other genre that affords dialogue.*

*Task can be adapted to suit undergraduate, postgraduate and doctoral requirements and can be set as individual or collaborative.

** Recalling the example of Lucia, the psychology student who was excluded from her class because she was unfamiliar with the jargon of academic psychology, this writing task would provide an opportunity for her to remain in her psychology class and work with other students to mutually explain their understanding of psychology. The benefit to Lucia would be that she remains in the psychology class and in so doing, develops her understanding of the discipline through written dialogue. The benefit to her more academically-trained peers would be that they learn about situated experiences of psychology from Lucia and hone their own academic skills of communicating complex knowledge through dialogue with readers who have different understandings.

Example assessment criteria

Learning Outcomes: to critically explain disciplinary concepts to different audiences		
Impact of text	Semiotic resources	Reflection
Did the text lead to change? What kind and for whom?	Were the most fitting resources used for your readership?	What did you learn? What worked and why?
Who did it benefit, harm, include, exclude?	Was the communicative aim achieved? How?	What would you do differently?
How will you follow up/ build on this task?	What peer/readership feedback did you receive?	Did you enjoy this task? Why?

Educational principle: to understand and communicate complex ideas to those who are less familiar with them in order to understand them better yourself.

Critical realist principle: to mobilize the writer's linguistic skills (EMPIRICAL) in creating a text (ACTUAL) that demonstrates knowledge of reader expectations in the textual environment (REAL) in order to bring about mutual understanding of complex ideas (EMERGENT ACADEMICNESS). See Figure 1 on page 105.

Pedagogic principle: increase awareness of the communicative affordances of the dialogue as an academic genre.

Scholarship: task ideas and rationales inspired by English (2011, 2015).

What makes the text and task academic: it fulfils the socio-academic practice (SAP) of writing for an authentic audience and is motivated by the epistemic virtue (EV) of transforming understandings of existing knowledge.

Pedagogies as Levers of Change: Investment in Scholarship and Pedagogy

Resistance to change has many causes. It includes a toxic mix, or perfect storm, of contentment with the *status quo*, fear of the unknown, unfamiliarity with the alternatives, lack of resources and opportunities and lack of agency. To paraphrase Laurel Richardson, resistance can also take the form of defensiveness:

> If comics and rap count as academic writing and I can't do it, what happens to my identity, my prestige, my status – my place in the pecking order – ME?

Richardson took her academic field of sociology to task for writing in boring, linear and de-personalized prose suggesting instead that poetry better captured the rhythms and voices of the sociological reality she was investigating (see Chapter 1). Her fellow sociologists argued that poetry was not an appropriate method of enquiry because it lacked validity. What they overlooked, though, was that all methods of representing reality are proxies for that reality and, as such, they are all, to varying degrees, fallible. This is why different research methods and methodologies are chosen or discarded depending on the object of enquiry. In fact, Richardson had not suggested that they too adopt poetry as their preferred method of enquiry: she was simply making the point that it was one of *her* chosen methods and that it afforded validity as a methodological proxy for the social reality she was researching (namely as a way of transcribing her interview data so as to evoke as closely as possible the rhythms and emotions of the women she had been interviewing). Similarly, advocating for a re-configuration of what makes writing academic, based on the warrants afforded throughout this book, does not imply that all academic writers should rap or draw their research or that teachers of academic writing, trained to teach the genre of linear prose, should lose their jobs because their skills are no longer required: those skills will be required for many futures to come, but they are likely to become part of a broader ecology of skills as new forms of writing emerge. As Sousanis reminds us in opening this chapter, 'linear sequences have their strengths, but they are not the only possibility'. The visual argument of his graphic dissertation can be read through the theoretical lens proposed by Jude Fransman, who shares her rationale for re-imagining the conditions of possibility for the PhD by mobilizing the metaphor of a map. Maps are 'open systems' that allow us to organize reality rather than reproduce it; they are open to change because they are not determined by a single use or purpose (Fransman, 2012, p. 140):

> The map is [...] detachable, reversible, susceptible to constant modification. It can be torn, reversed, adapted to any kind of mounting, reworked by an individual, group or social formation.

Although she does not draw on critical realist philosophy to argue this, she is nevertheless describing what is one of the defining properties of an open system, namely their permeability, which is what makes them 'susceptible to modification' and, therefore, open to change.

What I am similarly suggesting is that we harness the permeability afforded by academic texts understood as open systems to *open up possibilities* for re-configuring what makes them academic based on our values, on a range of SAPs and EVs that extend beyond tired and anachronistic notions of 'objectivity', 'linearity' and 'reliability'. For change to happen, university leadership, teachers and students need to democratically activate the judgemental rationality of their agencies to trigger change at the level of the ACTUAL, which is the transitive and epistemological level of reality agents have direct access to and which requires deep knowledge at the level of the REAL to be effective. Writing pedagogies can be the levers of change that teachers, students and academic writers can activate to open the spaces needed for these possibilities to emerge. I argued in Chapter 4 that academic texts are open systems in virtue of their social complexity. This makes them porous whilst still remaining stable enough to warrant their status as 'systems'. By being porous, they have the inbuilt capacity to allow new skills and practices to enter their systems without the system collapsing. For this reason, academic texts are located at the level of the ACTUAL, where change is possible. When new academic texts emerge, they do not replace the old ones: a graphically drawn or musically performed thesis does not pose a threat to the traditional monograph, but remains very much within the system of academic knowledge production because it still has to comply with reality at the level of the REAL within which university structures are historically, economically and socially bound to enacting specific SAPs. This includes, for example, the requirement to reference research, gain ethics committee approvals and justify methodological frameworks, none of which rule against using comics, to mention one of any number of semiotic resources, as a scientific research method (Al-Jawad, 2015).

Levers of change include new pedagogies and access to relevant scholarship. They can be understood as 'cracks in the system' that need to be both pro-actively and collectively created and then picked away at so that the old foundations either collapse or become replaced by the new ones. Levers require several structural conditions for agents to activate them. The next section limits itself to considering the two conditions with which I am most familiar and have had access to as a salaried permanent teacher of academic writing with no contractual obligation to do research: these levers are scholarship and pedagogy. It is important to declare my positionality because my own agency to enact pedagogical change at the level of the ACTUAL is also subject to material opportunities and constraints afforded at the level of the REAL. These differ from the material opportunities and constraints of someone who is casually employed or of an academic manager or professor, for example, each of whom is likely to have varying degrees of agency, such as access to budgets, and varying degrees of autonomy to activate a range of levers of change, such as research time built into their workloads or membership of committees where they can contribute to making decisions about scholarship and pedagogy. Positionality with regard to agency is crucial because each level of professional status comes with different opportunities and constraints that agents are more or less free to act upon.

Change through Scholarship

If teachers and assessors of academic writing are to be equal partners in laying the foundation of a future and open academic writing pedagogy that transforms practices and closes the theory *versus* practice gulf between 'what goes on in the classroom' and 'what is said in the research journals', then writers and teachers of academic writing at all levels and across all disciplines must have access to scholarship. I locate scholarship at the level of the REAL because it is part of the intransitive ontological reality, i.e. it exists whether or not we choose to or can engage with it. As agents, we can choose to ignore this reality, but that doesn't change its ontological realness. By 'access' I mean material access in the form of access to a library and to open resources but I also mean 'access' in the form of contractual terms, whereby employers support and value the scholarship of teaching and learning (SoTL) as part of employment terms and conditions at the level of the REAL that enable academic staff to flourish through professional growth and fulfilment (Braxton et al., 2002; Hutchings & Shulman, 1999). Material investment in SoTL is likely to inspire teachers who have the curiosity and the disposition to bridge the theory–practice divide to join communities of writing practitioners and researchers engaged in sharing and disseminating their work. This would also serve to bridge the knowledge gap between teachers of academic writing working on the 'edge of academia' and those teaching and researching 'the proper disciplines'.

But it is not just access to knowledge that practitioners need: however much scholarship one engages with, a teacher of academic writing is unlikely to be knowledgeable of every academic genre at the level of the REAL. This is why Sam, my semi-fictitious student from Chapter 1, was confused. She had clearly been taught, to the best of her teachers' knowledge, that academic writing was pretty much the same, formulaic and transferable across the disciplinary board. This is why Sam was unable to then make sense of the differences in standards and expectations that they ended up encountering on their degree programme. Even when teachers do become familiar with studies that have identified some of the skills and practices students need to write at university, it remains difficult to decide what a general academic writing course, such as those taught by EAP or in Academic Writing Centres and Library Services, should select, prioritize and then teach. One answer to the general *versus* specific academic writing conundrum is provided by Wardle (2017). She argues that students be taught general principles about writing and what it means to be an author so that they can critically transfer *knowledge of writing*, rather than skills, to other contexts. This would avoid the 'rigid' and 'inappropriate' application of rules from one context to another and would educate students in a reflective and mindful approach to writing whereby they notice disciplinary conventions in their readings and are able to then infer relevant patterns rather than accumulate a set of rules. But who can teach the teachers to teach their students in this way? The solution, for Elizabeth Wardle, is to create MA (Master's)-level degree programmes that teach university teachers about both the theory *and* practice of academic writing. As Downs and Wardle (2007, p. 554) claim: 'Having a major … dramatically changes a field's standing in the academy'. Indeed, as argued in Molinari (2013), MAs in Creative Writing abound yet those in Academic Writing do not.[1] This seems highly incongruous given the challenges that all academic writers deal with and the high-stakes audit culture that academic writing is invested in, from undergraduate writing assignments all the way to the high-impact writing that academics are expected to publish in order to fulfil the requirements of the REF (the 4-yearly UK Research Excellence Framework that determines the extent to which research departments receive government funding and that creates promotion pathways).

In addition to the more traditionally published literatures on academic writing referenced throughout this book, there are online communities of scholars whose work is possibly more readily and freely accessible to anybody with an internet connection. These scholars freely share their own and each other's knowledge and resources, they form reading groups and organize seminars, have journals and blogs and, via social media, fulfil the prophecy of the 'networked university' described by Nicolas Standaert in Barnett (2012). There are simply too many of these 'networked resources' to list and any selection is necessarily at the expense of equally generous and thorough scholarship, but three examples of where scholarship on a more nuanced, creative and socially just approach to academic writing is regularly evidenced, updated and shared are:

- the blog of independent writing scholar Dr Helen Kara (https://helenkara.com/), who publishes research on creative methods and indigenous knowledges;

[1] Notable exceptions in the UK are an MSc in Chemistry and Scientific Writing [accessed 27 December 2018] at the University of Warwick and an MA in Academic Writing Development and Research [accessed 27 December 2018] at Coventry University.

- the blog of The Hidden Curriculum Team (https://drhiddencurriculum. wordpress. com/), whose book on the hidden landscape of doctoral writing chronicles opportunities and possibilities for writers rather than foregrounding rules and conventions (Elliot et al., 2020);
- the blog of Professor Pat Thomson (https://patthomson. net/), who enacts her agency by triggering the levers of change that her status as an academic supervisor, writer, teacher and tenured professorship affords her.

Change in academic writing practices that re-configures what makes writing academic can be actioned via access to such and other scholarship and by giving degree-level status to the complex intellectual and methodological work carried out by the practice of writing as a method of enquiry. Change is also actioned when scholars join collectively to build communities of knowledge and practice (Lave & Wenger, 1991) that are networked and therefore amplify the chances of triggering levers of change that an individual alone would not have the power to do. Through scholarship, agents can become invested with the agency needed to action the levers of change between the levels of the EMPIRICAL and the ACTUAL of a critical realist stratified reality. What this means in practice is that knowledge of academic writing scholarship at the level of the REAL can enable a writer at the level of the EMPIRICAL to mobilize their knowledge of all the possible genres (at the level of the REAL) that can then become available at the level of the ACTUAL.

Change through Pedagogy

If you teach academic writing or if you are a student of academic writing, at any level of university instruction, you will hopefully have experienced some very good practice. You may have had a mentor or tutor or supervisor or even have read some inspiring and liberating work on teaching that spurred you on to become the best writer, or composer of texts, that you could be. Equally, like Sam, you may have had some frustrating, confusing and unnecessarily time-consuming experiences. Either way, you will have become aware of how important pedagogy is to becoming a happy, fulfilled and confident academic writer. Several such pedagogies exist. What they tend to have in common is a meaningful purpose, authentic content and a genuine commitment to your flourishing. From a critical realist perspective, this also means writing and teaching writing from a position of knowledge that ensures these three qualities – meaningfulness, authenticity and genuineness – enact a socially just pedagogy. Without these three qualities, academic writing is unable to fulfil its transformative educational imperative, which is to change the world for the better. Meaningfulness can be understood as writing that is knowledge or content-informed, writing that means something to someone somewhere; authenticity can be understood as writing that has a purpose, such as a newsletter to inform a community, a blog to share scholarship, or a PhD thesis that is inclusive because it broadens its readership (Harron, 2016); and genuineness can be understood as the opposite of 'performativity', that hollowed-out semblance of an academic text that is more akin to *écriture* than to *écrire*.

As part of his critical realist pedagogy to enact change for social justice, Donald Judd triggers the levers of change by cautioning against generic academic writing instruction that lacks a subject matter and that purports to teach transferable skills. Specifically, Judd takes the socio-academic practice of critical thinking to task, arguing that in order to write well, we must also understand what we are reading. This is because change in the social world cannot take place without a deep understanding of the REAL social structures that constitute the world (Judd, 2003, pp. 126):

> The traditional lack of a subject matter in writing courses is both a strength and a weakness. Sophisticated writing cannot be divorced from a degree of sophisticated understanding of a concrete subject matter. Even if you apply formal logic to your writing and detect logical fallacies and conflicting assertions in an argument, while important, this will not necessarily lead to a more sophisticated understanding and, thus, to more sophisticated writing. 'How could someone learn', asks Frank Smith (1990: 97) 'to detect conflicting assertions in a chemistry text, an article on chess, or to estimate for repairs to an automobile, without an understanding of chemistry, chess or automobile mechanics, in which case contradictions would be immediately apparent?'. The answer of course, is that one cannot. A pre-requisite to using critical thinking skills is an adequate grounding in the subject matter about which one is thinking critically. …. It may be unrealistic to expect that your writing will get progressively better when you are writing about several unrelated topics over the course of an academic term because little opportunity is given to you to develop a more sophisticated understanding of those topics.

Since most generic academic writing instruction, such as IELTS, EAP and other academic writing services, tends to teach writing about 'several unrelated topics', it is no surprise that students do not develop sufficient disciplinary knowledge to be exposed to the genres of their disciplines and to become confident critical academic writers.

Judd goes on to make the case for an interdisciplinary approach to the teaching of academic writing because this is the only way that a deep understanding of social phenomena can be gained. Without this understanding, the levers of change cannot be activated (Judd, 2003, p. 132):

> Critical thinking involves understanding a process/product as simultaneously interconnected to or interpenetrating multiple structures, both social and natural. Students often have a tendency to see the workings of the world as fragmented and disconnected. For example, if we consider a phenomenon like 'homelessness' we might say that is only a social problem, not an economic or medical one. By ignoring the impact of the economic system on unemployment, the connection between homelessness and the economic system is lost. By seeing the interconnections between homelessness, the economic system, the welfare system, the health system, the educational system, etc. students begin to understand the issue in a much more complex fashion than before.

Both Judd (2003) and Bernard-Donals (1998) refer to writing as 'an agent of change' because it is a transitive method of enquiry. Like all methods of enquiry, it aims to understand reality in order for something to happen to that reality (which can include anything from publishing it, to sharing it and transforming it). For writing to be an agent of change, writers must understand the structural realities at the ontological level of the REAL. This understanding is likely to ensure they write meaningful, authentic and genuine texts, which, in turn, can have a material and transformative impact on the world. In this sense, a critical realist understanding of what makes writing academic is its capacity to 'mediate activity' (Threshold concept 1. 5) because it enables *things to happen*.

The references to 'interconnectedness' and 'complexity' in the above quotation further align with the critical realist approach to curriculum design discussed in Mirzaei Rafe et al. (2020). Indeed, interdisciplinary praxis is the foundation of a critical realist pedagogy because only an interdisciplinary praxis founded on knowledge of science, sociology and philosophy can realistically enhance the agency required to trigger the levers of change (Mirzaei Rafe et al., 2020, p. 3): 'The thinking curriculum of CR [Critical Realism] is therefore a dynamic, predominantly collective interdisciplinary enquiry between "the real", "the actual" and the "empirical".'

I conclude this section with reference to two more fully developed pedagogies that have the potential to trigger the levers of change needed to reconfigure what makes a text academic. This is because they engage students with knowledge at the level of the REAL, thus empowering them to make writing choices such as those advocated by Carmichael-Murphy (2021), who argues for a de-colonial re-configuring of what and whose knowledge writers should be allowed to represent and how they should represent it. The first pedagogy is by UK scholars Lomer and Anthony-Okeke (2019) and the second is by Australian scholar Manathunga (2017, 2020a).

An Active Blended Learning Model

In their article on 'ethically engaging international students' in higher education, Lomer and Anthony-Okeke (2019) push back against the deficit model discussed in Chapter 1 by proposing an 'engaged' and 'ethical' pedagogy based on the work of Madge et al. (2009). This pedagogy seeks to dismantle imperialist and colonialist ideologies about what students should know and how they should represent their knowledge. Instead of asking students to demonstrate their knowledge via the traditional academic essay format, students' knowledge and critical thinking was assessed on their blog writing and their level of interaction and engagement with other students. Students were required to share, comment, explain and analyse their chosen topics via a series of posts that they managed and curated creatively. This pedagogic choice speaks directly to laying the foundation of a future pedagogy that reconfigures what makes writing academic on at least two fronts: first, it indexes teacher agency in identifying the levers of pedagogical change needed to enact such an assessment; and secondly, it empowers students by developing their own creative agencies as knowers and writers. In the spirit of sharing scholarship that builds networked communities that can collectively activate the levers of change, information about the authors' 'pedagogies for internationalization' has been made available here: https://internationalpedagogies. home. blog/

Creating Space for Southern Knowledge Systems

Mindful of what de Sousa Santos (2009) refers to as the 'ecology of knowledge' and of the sociologies of absence that this ecology exposes when it becomes apparent that only some knowledges make it into the curriculum, Manathunga (2020b) enacts her agency as a doctoral supervisor by modelling and encouraging in her students 'gentle reflection, deep listening and courageous radical action' as a way for Southern, Transcultural and Indigenous knowledge systems to emerge and become visible. This involves a series of pedagogical, as well as epistemological, commitments, such as defining your standpoint as a writer and knower (what I referred to earlier as 'positionality') and knowing history, what

Manathunga refers to as 'deep', 'slow' and 'ancient' time. This ensures writers are able to identify the events, violences, values and cultures that have led to what is visible in the present. Her blog post on 'decolonising doctoral education' shares examples of doctoral writers who have shaped their texts to fit the knowledge they are representing. For example, Manathunga refers to a Cambodian doctoral researcher who wrote her thesis as a memoir because she had to literally rely on her memory to allow the knowledge of her Cambodian grandmother's memory to emerge as knowledge. All this has been shared via the Hidden Curriculum team and further signals the power of networked communities to trigger change by making this kind of knowledge visible: https://drhiddencurriculum.wordpress.com/2020/07/09/decolonising-doctoral-education-sociologies-of-emergence

Conclusions

For academic writers and their teachers to become agents of change in both their own practices and in re-configuring what makes writing academic, new pedagogies need to emerge. The foundations of such pedagogies require writers and teachers to have the agency and material conditions to be able to lay them in the first place: one way of ensuring that teachers of academic writing are empowered to lay such foundations is to ensure they are securely employed and that they are supported in scholarly enquiry. I have identified two key levers that can help activate this agency: scholarship and pedagogy itself. Scholarship can act as a lever of change because it affords deep knowledge of the structures operating at the level of the REAL. This knowledge is needed if agents are to engage in transformative practices that allow for change at the level of the ACTUAL. Pedagogy can act as a lever of change because it can provide opportunities for interdisciplinary knowledge, which is REAL knowledge (in critical realist terms), to be the focus of a writing curriculum. Interdisciplinary knowledge enables writers as knowers to create texts that are more likely to become 'agents of change' because they represent the knowledge needed to transform reality for the better at the level of the ACTUAL. Examples of pedagogies that might engage students with this kind of deep learning were given together with examples of the kinds of academic texts that would allow this knowledge to emerge. I have suggested that what makes writing academic are texts that afford the emergence of socio-academic practices (SAPs) and epistemic virtues (EVs) aimed at transforming knowledge in the interests of social justice.

Signing Off

So, where does all this leave us?

Before I answer this, let me first summarise the gist of these five chapters.

The Gist

Set in the context of twenty-first-century neoliberal educational practices and commodification, I have argued that what makes writing academic are its emerging SAPs, not the unhinged will of the writer or the decontextualized rules and surface features of the textual environment. Having framed academic writing in the tradition of EAP and American Composition Studies, both of which are influential in shaping academic writing discourses and have spawned a highly lucrative textbook industry, I endorsed the view that academic writing is a social practice that has a history and is therefore contingent. This contingency implies that it can be different to how it is conventionally portrayed by EAP and other study skill approaches to academic writing.

The Detail

Reductive approaches to writing have undesirable aesthetic, socio-cultural and ethical implications, including the denial of a writer's humanity, understood in terms of the literacies, backgrounds and range of knowledge repertoires that they (could) bring to their academic texts. Specifically, I have challenged the histories that conflate writing with the alphabet and with higher-order thinking, arguing instead that writing did not have to be conflated with the alphabet and that although it has been, this does not mean that alphabetic cultures are better at thinking than oral or visual cultures. I have also highlighted that within academic writing cultures there is a thriving diversity of genres, yet modern-day standards of English academic writing seem to have evolved from and reified only one, the experimental article. Cherry-picking the histories that have colluded with the idea that writing raises consciousness and that academic writing is 'objective' amounts to an ideological stance, and ontological complicity, that leads to unjust practices, such as the exclusion of knowledge that is not presented 'objectively' in alphabetically written forms. Moreover, reductive approaches that reify a particular paradigm of academic writing – the alphabetic and 'encapsulated' one that reduces writing to specific terminologies and genres – allow hoaxes and IELTS essays to count as academic. These are not academic because they transgress the values of academic integrity – such as a commitment to the truth – which is an emergent SAP. Rather, what makes writing academic are the ways in which writers knowledgeably interact with their textual environments to allow SAPs to emerge. These environments include threshold concepts that trouble and re-configure what we think makes writing academic. In considering the role that argument also plays in our understandings of what makes writing academic, I claimed that whilst arguments can make writing academic, there is no requirement for them to be propositional (i.e. linguistic) or logical because most academic arguments are substantive and inductive. Because of this non-reductive nature, argument, too, can be considered as a socio-academic practice SAPs that emerges from the interaction of the writer with their textual environment.

In Chapter 4, I introduced the philosophy of critical realism as a macro theory to argue that academic writing is a transitive and epistemological method of enquiry that belongs to the realm of empirical reality. This makes it as (in)fallible as any other method of enquiry that is essentially a proxy for reality because it is not reality itself. This commits us to the conclusion that academic writing can never be 'objective' because it is a method of *human* enquiry and representation and is, therefore, by definition, always subjective. This is why I have also located the writer within the realm of the empirical alongside their various other methods of enquiry. This level of reality is epistemologically real. In other words, it exists, but it can vary, in the sense that writers have relative freedoms to choose their methods of enquiry, have different values, skills and abilities, and diverse worldviews (ideologies).

The specific genres that are in circulation at the level of the ACTUAL, such as traditional genres and those discussed in Chapter 3, are also epistemologically real because they are the result of human agents who have chosen to make them manifest by bringing them in, so to speak, from the infinite pool of genres available in the textual environment (REAL). The level of the ACTUAL contains the texts that actually exist in academia and that have to varying degrees been sanctioned as 'academic'. For example, Sousanis, Carson and Harron all received their doctorates, despite them having been drawn, rapped and written for three different audiences. These, despite being wildly different in their forms, are considered to be academic not in virtue of their surface features but in virtue of their compliance with the deep institutional requirements at the structural level of the textual environment, which is ontologically REAL. By contrast, the level of the EMPIRICAL is epistemologically real because it is a transitive level of reality, one that can change according to the choices of the agent.

Where change is much slower and even impossible is at the level of the REAL. This is the ontological level of reality. In critical realism, this is the level of deep structures, ones that are historical, institutionally embedded and entangled in the deep-seated disciplinary traditions of academic institutions. It includes institutional practices that no amount of agency can change, such as the need to do research in order to be awarded a PhD or the fact that language and the alphabet are here to stay.

The three realms of reality – the REAL, the ACTUAL and the EMPIRICAL – form an open system. In virtue of being porous and permeable, meaning that new knowledge can 'filter through' at each level, opportunities for change become possible at the level of the ACTUAL. This requires agents to identify those opportunities for change, which I have referred to as 'levers' and 'cracks', following Mason and Street. In order for agents to identify and action these levers, they must exert their rational judgement and have deep knowledge of the level of the REAL because they need to know what is available at the ontological level in order to introduce meaningful change at the epistemological level. For academic writers and their teachers to become agents of change in both their own practices and in re-configuring what makes writing academic, new pedagogies need to emerge. The foundations of such pedagogies require writers and teachers to have agency to be able to lay them. I have identified two key levers that can help activate this agency: scholarship and pedagogy itself. Scholarship can act as a lever of change because it affords deep knowledge of the structures at the level of the REAL. This knowledge is needed if agents are to engage in transformative practices that allow for change at the level of the ACTUAL to take place. Pedagogy can act as a lever of change because it can provide opportunities for interdisciplinary knowledge, which is knowledge at the level of the REAL, to be the focus of a writing curriculum. Interdisciplinary knowledge enables writers as knowers to create texts that are more likely to become 'agents of change' because they represent the knowledge needed to transform reality at the level of the ACTUAL. In Chapter 5, several examples of pedagogies that engage students with this kind of deep learning were given with an indication of how, at the level of the ACTUAL, each pedagogy has the potential to bring about change that is socially just: twelve reasons for change and pedagogic examples were given. I then referred the reader to an ethical pedagogy for international students whereby postgraduate researchers were assessed on their collaborative blog writing rather than on their ability to write an academic essay; and the choice of a memoir for the genre of the doctorate meant that a Cambodian doctoral researcher's knowledge could emerge in ways that would otherwise not have been possible had she been required to write her thesis for the traditional IMRAD structure, for example.

Overall, I encouraged writers and their teachers to engage with academic writing communities led by writing scholars who generously share their knowledge and resources as part of a collective and collegial project dedicated to helping academic writers flourish.

Where to Next?

Because of its focus on change and its commitment to transformative practices that further the mission of education, which is to be emancipatory and transformative, critical realist theory lends itself to providing a rationale for continuing to transform pedagogies in the interests of ethics and social justice. This is because it theorizes academic writing as an open system – not a straight-jacket, a pigeon hole, a skill, a generic practice, or a subservient 'handmaiden to the disciplines', but as a full-blown agent of change. This is powerful. And scary. Open systems are potentially unpredictable and unwieldy: 'I've created a monster,' comes to mind because the possibilities at the level of the REAL are infinite and those at the level of the ACTUAL are simply the tip of the ice-berg. Critical realism allows us the freedom to imagine what else might be possible at the level of the ACTUAL in a future university, similar to those imagined in Barnett (2012).

Writing understood as a method of enquiry and agent of change is clearly already being enacted at the level of the ACTUAL, as the many doctoral theses referred to indicate. But critical realism is a complex theory and it is perhaps for this reason that it has had such little uptake in academic writing pedagogies. Another reason might be that, as already highlighted, resistance to change is common for a range of reasons, including ideological ones: transforming academic writing practices means relinquishing some of our deeply held beliefs about professional standards, identities and competencies. In her book *Fields of Play*, Laurel Richardson articulates this resistance well.

Arguing that what makes writing academic are its SAPs has raised as many questions as I hope it has resolved. I leave you with the questions that I would like further research to investigate:

- What are the limitations of critical realist theory as a *praxis* for writing in the academy? For example, how and who classifies what belongs to the level of the EMPIRICAL, the ACTUAL and the REAL?
- Who judges the 'judgmental rationality' of agents who are invested with the power to trigger the levers of change needed to transform what happens at the level of the ACTUAL? And who 'invests them' with this power?
- And, related to the above, what are the generative mechanisms of the transitive epistemological realities of the REAL and the ACTUAL, i.e. can change ever occur at the intransitive ontological level of the REAL? For example, what are the levers that might change existing threshold concepts or technologies or institutional practices? How and who could trigger these levers? Roy Bhaskar's alethic version of the truth might hold the key to this as it is an attempt to bridge the objective truth at the level of the REAL and the subjective interpretivist truth at the level of the ACTUAL (Groff, 2000);
- What new SAPs (Socio-Academic Practices), EVs (Epistemic Virtues) and TCs (Threshold Concepts) might emerge from the open system that academic writing is, especially with regard to the epistemologies of the South, but also to other epistemologies, such as technological and algorithmic ones (Introna, 2016)?
- What, if any, pedagogical differentiations might be needed at undergraduate, Master's and doctoral levels with regard to choice of genres at the ACTUAL level? For example, are the possibilities at the level of the ACTUAL suitable for all levels of knowledge communication?
- What, if any, disciplinary differentiations are needed with regard to choice of genres at the ACTUAL level? For example, could a scientist write a memoir to explain scientific theories?
- And, finally, what might be the constraints on what makes writing academic? Would these all be at the level of the REAL, as I seem to have implied, or are there constraints at the level of the ACTUAL and EMPIRICAL?

These questions are the beginnings of new conversations that I hope to be part of.

Thank you for reading me,
Julia

Afterword

Suresh Canagarajah

> In every society the production of discourse is at once controlled, selected, organized and redistributed according to a certain number of procedures, whose role is to avert its powers and its dangers, to cope with chance events, to evade its ponderous, awesome materiality.
>
> (Foucault 1972b, p. 216)

Academic publishing conventions are treated as normative by most scholars. They think of the existing textual and publishing conventions as perhaps the most logical for learned or research discourse. Some scholars talk of these conventions as universally valid for that reason. Others justify them as merely instrumental. That is, these conventions are treated as value-free and neutral, simply a means to an end – presumably the rich and diverse ends of scholars around the world. However, scholars who work from non-privileged contexts almost always realize that these writing and publishing conventions are not innocent. I had to learn this the hard way. After my doctoral studies in the United States, I returned to teaching in my native Sri Lanka, thinking that my training in academic research and writing conventions would help me contribute to the wider scholarly community on local knowledge. I quickly found that an expertise in academic writing conventions was not sufficient for me to engage in publishing. Access to the resources required for publishing according to those conventions was not equally available to everyone. Also, the conventions didn't favour the communication of knowledge that mattered to us in terms of how we wanted them conveyed. Finally, the conventions distorted our voices and identities, and compelled us to write according to an ethos that was alien to us and to our scholarly persona.

Foucault's statement in the epigraph points to the politics of academic writing conventions. Firstly, the conventions are not a neutral medium. They constrain and control the messiness, unpredictability, and complexity of life and experiences. This inevitably leads to some distortions. Not surprisingly, this distortion is skewed to favour certain social groups. That is because it is the privileged who do the selection, organization and redistribution of these discourse conventions. There is therefore a relationship between the groups that define these conventions, their knowledge and their power; hence, the troubling nexus between knowledge and power, with academic writing/publishing conventions playing a critical role in sustaining this unfair nexus.

I like to add a personal touch and embodied voice in this afterword in support of Julia Molinari's project to democratize and pluralize academic writing. I draw from the experiences of my colleagues and myself in trying to publish from Sri Lanka, which I have narrated more elaborately in my book *A Geopolitics of Academic Writing* (Canagarajah, 2002b).

Consider the requirement to frame one's research or scholarly contribution in terms of the state of the art. The obligatory literature review. It often appears in the beginning of an article, before one develops one's own argument or findings, and is supposed to demonstrate the importance of one's research findings. It is presented as a harmless convention of 'joining the conversation'. How can readers assess if one's knowledge is new or significant if authors don't demonstrate how it fits the current disciplinary discourses, it is argued. In the canonical definition of research articles, John Swales (1990) considers the literature review the burden of the opening move, which he calls 'Create a Research Space'. It involves 'Establishing a Territory' (identifying the body of discourse framing the study), 'Establishing a Niche' (showing a gap in the existing literature), and then 'Occupying the Niche' (showing how one's contribution furthers this discourse). In Sri Lanka, we had many problems in meeting this requirement. To begin with, we didn't have the latest publications in any discipline to be able to review them closely for our articles. Journals and books are expensive, as a few multinational publishers monopolize academic publishing and raise the prices to favour their profit motivation. If journals and books are expensive for libraries in the United States and United Kingdom, they are beyond reach for scholars in the Global South. Therefore, when my colleagues and I submit articles from Sri Lanka, reviewers and editors in the West often turn them back by saying that they are 'inappropriately framed'. What this means is that we failed to start our article by entering the current state of the knowledge as scholars in the West understand it. They compel us to frame our research in relation to a list of publications they consider critical for that area of scholarship.

Even in the cases where we gain access to some of the publications the editors and reviewers helpfully suggest for our consideration, we find that they pose rhetorical and ideological constraints on what we want to write about. Consider the example when I first wanted to publish about publishing inequalities as shaped by material inequalities and unequal access to scholarly resources. 'Publishing on publishing' was not a thing in any discipline at that time in the 1990s! There was no literature to review. So I started off with a personal narrative on how I returned from the United States with a knowledge of academic conventions, but couldn't adopt them because of material inequalities in Sri Lanka. I cited from news media and popular journals that had reported on the dire academic conditions for scholars in the Global South. I also didn't know under which discipline a publication on academic publishing would fall. So I sent the article to a journal on writing scholarship. The reviewers turned back my submission saying that the focus of my argument was not clear because it was not framed in terms of any existing scholarly literature. What they forgot was that there was no scholarship on such a topic at that time. Finally, on the suggestion of the reviewers, I tried to frame my article on the studies in writing scholarship on the differences and difficulties for second-language students. However, I realized how this literature distorted my argument. My article was not about language differences. It was actually about material differences that exceeded language or cultural diversity. Framing publishing inequalities as a linguistic or cultural problem can actually end up blaming the victim. It will appear as if scholars in the periphery are unable to publish simply because they adopt grammatical or discoursal conventions that are different. If they only learn the proper language and conventions they will be successful, it might be interpreted. In that sense, this would not be the problem of the publishing industry, but of the individual scholars. Thus, framing local knowledge in terms of publications available in the field involves filtering out the critical edge in our argument, distorting the significance or compromising our positions.

If we adopt a longer historical lens on academic writing conventions, we will find that they have not been static, absolute or universal. They have been changing in relation to material conditions, even in the West. In the earliest scientific publications in the *Philosophical Transactions of the Royal Society of London* in the seventeenth century, the research articles started with a 'Dear Editor', written in first person, and narrating the experiment that the scholar undertook (see Atkinson, 1996). The writing adopted a narrative and temporal progression. There was no literature review to speak of, because it took many more years for findings to sediment into established knowledge and states of the art. The bulk of the articles at this time related to methodology, as research instruments were not universal or universally accessible. In what Shapin (1984) calls 'communal witnessing', the authors had to narrate the assembling of the research instrument and experimental procedures so that they could satisfy the empirical requirement of making their research visible for replication. As research progressed, literature review became more critical to demonstrate one's own unique contribution. The methodology section became reduced in significance and space as instruments and methods became standardized.

The literature review is now undergoing further changes. John Swales (1990) observes that the explosion of journals and disciplines has created some confusion about what exactly is the state of the art. There are multiple conversations going on from different theoretical perspectives on the same topic or subject. Furthermore, the disciplinary discourses are more layered, with bodies of work or states of the art on every subtopic or sub-discipline. The confusion is quite evident in novice scholars even in the West. They often cite the publications they are most familiar with or have immediate access to, unaware of the pedigree of a term, construct or paradigm. Swales (1990) and Bazerman (1988) therefore observe a structural change underway in the genre of research articles. They observe that literature review is now not limited to one place in the article (i.e. in the opening section, as it was traditional), but occurs in more diversified manner at different points in the text as relevant to the ongoing discussion. That is, authors see the need to bring up a relevant body of literature as it pertains to the subtopics or themes both in the framing section and the concluding discussion on the significance and interpretation of their findings.

What this example of the literature review suggests is that genre conventions have continued to change in relation to material and historical conditions. Not only did the academic writing conventions evolve under different conditions at different historical periods, it is still changing. This illustration of the trajectory of the literature review is one among many genre conventions I can suggest for their diverse realizations and evolutions over time. Such examples demystify academic publishing conventions. There is nothing universal or absolute about the academic genre. It has changed before, and it is still changing in relation to diverse social and historical conditions.

Other conditions such as technological, rhetorical and epistemological shifts are also initiating dramatic changes in academic writing currently. However, it is important for all of us to engage in these changes to nudge them in favour of greater democratization and inclusivity in academic communication and publishing. We cannot treat such genre changes as impersonal, neutral or automatic. Foucault would remind us that there is always a politics in knowledge construction, even if the social players, media, and platforms are different. It is for this reason that books such as this that theorize diversification and chart new ways forward are much needed. I am in solidarity with scholars like Julia who are working to diversify academic writing so that all scholars can have a voice, share knowledge more equitably, and conduct a healthy and fair exchange of knowledge. If there is one thing that the recent pandemic teaches us, it is that any activity that doesn't assume human interdependence is going to be costly for all of us. Monopolization of knowledge, isolation of certain communities from networks of knowledge production, and deliberate or unwitting distortion of knowledge that favours one's own values and interests will have dire implications for our collective human future. Let us work towards more open and fair scholarly exchanges through academic publishing.

References

Abdulrahman, H. K., Adebisi, F., Nwako, Z., & Walton, E. (2021). Revisiting (inclusive) education in the postcolony. *Journal of the British Academy*, 9(s1), 47–75. https://doi.org/10.5871/jba/009s1.047

Adler-Kassner, L., & Wardle, E. A. (Eds.). (2015). *Naming what we know: Threshold concepts of writing studies*. Utah State University Press.

Aitchison, C. (2017, 27 July 2017). How are we to understand plagiarism in doctoral writing? *Doctoral Writing SIG*. https://doctoralwriting.wordpress.com/2017/07/27/how-are-we-to-understand-plagiarism-in-doctoral-writing/

Al-Jawad, M. (2015). Comics are research: Graphic narratives as a new way of seeing clinical practice. *Journal of Medical Humanities*, 36(4), 369–74. https://doi.org/10.1007/s10912-013-9205-0

Alexander, O., Argent, A., & Spencer, J. (2008). *EAP essentials: A teacher's guide to principles and practice*. Garnet Education.

Allen, S. (2015). *Beyond argument: Essaying as a practice of exchange* (S. H. McLeod, Ed.). The WAC Clearinghouse and Parlor Press. wac.colostate.edu and www.parlorpress.com

Alvesson, M., Gabriel, Y., & Paulsen, R. (2017). *Return to meaning: A social science with something to say*. Oxford University Press. https://doi.org/10.1093/oso/9780198787099.001.0001

Alvesson, M., & Sandberg, J. (2013). *Constructing research questions doing interesting research*. SAGE Publications Ltd.

Andrews, R. (2003). The end of the essay. *Teaching in Higher Education*, 8(1), 117–28.

Andrews, R. (2010). *Argumentation in higher education: Improving practice through theory and research*. Routledge.

Andrews, R., Borg, E., Davis Boyd, S., Domingo, M., & England, J. (Eds.). (2012). *The SAGE handbook of digital dissertations and theses*. SAGE.

Anson, C. M., & Moore, J. L. (Eds.). (2016). *Critical transitions: Writing and the question of transfer*. Fort Collins: The WAC Clearinghouse and University Press of Colorado. http://wac.colostate.edu/books/ansonmoore/

Appiah, K. A. (2016a). *Mistaken identities* [Radio Broadcast]. J. Frank; BBC Radio 4. http://www.bbc.co.uk/programmes/b07z43ds

Appiah, K. A. (2016b, 9 November 2016). There is no such thing as Western civilisation. *The Guardian*. https://www.theguardian.com/world/2016/nov/09/Western-civilisation-appiah-reith-lecture

Archer, A. (2016). Multimodal academic argument: Ways of organising knowledge across writing and image. In A. Archer & E. O. Breuer (Eds.), *Multimodality in*

Higher Education (Vol. 33, pp. 93–113). Brill. 1850–9999. http://booksandjournals. brillonline.com/ BLDSS

Archer, A., & Breuer, E. (Eds.). (2015). *Multimodality in writing: The state of the art in theory, methodology and pedagogy*. Brill, 1850–9999. http://booksandjournals. brillonline.com/ BLDSS.

Archer, A., & Breuer, E. (Eds.). (2016). *Multimodality in higher education* (Vol. 33). Brill. 1850–9999 http://booksandjournals.brillonline.com/ BLDSS.

Archer, M. (1995). *Realist social theory: The morphogenetic approach*. Cambridge University Press.

Archer, M. (1998). *Critical realism: Essential readings*. Routledge.

Archer, M. (2000). *Being human: The problem of agency*. Cambridge University Press.

Archer, M. (2002). Realism and the problem of agency. *Alethia*, 5(1), 11–20. https://doi.org/10.1558/aleth.v5i1.11

Archer, M. (2003). *Structure, agency, and the internal conversation*. Cambridge University Press.

Arendt, H. (1953). Ideology and terror: A novel form of government. *The Review of Politics*, 15(3), 303–27. http://www.jstor.org/stable/1405171

Arnheim, R. (1969). *Visual thinking*. University of California Press.

Arnheim, R. (1974). *Art and visual perception: A psychology of the creative eye* (Expanded and rev. ed.). University of California Press.

Atkinson, D. (1996). The philosophical transactions of the Royal Society of London, 1675–1975: A sociohistorical discourse analysis. *Language in Society*, 25(1), 333–72.

Atkinson, P. (2013). Ethnographic writing, the avant-garde and a failure of nerve. *International Review of Qualitative Research*, 6(1), 19–35. https://doi.org/10.1525/irqr.2013.6.1.19 %J

Ávila Reyes, N., Navarro, F., & Tapia-Ladino, M. (2020). Identidad, Voz y Agencia: Claves para una Enseñanza Inclusiva de la Escritura en la Universidad. *Archivos Analíticos de Políticas Educativas*, 28(98). https://epaa.asu.edu/ojs/article/view/4722

Baber, Z. (1995). The new production of knowledge: The dynamics of science and research in contemporary societies., Michael Gibbons, Camille Limoges, Helga Nowotny, Simon Schwartzman, Peter Scott, Martin Trow. *Contemporary Sociology*, 24(6), 751–2. https://doi.org/10.2307/2076669

Back, L. (2016). *Academic diary: Or why higher education still matters*. Goldsmiths Press.

Badenhorst, C., Amell, B., & Burford, J. (Eds.). (2021). *Re-imagining doctoral writing*. Colorado: The WAC Clearinghouse; University Press of Colorado. https://doi.org/10.37514/INT-B.2021.1343

Bailey, S. (2006). *Academic writing: A handbook for international students* (2nd ed.). Routledge.

Bakhtin, M., & Holquist, M. (1981). *The dialogic imagination: Four essays*. University of Texas Press.

Ball, C. E., & Charlton, C. (2015). All writing is multimodal. In L. Adler-Kassner & E. A. Wardle (Eds.), *Naming what we know: Threshold concepts of writing studies* (pp. 42–3). Utah State University Press.

Ball, C. E., & Loewe, D. M. (Eds.). (2017). *Bad ideas about writing*. WVU Libraries. https://textbooks.lib.wvu.edu/badideas/

Ball, P. (2004). *Critical mass: How one thing leads to another*. Heinemann.

Bammer, A., & Joeres, R.-E. B. (Eds.). (2015). *The future of scholarly writing: Critical interventions* (1st ed.). Palgrave Macmillan.

Barber, C. (1993). *The English language: A historical introduction*. Cambridge University Press.

Barnett, R. (1990). *The idea of higher education*. The Society for Research into Higher Education & Open University Press.

Barnett, R. (2012). *The future university: Ideas and possibilities*. Routledge.

Barnett, R. (2013). *Imagining the university*. New York, NY: Routledge.

Barthes, R. (1967, Web. 3 December 2012). The death of the author. *Aspen: The Magazine in a Box 5+6. ubu.com*. http://www.tbook.constantvzw.org/wp-content/death_authorbarthes.pdf

Bazerman, C. (1988). *Shaping written knowledge: The genre and activity of the experimental article in science*. University of Wisconsin Press.

Bazerman, C. (Ed.). (2007). *Handbook of research on writing history, society, school, individual, text* (1st ed.). Routledge.

Bazerman, C. (2015). Social changes in science communication: Rattling the information chain. In A. G. Gross & J. Ruehl (Eds.), *Science and the Internet: communicating knowledge in a digital age* (pp. 267–81). Baywood Publishing Company Inc.

Becker, H. S. (1986). *Writing for social scientists: How to start and finish your thesis, book, or article* (2nd ed.). University of Chicago Press.

Beckett, D., & Hager, P. (2018). A complexity thinking take on thinking in the university. In S. S. E. Bengtsen & R. Barnett (Eds.), *The thinking University: A philosophical examination of thought and higher education* (pp. 137–53). Springer. http://ebookcentral.proquest.com/lib/nottingham/detail.action?docID=5376066

Bengtsen, S. S. E., & Barnett, R. (2017). Realism and education: A philosophical examination of the 'realness' of the university. In Y. H. Waghid (Ed.), *Reader in philosophy of education* (pp. 121–37). JUTA & Company, Ltd.

Bengtsen, S. S. E., & Barnett, R. (2018). *The thinking university: A philosophical examination of thought and higher education*. Springer. http://ebookcentral.proquest.com/lib/nottingham/detail.action?docID=5376066

Bennett, K. (2009). English academic style manuals: A survey. *Journal of English for Academic Purposes*, 8(1), 43–54. https://doi.org/10.1016/j.jeap.2008.12.003

Bennett, K. (2010). Academic discourse in Portugal: A whole different ballgame? *Journal of English for Academic Purposes*, 9, 21–32.

Bennett, K. (2015). The transparency trope: Deconstructing English academic discourse. *Discourse and Interaction*, 5–19. https://doi.org/10.5817/DI2015-2-5

Bereiter, C., & Scardamalia, M. (1987). *The psychology of written composition*. Lawrence Erlbaum Associates.

Bernard-Donals, M. F. (1998). *The practice of theory: Rhetoric, knowledge, and pedagogy in the academy*. Cambridge University Press.

Bernstein, S. N., & Lowry, E. (2017). The five-paragraph essay transmits knowledge. In C. E. Ball & D. M. Loewe (Eds.), *Bad ideas about writing* (pp. 214–9). WVU Libraries. https://textbooks.lib.wvu.edu/badideas/

Besley, T. A., & Peters, M. A. (Eds.). (2013). *Re-imagining the creative university for the 21st century*. Sense Publishing.

Bezemer, J., & Kress, G. (2008). Writing in multimodal texts: A social semiotic account of designs for learning. *Written Communication*, 25(2), 166–95.

Bhaskar, R. (1989). *Reclaiming reality: A critical introduction to contemporary philosophy*. Verso.

Bhaskar, R. (1998). *The possibility of naturalism: A philosophical critique of the contemporary human sciences* (3rd ed.). Routledge.

Biesta, G., Filippakou, O., Wainwright, E., & Aldridge, D. (2019). Why educational research should not just solve problems, but should cause them as well. *British Educational Research Journal*, 45(1), 1–4. https://doi.org/10.1002/berj.3509

Björkvall, A. (2016). Ploughing the field of higher education: An interview with Gunther Kress. In A. Archer & E. O. Breuer (Eds.), *Multimodality in higher education* (Vol. 33, pp. 21–30). Brill.

Blair, A., J. (2008). The rhetoric of visual arguments. In C. A. Hill & M. H. Helmers (Eds.), *Defining visual rhetorics* (pp. 41–62). Lawrence Erlbaum; Taylor and Francis e-Library.

Blommaert, J. (2010). *The sociolinguistics of globalization*. Cambridge University Press. http://ebookcentral.proquest.com/lib/nottingham/detail.action?docID=542831

Blommaert, J. (2013). *Ethnography, superdiversity and linguistic landscapes: Chronicles of complexity*. Multilingual Matters.

Blommaert, J., & Horner, B. (2017). Mobility and academic literacies: An epistolary conversation. *London Review of Education*, 15(1), 2–20. https://doi.org/https://doi.org/10.18546/LRE.15.1.02

Bond, B. (2020). *Making language visible in the University: English for academic purposes and internationalisation*. Channel View Publications. http://ebookcentral.proquest.com/lib/nottingham/detail.action?docID=6267101

Boughey, C. (2013). The significance of structure, culture and agency in efforts to support and develop student learning at South African universities. In R. Dunpath & R. Vithal (Eds.), *Access and success in higher education*. Pearson Educational.

Boughey, C., & McKenna, S. (2021). *Understanding higher education: Alternative perspectives*. African Minds. https://www.africanminds.co.za/understanding-higher-education/

Bourdieu, P., & Thompson, J. B. (1991). *Language and symbolic power*. Polity.

Bovill, C. (2020). Co-creation in learning and teaching: The case for a whole-class approach in higher education. *Higher Education*, 79(6), 1023–37. https://doi.org/10.1007/s10734 019 00453 w

Braxton, J., Luckey, W., & Helland, P. (2002). *Institutionalizing a broader view of scholarship through Boyer's four domains. ASHE-ERIC higher education report. Jossey-Bass higher and adult education series.*

Bretag, T. (2018). Academic integrity. *Oxford Research Encyclopedia of Business and Management.* https://oxfordre.com/business/view/10.1093/acrefore/9780190224851.001.0001/acrefore-9780190224851-e-147

Cameron, L., & Larsen-Freeman, D. (2007). Complex systems and applied linguistics. *International Journal of Applied Linguistics,* 17(2), 226–40. https://doi.org/10.1111/j.1473-4192.2007.00148.x

Canagarajah, S. (2002a). *Critical academic writing and multilingual students.* University of Michigan Press.

Canagarajah, S. (2002b). *A geopolitics of academic writing.* University of Pittsburgh Press.

Canagarajah, S. (2011). Codemeshing in academic writing: Identifying teachable strategies of translanguaging. *The Modern Language Journal,* 95(iii), 401–17. https://doi.org/10.1111/j.1540-4781.2011.01207.x 0026-7902/11/401–417

Canagarajah, S. (2013a). The end of second language writing? *Journal of Second Language Writing,* 22, 440–1. https://doi.org/http://dx.doi.org/10.1016/j.jslw.2013.08.007

Canagarajah, S. (2013b). *Literacy as translingual practice: Between communities and classrooms.* Routledge.

Canagarajah, S. (2013c). *Translingual practice: Global Englishes and cosmopolitan relations.* Routledge.

Canagarajah, S. (2018). Materializing 'competence': Perspectives from international STEM scholars. *The Modern Language Journal,* 102(2), 268–91. https://doi.org/https://doi.org/10.1111/modl.12464

Canagarajah, S. (2019). *Transnational literacy autobiographies as translingual writing.* Routledge.

Canagarajah, S. (2021, 27–28 May 2021). *Negotiating norms in academic writing* [Lecture]. Stockholm University (online). https://www.youtube.com/watch?v=KS_ktq2GkQ4

Canagarajah, S., & Lee, E. (2013). Negotiating alternative discourses in academic writing and publishing: Risks with hybridity. In L. Thesen & L. Cooper (Eds.), *Risk in academic writing: postgraduate students, their teachers and the making of knowledge* (pp. 59–99). Multilingual Matters.

Carel, H., & Kidd, I. J. (2014). Epistemic injustice in healthcare: A philosophical analysis [journal article]. *Medicine, Health Care and Philosophy,* 17(4), 529–40. https://doi.org/10.1007/s11019-014-9560-2

Carmichael-Murphy, P. (2021). It's time to decolonise the doctoral degree. *WONKHE.* https://wonkhe.com/blogs/its-time-to-decolonise-the-doctoral-degree/

Carr, W. (1998). What is an educational practice? In M. Hammersley (Ed.), *Educational research: Current issues* (Vol. 1, pp. 160–76). The Open University/Paul Chapman Publishing.

Carson, A. D. (2017). *Owning my masters: The rhetorics of rhymes & revolutions* [Rap Podcasts, Clemson University]. Preme & Truth. https://aydeethegreat.bandcamp.com/

Case, J. M. (2013). *Researching student learning in higher education: A social realist approach*. Routledge.

Chalmers, D. J. (1996). *The conscious mind: In search of a fundamental theory*. Oxford University Press.

Chalmers, D. J. (2006). Strong and weak emergence. In P. Clayton & P. Davies (Eds.), *The Re-emergence of emergence: The emergentist hypothesis from science to religion*. Oxford University Press. http://ebookcentral.proquest.com/lib/nottingham/detail.action?docID=430431

Chanock, K. (2014). *'Telling' insights from experience: Establishing resonance with readers, theory, and participants* [cases, learning advisers, narrative]. http://journal.aall.org.au/index.php/jall/article/view/316

Choudry, A. (2020). Reflections on academia, activism, and the politics of knowledge and learning. *The International Journal of Human Rights*, 24(1), 28–45. https://doi.org/10.1080/13642987.2019.1630382

Clark, W. (2006). *Academic charisma and the origins of the research university*. University of Chicago Press; University Presses Marketing [distributor]. Table of contents http://www.loc.gov/catdir/toc/ecip0513/2005015152.html

Cocteau, J. (1957). *La Difficulté d'être*. Editions du Rocher.

Coleman, D., Starfield, S., & Hagan, A. (2003). *The attitudes of IELTS stakeholders: Student and staff perceptions of IELTS in Australian, UK and Chinese tertiary institutions*.

Collier, A. (1994). *Critical realism: An introduction to Roy Bhaskar's philosophy*. Verso.

Collini, S. (2012). *What are universities for?* Penguin.

Collins, H. (2019, 9 May2019). Deat of the author? AI generated books and the production of scientific knowledge. *LSE Impact Blog*. https://blogs.lse.ac.uk/impactofsocialsciences/2019/05/09/death-of-the-author-ai-generated-books-and-the-production-of-scientific-knowledge/

Collyer, F., Connell, R., Maia, J., & Morrell, R. (2019). *Knowledge and global power making new Sciences in the South*. Monash University Publisher.

Connell, R. (2013). The neoliberal cascade and education: An essay on the market agenda and its consequences. *Critical Studies in Education*, 54(2), 99–112. https://doi.org/10.1080/17508487.2013.776990

Connell, R. (2019). *The good university: What universities actually do and why its time for radical change* (1st ed.). JM: Zed Books.

Costelloe, T. (2018). Giambattista Vico. In E. N. Zalta (Ed.), *The Stanford Encyclopedia of Philosophy*.

Coulmas, F. (1989). *The writing systems of the world*. Basil Blackwell.

Cousin, G. (2006). An introduction to threshold concepts. *Planet*, 17(1), 4–5. https://doi.org/10.11120/plan.2006.00170004

Cox, M. (2014). In response to today's 'felt need': WAC, faculty development, and second language writers. In T. Myers Zawacki & M. Cox (Eds.), *WAC and second language writers: Research towards linguistically and culturally inclusive programs and practices* (pp. 299–326). The WAC Clearinghouse Parlor Press. http://wac.colostate.edu/books/l2/wac.pdf

Coxhead, A. (2011). The academic word list 10 years on: Research and teaching implications. *TESOL Quarterly*, 45(2), 355–62.

Crystal, D. (1988). *The English language*. Penguin.

Crystal, D. (2003). *The Cambridge encyclopedia of the English language* (2nd ed.). Cambridge University Press.

Cuthbert, R. (2018, 26 November 2018). Fake research and trust in the social sciences. *SRHE News Blog*. https://srheblog.com/2018/11/26/fake-research-and-trust-in-the-social-sciences/

d'Agnese, V. (2017). The eclipse of imagination within educational 'official' framework and why it should be returned to educational discourse: A Deweyan perspective. *Studies in Philosophy of Education*, 36, 443. https://doi.org/https://doi.org/10.1007/s11217-016-9511-x

D'Agostino, F. (2012). Disciplinarity and the growth of knowledge. *Social Epistemology*, 26(3–4), 331–50. https://doi.org/10.1080/02691728.2012.727192

Daston, L., & Galison, P. (2007). *Objectivity*. Zone Books.

Daston, L., & Galison, P. (2010). *Objectivity*. Zone Books.

Davis, M. (2019). Publishing research as an EAP practitioner: Opportunities and threats. *Journal of English for Academic Purposes*, 39, 72–86. https://doi.org/https://doi.org/10.1016/j.jeap.2019.04.001

Dawkins, R. (1998). Intellectual impostures: Book review. *Nature*, 394(9 July), 141–3.

DBIS (2016). Success as a *Knowledge Economy: Teaching Excellence, Social Mobility and Student Choice. D. f. B. I. a. Skills*. https://www.gov.uk/government/publications/higher-education-success-as-a-knowledge-economy-white-paper.

de Sousa Santos, B. (2009). A non-occidentalist West?: Learned ignorance and ecology of knowledge. *Theory, Culture & Society*, 26(7–8), 103–25. https://doi.org/10.1177/0263276409348079

de Sousa Santos, B. (2017). *Decolonising the university: The challenge of deep cognitive justice*. Cambridge Scholars Publishing. www.cambridgescholars.com

DeFrancis, J. (1989). *Visible speech: The diverse oneness of writing systems*. University of Hawaii Press.

Derrida, J., & Spivak, G. C. (1976). *Of grammatology*. Johns Hopkins University Press.

Devitt, A. J. (1996). Genres and the teaching of genre. *College Composition and Communication*, 47(4), 605–15.

Dewey, J. (1916). *Democracy and education: An introduction to the philosophy of education*. The Free Press Simon and Schuster.

Dewey, J. (1938). *Experience and education*. Touchstone, Kappa Delta Pi, Simon & Schuster.

Ding, A. (2016, 25 January 2016). Neoliberal EAP: Are we all neoliberals now? *Teaching EAP: Polemical. Questioning, debating and exploring issues in EAP.* https://teachingeap.wordpress.com/2016/01/25/neo-liberal-eap-are-we-all-neoliberals-now/

Ding, A., & Bruce, I. (2017). *The English for academic purposes practitioner: Operating on the edge of academia* (P. Macmillan ed.). Palgrave.

Donati, P., & Archer, M. (2015). *The relational subject.* Cambridge University Press. Cover image http://assets.cambridge.org/97811071/06116/cover/9781107106116.jpg

Donnelly, M., Baratta, A., & Gamsu, S. (2019). A sociolinguistic perspective on accent and Social mobility in the UK teaching profession. *Sociological Research Online*, 24(4), 496–513. https://doi.org/10.1177/1360780418816335

Doody, A., Follinger, S., & Taub, L. (2012). Structures and strategies in ancient Greek and Roman technical writing: An introduction. *Studies in History and Philosophy of Science*, 43, 233–6.

Downs, D., & Wardle, E. (2007). Teaching about writing, righting misconceptions: (Re)envisioning 'first-year composition' as 'introduction to writing studies'. *College Composition and Communication*, 58(4), 552–84. http://www.jstor.org/stable/20456966

Eaton, M. M. (1994). The intrinsic, non-supervenient nature of aesthetic properties. *The Journal of Aesthetics and Art Criticism*, 52(4), 383–97. https://doi.org/10.2307/432026

Eco, U. (2015). *How to write a thesis.* The MIT Press.

Eisenstein, E. L. (1983). *The printing revolution in early modern Europe.* Cambridge University Press.

Elbow, P. (1994). What do we mean when we talk about voice in writing? In K. Yancey (Ed.), *Voices on voice. Perspectives, definition, inquiry* (pp. 1–35). National Council of Teachers of English.

Elliot, D. L., Bengtsen, S. S. E., Guccione, K., & Kobayashi, S. (2020). *The hidden curriculum in doctoral education.* Palgrave Pivot. https://doi.org/10.1007/978-3-030-41497-9

Emig, J. (1977). Writing as a mode of learning. *College Composition and Communication*, 28(2), 122–8. https://doi.org/10.2307/356095

English, F. (2011). *Student writing and genre: Reconfiguring academic knowledge.* Continuum.

English, F. (2015). Writing differently: Creating different spaces for student learning. In A. Chik, T. Costley, & M. C. Pennington (Eds.), *Creativity and discovery in the University writing class: a teacher's guide.* Equinox.

Erard, M. (2018). The deep roots of writing: Was writing invented for accounting and administration or did it evolve from religious movements, sorcery and dreams? *Aeon*.

EUROSTAT (2019). Disability Statistics. P. a. s. conditions. Online publications https://ec.europa.eu/eurostat/statistics-explained/index.php?title=Disability_statistics, European Union

Evans, V. (2009). *How words mean: Lexical concepts, cognitive models, and meaning construction.* Oxford University Press.

Evans, V. (2014). *The language myth: Why language is not an instinct.* Cambridge University Press.

Fairclough, N. (1992). *Discourse and social change.* Polity.

Fairclough, N. (2001). *Language and power.* Pearson Education.

Fantl, J. (2017). Knowledge How. In Edward N. Zalta (Ed.), *The Stanford Encyclopedia of Philosophy* (Fall 2017 Edition). https://plato.stanford.edu/archives/fall2017/entries/knowledge-how/

Feak, C., & Swales, J. (2013). Tensions between the old and the new in EAP textbook revision: A tale of two projects. In N. Harwood (Ed.), *English language teaching textbooks: Content, consumption, production* (pp. 299–319). Palgrave Macmillan Limited. http://ebookcentral.proquest.com/lib/nottingham/detail.action?docID=1588738

Fischer, A. (2015). 'Hidden features' and 'overt instruction' in academic literacy practices: A case study in engineering. In T. Lillis, K. Harrington, M. R. Lea, & S. Mitchell (Eds.), *Working with academic literacies: Case studies towards transformative practices* (pp. 75–85). The WAC Clearinghouse/Parlor Press. http://wac.colostate.edu/books/lillis/

Fischer, R. S. (2005). *A history of writing.* London: Reaktion Books.

Fish, S. E. (2017). *Winning arguments: What works and doesn't work in politics, the bedroom, the courtroom, and the classroom.* HarperCollins.

Fitzmaurice, M. (2010). Considering teaching in higher education as a practice. *Teaching in Higher Education*, 15(1), 45–55. https://doi.org/10.1080/13562510903487941

Flores, N., & Rosa, J. (2015). Undoing appropriateness: Raciolinguistic ideologies and language diversity in education. *Harvard Educational Review*, 85(2), 149–71. https://doi.org/10.17763/0017-8055.85.2.149

Fodor, J. (1974). Special sciences (Or: The disunity of science as a working hypothesis). *Synthese*, 28(2), 97–115. http://www.jstor.org.ezproxy.nottingham.ac.uk/stable/20114958

Fodor, J. (1997). Special sciences: Still autonomous after all these years. *Philosophical Perspectives*, 11, 149–63. http://www.jstor.org.ezproxy.nottingham.ac.uk/stable/2216128

Foucault, M. (1969). What is an author. *Lecture presented to the Société française de Philosophie on 22 February 1969.* http://seas3.elte.hu/coursematerial/HarasztosAgnes/Foucault_WhatIsAnAuthor.pdf

Foucault, M. (1972a). *The archaeology of knowledge.* Routledge.

Foucault, M. (1972b). The discourse on language. In *The Archaeology of Knowledge* (pp. 215–37). Pantheon.

Fox, K. (2021). A funny turn. In R. Phillips & H. Kara (Eds.), *Creative Writing for Social Research* (pp. 159–66). Policy Press.

Franca, L., & Lloyd, E. (2000). *Sokal hoax: The sham that shook the academy*. University of Nebraska Press. http://ebookcentral.proquest.com/lib/nottingham/detail.action?docID=3039287

Fransman, J. (2012). Re-imagining the conditions of possibility of a PhD thesis. In R. B. Andrews, Erik; Boyd Davis, Stephen, Domingo, Myrrh and England, Jude (Eds.), *The SAGE handbook of digital dissertations and theses* (pp. 138–56). SAGE.

Freire, P. (2000). *Pedagogy of the oppressed* (30th anniversary ed.). Continuum.

Fricker, M. (2007). *Epistemic injustice: Power and the ethics of knowing*. Oxford University Press. Table of contents only http://www.loc.gov/catdir/toc/ecip0710/2007003067.html

Friesen, N. (2017). *The textbook & the lecture: Education in the age of new media*. Johns Hopkins University Press.

Galtung, J. (1981). Structure, culture, and intellectual style: An essay comparing saxonic, teutonic, gallic and nipponic approaches. *Theory and Methods/Théorie et méthode*, 20(6), 817–56. https://doi.org/http://journals.sagepub.com/doi/abs/10.1177/053901848102000601

Gelb, I. J. (1952). *A study of writing. The foundations of grammatology*. Routledge & Kegan Paul.

Gelb, I. J. (1963). *The study of writing* (2nd rev. ed.). University of Chicago Press.

Good, G. (1988). *The observing self: Rediscovering the essay*. Routledge.

Goody, J. (1977). *The domestication of the savage mind*. Cambridge University Press.

Gourlay, L. (2012). Media systems, multimodality and posthumanism: Implications for the dissertation? In R. B. Andrews, Erik; Boyd Davis, Stephen, Domingo, Myrrh and England, Jude (Eds.), *The SAGE handbook of digital dissertations and Theses* (pp. 85–100). SAGE.

Gourlay, L. (2016). Multimodality, argument and the persistence of the written text. In A. Archer & E. O. Breuer (Eds.), *Multimodality in higher education* (Vol. 33, pp. 79–90). Brill.

Graff, G., & Birkenstein, C. (2006). *'They say/I say': The moves that matter in academic writing* (1st ed.). W. W.Norton & Company.

Grafton, A. (1997). *The footnote: A curious history* (New ed.). Harvard University Press.

Groarke, L. (2015). Going multimodal: What is a mode of arguing and why does it matter? *Argumentation*, 29, 133–55. https://doi.org/DOI-10.1007/s10503-014-9336-0

Groff, R. (2000). The truth of the matter: Roy Bhaskar's critical realism and the concept of alethic truth. *Philosophy of the Social Sciences*, 30(3), 407–35. https://doi.org/10.1177/004839310003000304

Grove, J. (2016, 29 September 2016). Mature students 'do better with non-written assessment': Academic attainment of disadvantaged students can be improved if they can decide how they are assessed, study claims. *Times Higher Education*. https://www.timeshighereducation.com/news/mature-students-do-better-non-written-assessment

Gutkind, L. (1997). *The art of creative nonfiction: Writing and selling the literature of reality*. Wiley.

Hadley, G. (2015). *English for academic purposes in neoliberal universities: A critical grounded theory*. Springer. 1850–9999. http://www.springer.com/gb/ BLDSS

Halverson, J. (1992). Havelock on Greek orality and literacy. *Journal of the History of Ideas*, 53(1), 148–63. http://www.jstor.org/stable/2709915

Hamilton, M., & Pitt, K. (2009). Creativity in academic writing: Escaping from the straightjacket of genre. In A. Carter, T. Lillis, & S. Parkin (Eds.), *Why writing matters: Issues of access and identity in writing research and pedagogy* (pp. 61–79). John Benjamins Publishing Company. https://doi.org/10.1075/swll.12.12ham

Hanauer, D. I., Sheridan, C. L., & Englander, K. (2019). Linguistic injustice in the writing of research articles in English as a second language: Data from Taiwanese and Mexican researchers, 36(1), 136–54. https://doi.org/10.1177/0741088318804821

Hancock, S. (2020, 17 February 2020).The employment of PhD graduates in the UK: what do we know? *HEPI: Higher Education Policy Institute*. https://www.hepi.ac.uk/2020/02/17/the-employment-of-phd-graduates-in-the-uk-what-do-we-know/

Hanna, J. (2014). Manifestos: A Manifesto. The 10 traits of effective public declarations, an Object lesson. *The Atlantic*. https://www.theatlantic.com/entertainment/archive/2014/06/manifestos-a-manifesto-the-10-things-all-manifestos-need/372135/

Haraway, D. (1988). Situated knowledges: The science question in feminism and the privilege of partial perspective. *Feminist Studies*, 14(3), 575–99. https://doi.org/10.2307/3178066

Harding, S. (1995). 'Strong objectivity': A response to the new objectivity question. *Synthese*, 104(3), 331–49. http://www.jstor.org/stable/20117437

Harper, R., Bretag, T., Ellis, C., Newton, P., Rozenberg, P., Saddiqui, S., & van Haeringen, K. (2019). Contract cheating: A survey of Australian university staff. *Studies in Higher Education*, 44(11), 1857–73. https://doi.org/10.1080/03075079.2018.1462789

Harris, R. (1986). *The origin of writing*. Duckworth.

Harris, R. (1989). How does writing restructure thought? *Language and Communication*, 9(2/3), 99–106.

Harris, R. (2000). *Rethinking writing*. Athlone.

Harris, R. (2011). *Integrationist notes and papers 2009–2011*. Bright Pen.

Harris, R., & Taylor, T. J. (1989). *Landmarks in linguistic thought: The Western tradition from Socrates to Saussure*. Routledge.

Harron, P. A. (2016). *The equidistribution of lattice shapes of rings of integers of cubic, quartic, and quintic number fields: An artist's rendering: Based on the original story by Manjul Bhargava and Piper Harron* [A Dissertation presented to the faculty of Princeton University in Candidacy for the Degree of Doctor of Philosophy, Princeton University].

Harwood, N. (2005). What do we want EAP teaching materials for? *Journal of English for Academic Purposes*, 4(2), 149–61. https://doi.org/http://dx.doi.org/10.1016/j.jeap.2004.07.008

Hathaway, J. (2015). Developing that voice: Locating academic writing tuition in the mainstream of higher education. *Teaching in Higher Education*, 20(5), 506–17. http://dx.doi.org/10.1080/13562517.2015.1026891

Havelock, E. A. (1976). *Origins of Western literacy*. Ontario Institute for Studies in Education.

Havelock, E. A. (1982). *The literate revolution in Greece and its cultural consequences*. Princeton University Press.

Hayot, E. (2014). *The elements of academic style: Writing for the humanities*. Columbia University Press.

Healey, M., Matthews, K. E., & Cook-Sather, A. (Eds.). (2020). *Writing about learning and teaching in higher education: Creating and contributing to scholarly conversations across a range of genres*. Elon University.

Helms-Park, R., & Stapleton, P. (2003). Questioning the importance of individualised voice in undergraduate L2 argumentative writing: An empirical study with pedagogical implications. *Journal of Second Language Writing*, 12, 245–65.

Henderson, J. (2018). Styling writing and being styled in university literacy practices. *Teaching in Higher Education*, 1–17. https://doi.org/10.1080/13562517.2018.1527765

HESA (2020a). Widening participation: UK domiciled full-time HE undergraduate student enrolments by participation characteristics, academic years 2018/19 to 2019/20. H. Education. https://www.hesa.ac.uk/data-and-analysis/students

HESA (2020b). Higher Education Student Statistics: UK, 2018/19. H. Education. https://www.hesa.ac.uk/news/16-01-2020/sb255-higher-education-student-statistics/numbers

Hirst, P. H. (1998). Educational theory. In M. Hammersley (Ed.), *Educational research: current issues* (Vol. 1, pp. 149–59). The Open University/Paul Chapman Publishing.

Hocking, D., & Toh, G. (2010). EAP writing: Reflections on divergent perceptions and expectations among tutors and students. *Asian Journal of English Language Teaching*, 20, 161–83.

Hodgson, N., Vlieghe, J., & Zamojski, P. (Eds.). (2018). *Manifesto for a post-critical philosophy*. Punctum books. https://doi.org/https://www.doi.org/10.21983/P3.0193.1.00

Hogan, P. (2015). Recovering the lost métier of philosophy of education? Reflections on educational thought, policy and practice in the UK and farther afield. *Journal of Philosophy of Education*, 49(3), 366–81.

Hohwy, J., & Kallestrup, J. (2008). *Being reduced: New essays on reduction, explanation, and causation*. Oxford University Press.

Holbrook, A., Burke, R., & Fairbairn, H. (2020). Linguistic diversity and doctoral assessment: Exploring examiner treatment of candidate language. *Higher Education Research & Development*, 1–15. https://doi.org/10.1080/07294360.2020.1842336

Holmes, J. (1992). *An introduction to sociolinguistics*. Longman.

Horner, B., & Lu, M.-Z. (2013). Translingual Literacy, Language Difference, and Matters of Agency. *College English* 75(6), 586–611.

Hountondji, P. J. (1995). Producing knowledge in Africa today the second Bashorun M. K. O. Abiola distinguished lecture. *African Studies Review*, 38(3), 1–10. https://doi.org/10.2307/524790

Hurley, P. J. (2000). *A concise introduction to logic* (7th ed.). Wadsworth/Thomson Learning.

Hutchings, P., & Shulman, L. (1999). The scholarship of teaching: New elaborations, new developments. *Change*, 31(5), 10–15. http://www.jstor.org/stable/40165542

Hyland, K. (2002). Options of identity in academic writing. *ELT Journal*, 56(4), 351–8.

Hyland, K. (2006). The 'Other' English: Thoughts on EAP and academic writing. *The European English Messenger*, 15(2), 34–57.

Hyland, K. (2016). *Teaching and researching writing* (3 ed.). Routledge.

Hyland, K., & Feng (Kevin), J. (2017). Is academic writing becoming more informal? *English for Specific Purposes*, 45, 40–51. https://doi.org/http://dx.doi.org/10.1016/j.esp.2016.09.001

Hyland, K., & Hamp-Lyons, L. (2002). EAP: Issues and directions. *Journal of English for Academic Purposes*, 1(1), 1–12.

Ingraham, B. D. (2005). Ambulating with mega-fauna: A scholarly reflection on *Walking with Beasts*. In R. Land & S. Bayne (Eds.), *Education in cyberspace* (pp. 45). Routledge Falmer.

Introna, D. L. (2016). Algorithms, governance, and governmentality: On governing academic writing. *Science, Technology, and Human Values*, 4(1), 17–49. https://doi.org/DOI:-10.1177/0162243915587360

Ivanič, R. (1998). *Writing and identity: The discoursal construction of identity in academic writing*. John Benjamins.

Jenkins, J. (2016). Correspondence from Jennifer Jenkins. *English Language Teaching Journal*, 70(1), 122. https://doi.org/10.1093/elt/ccv063

Jones, J. (2014). *Slavoj Žižek charged with plagiarizing: A white nationalist magazine article*. Retrieved 23 March 2016 from http://www.openculture.com/2014/07/slavoj-zizek-charged-with-plagiarizing-a-white-nationalist-magazine-article.html

Judd, D. (2003). *Critical realism and composition theory*. Routledge.

Kaidesoja, T. (2009). Bhaskar and Bunge on social emergence. *Journal for the Theory of Social Behaviour*, 39(3), 300–22. https://doi.org/https://doi.org/10.1111/j.1468-5914.2009.00409.x

Kamler, B., & Thomson, P. (2006). *Helping doctoral students write: Pedagogies for supervision*. Routledge. Table of contents only. http://www.loc.gov/catdir/toc/ecip0610/2006007398.html

Kaplan, R. B. (1980 [1966]). Cultural thought patterns in inter-cultural education. In K. Croft (Ed.), *Readings on English as a second language* (pp. 399–418). Winthrop.

Kara, H. (2015). *Creative research methods in the social sciences: A practical guide*. The Policy Press.

Kiley, M., & Wisker, G. (2009). Threshold concepts in research education and evidence of threshold crossing. *Higher Education Research & Development*, 28(4), 431–41. https://doi.org/10.1080/07294360903067930

Kim, J. (2006). Emergence: Core ideas and issues. *Synthese*, 151(3), 547–59.

King, A. (2010). The odd couple: Margaret Archer, Anthony Giddens and British social theory. *The British Journal of Sociology*, 61, 253–60. https://doi.org/10.1111/j.1468-4446.2009.01288.x

King, B. (1991). Reviewed Work(s): Visible speech: The diverse oneness of writing systems by John DeFrancis. *Linguistic Society of America*, 67(2), 377–9. http://www.jstor.org/stable/415119

Knapp, S., & Michaels, W. B. (1982). Against theory. *Critical Inquiry*, 8(4), 723–42. http://www.jstor.org/stable/1343194

Knorr Cetina, K., Schatzki, T. R., & Von Savigny, E. (Eds.). (2001). *The practice turn in contemporary theory*. Routledge. http://ebookcentral.proquest.com/lib/nottingham/detail.action?docID=235322.

Kripke, S. A. (1972). *Naming and necessity*. Blackwell.

Krishnan, A. (2013). Organizing Science: A Further Reply to Fred D'Agostino. *Social Epistemology Review and Reply Collective*, 2(3), 19–21.

Kruse, O. (2006). The origins of writing in the disciplines: Traditions of seminar writing and the humboldtian ideal of the research university. *Written Communication*, 23(3), 331–52. https://doi.org/10.1177/0741088306289259

Kuhn, L. (2008). Complexity and educational research: A critical reflection. *Educational Philosophy and Theory*, 40(1), 177–89. https://doi.org/10.1111/j.1469-5812.2007.00398.x

Kuhn, T. (1962). *The structure of scientific revolutions*. University of Chicago Press.

Kunju, H. W. (2017). *IsiXhosa ulwimi lwabantu abangesosininzi eZimbabwe: ukuphila nokulondolozwa kwaso* [Rhodes University]. http://hdl.handle.net/10962/7370

Kuttner, P., Sousanis, N., & Weaver-Hightower, M. B. (2017). How to draw comics the scholarly way: Creating comics-based research in the academy. In P. Leavy (Ed.), *Handbook of arts-based research* (pp. 396–422). Guilford Press.

Labbé, C. (2010). Ike Antkare one of the greatest stars in the scientific firmament. *Université Joseph Fourier LIG Laboratory*, 1–14. http://hal.inria.fr/docs/00/71/35/64/PDF/TechReportV2.pdf

Labbé, C., & Labbé, D. (2012). Duplicate and fake publications in the scientific literature: How many SCIgen papers in computer science? *Scientometrics*, 1–19. https://doi.org/DOI-10.1007/s11192-012-0781-y

Latour, B., & Woolgar, S. (1986). *Laboratory life: The construction of scientific facts* (2nd ed.). Princeton University Press.

Laurillard, D., Stratfold, M., Luckin, R., Plowman, L., & Taylor, J. (2000). Affordances for learning in a non-linear narrative medium. *Journal of Interactive Media in Education*, 2 (Art. 2), 1–19. https://doi.org/http://doi.org/10.5334/2000-2

Lave, J., & Wenger, E. (1991). *Situated learning: Egitimate peripheral participation*. Cambridge University Press.

Law, J. (2003). *Making a mess with method*. 1–12. available online https://www.lancaster.ac.uk/fass/resources/sociology-online-papers/papers/law-making-a-mess-with-mcthod.pdf

Law, J. (2004). *After method: Mess in social science research*. Routledge. Table of contents. http://www.loc.gov/catdir/toc/ecip0413/2004001842.html

Law, S. (2014). Introduction. *Think*, 13(36), 5–9. https://doi.org/10.1017/S1477175613000274

Le Ha, P. (2009). Strategic, passionate, but academic: Am I allowed in my writing? *Journal of English for Academic Purposes*, 8(2), 134–46. https://doi.org/http://dx.doi.org/10.1016/j.jeap.2008.09.003

Lea, M., & Street, B. (1998). Student writing in higher education: An academic literacies approach. *Studies in Higher Education*, 23(2), 157–72.

Leedham-Green, E. (1996). *A Concise history of the University of Cambridge*. Cambridge University Press.

Leung, C., Lewkowicz, J., & Jenkins, J. (2016). English for academic purposes [Article]. *Englishes in Practice*, 3(3), 55–73. https://doi.org/10.1515/eip-2016-0003

Lillis, T. (2001). *Student writing: Access, regulation, desire*. Routledge.

Lillis, T. (2013). *The sociolinguistics of writing*. Edinburgh University Press.

Lillis, T., & Curry, M. J. (2010a). *Academic writing in a global context: The politics and practices of publishing in English*. Routledge.

Lillis, T., & Curry, M. J. (2010b). *Academic writing in a global context: The politics and practices of publishing in English*. Routledge.

Lillis, T., & Curry, M. J. (2015). The politics of English, language and uptake: The case of international academic journal article reviews. *AILA Review*, 28, 127–50.

Lillis, T., Harrington, K., Lea, M. R., & Mitchell, S. (Eds.). (2015). *Working with academic literacies: Case studies towards transformative practices*. The WAC Clearinghouse/Parlor Press. http://wac.colostate.edu/books/lillis/

Lillis, T., & Tuck, J. (2016). Academic literacies: A critical lens on writing and reading in the academy. In K. Hyland & P. Shaw (Eds.), *The Routledge handbook of English for academic purposes* (pp. 30–43). Routledge.

Little, D. (2018, 22 May 2018). Social generativity and complexity. *Understanding Society*. https://understandingsociety.blogspot.com/2018/05/social-generativity-and-complexity.html

Lomer, S., & Anthony-Okeke, L. (2019). Ethically engaging international students: Student generated material in an active blended learning model. *Teaching in Higher Education*, 24(5), 613–32. https://doi.org/10.1080/13562517.2019.1617264

Lunsford, A. A. (2015). 2.5 writing is performative. In L. Adler-Kassner & E. A. Wardle (Eds.), *Naming what we know: Threshold concepts of writing studies* (pp. 43–4). Utah State University Press.

Macfarlane, B. (2021a). The conceit of activism in the illiberal university. *Policy Futures in Education*, 19(5), 594–606. https://doi.org/10.1177/14782103211003422

Macfarlane, B. (2021b). Methodology, fake learning, and emotional performativity. *ECNU Review of Education*. https://doi.org/10.1177/2096531120984786

MacIntyre, A. (1985). *After virtue: A study in moral theory* (2nd ed.). Duckworth.

Madge, C., Raghuram, P., & Noxolo, P. (2009). Engaged pedagogy and responsibility: A postcolonial analysis of international students. *Geoforum*, 40(1), 34–45. https://doi.org/https://doi.org/10.1016/j.geoforum.2008.01.008

Malpas, J. (2002). The weave of meaning: Holism and contextuality. *Language & Communication*, 22(4), 403–19. https://doi.org/https://doi.org/10.1016/S0271-5309_02_00017-4

Manathunga, C. (2017). Intercultural doctoral supervision: The centrality of place, time and other forms of knowledge. *Arts and Humanities in Higher Education*, 16(1), 113–24. https://doi.org/10.1177/1474022215580119

Manathunga, C. (2020a, 9 July 2020). Decolonising doctoral education: Sociologies of emergence? *The hidden curriculum*. https://drhiddencurriculum.wordpress.com/2020/07/09/decolonising-doctoral-education-sociologies-of-emergence/amp/?__twitter_impression=true

Manathunga, C. (2020b). Decolonising higher education: Creating space for Southern knowledge systems. *Scholarship of Teaching and Learning in the South*, 4(1), 4–25. https://doi.org/10.36615/sotls.v4i1.138

Marin, L., Masschelein, J., & Simons, M. (2018). Page, text and screen in the university: Revisiting the Illich hypothesis. *Educational Philosophy and Theory*, 50(1), 49–60. https://doi.org/10.1080/00131857.2017.1323624

Mason, M. (2008). What is complexity theory and what are its implications for educational change? *Educational Philosophy and Theory*, 40(1), 35–49. https://doi.org/10.1111/j.1469-5812.2007.00413.x

Matsuda, P., & Tardy, C. (2008). Continuing the conversation on voice in academic writing. *English for Specific Purposes*, 27, 100–105.

Matthews, D. (2014). Focus on recruiting foreign students reveals 'mission drift'. *The Times Higher Education*. http://www.timeshighereducation.co.uk/news/focus-on-recruiting-foreign-students-reveals-mission-drift/2012240.article

Mays, C. (2017). Writing complexity, one stability at a time: Teaching writing as a complex system. *College Composition and Communication*, 68(3), 559–85. http://www.jstor.org/stable/44783580

Mbembe, A. (2008, 9 January 2008). What is postcolonial thinking? An interview with Achille Mbembe. *Eurozine*. https://www.eurozine.com/what-is-postcolonial-thinking/

McArthur, J. (2020). Assessment for social justice: Achievement, uncertainty and recognition. In C. Callender, W. Locke, & S. Marginson (Eds.), *Changing higher education for a changing World*. Bloomsbury.

Mcculloch, S. (2017). Hobson's choice: The effects of research evaluation on academics' writing practices in England. *Aslib Journal of Information Management*, 69(5), 503–15. https://doi.org/doi:10.1108/AJIM-12-2016-0216

McLuhan, M. (1964). *Understanding media: The extensions of man*. Ark, 1987.

Medway, D., Roper, S., & Gillooly, L. (2018). Contract cheating in UK higher education: A covert investigation of essay mills. 44(3), 393–418. https://doi.org/doi:10.1002/berj.3335

Mewburn, I. (2020, May 13). Where I call bullshit on the way we do the PhD. *The thesis whisperer.* https://thesiswhisperer.com/2020/05/13/stop-letting-the-ghosts-of-old-academia-haunt-you/

Meyer, J., & Land, R. (2006). *Overcoming barriers to student understanding: Threshold concepts and troublesome knowledge.* Routledge. Table of contents http://www.loc.gov/catdir/toc/ecip064/2005034793.html

Meyer, J., Land, R., & Baillie, C. (2010). *Threshold concepts and transformational learning.* Sense Publishers.

Mckenna, S. (2021). Technology should not stop us trusting students. *WONKHE* https://wonkhe.com/blogs/technology-should-not-stop-us-trusting-students/ (Accessed 30 September 2021).

Mirzaei Rafe, M., Noaparast, K. B., Hosseini, A. S., & Sajadieh, N. (2020). An examination of Roy Bhaskar's critical realism as a basis for educational practice. *Journal of Critical Realism,* 1–16. https://doi.org/10.1080/14767430.2020.1807799

Molinari, J. (2013). Holiday question 1: Why are there so few academic writing courses? *patter.* https://patthomson.wordpress.com/category/julia-molinari/

Molinari, J. (2014, 3 April 2014). Academic ghostwriting: To what extent is it haunting higher education? *The Guardian.* https://www.theguardian.com/higher-education-network/blog/2014/apr/03/academic-proofreading-write-essays-universities-students-ethics

Molinari, J. (2019). *What makes writing academic: An educational and philosophical response* Unpublished Ph.D. Thesis, University of Nottingham.

Molinari, J. (2021a). Playing with #acwri: A play on academic writing. In R. Phillips & H. Kara (Eds.), *Creative writing for social research: A practical guide* (pp. 20–4). Policy Press.

Molinari, J. (2021b). Re-imagining Doctoral Writings as Emergent Open Systems. In C. Badenhorst, B. Amell and J. Burford (Eds.), *Re-imagining doctoral writing* (pp. 49–69). The WAC Clearinghouse; University Press of Colorado. DOI: 10.37514/INT-B.2021.1343.2.02

Moore, T., & Morton, J. (2005). Dimensions of difference: A comparison of university writing and IELTS writing. *Journal of English for Academic Purposes,* 4, 43–66.

Morris, R. (2010). *Can the Subaltern Speak?: Reflections on the History of an Idea.* Columbia University Press. http://ebookcentral.proquest.com/lib/nottingham/detail.action?docID=895096

Moynihan, M. (2015, 24 September 2015). *Mafia author Roberto Saviano's plagiarism problem.* Retrieved 22 March 2016 from https://www.thedailybeast.com/mafia-author-roberto-savianos-plagiarism-problem?ref=scroll

Mulvey, B. (2021). Pluralist internationalism, global justice and international student recruitment in the UK. *Higher Education.* doi:10.1007/s10734-021-00750-3.

Myers Zawacki, T., & Cox, M. (Eds.). (2014). *and second language writers: Research towards linguistically and culturally inclusive programs and practices.* The WAC Clearinghouse, Parlor Press. http://wac.colostate.edu/books/l2/wac.pdf.

Naylor, R., Dollinger, M., Mahat, M., & Khawaja, M. (2020). Students as customers versus as active agents: Conceptualising the student role in governance and quality assurance. *Higher Education Research & Development*, 1–14. https://doi.org/10.1080/07294360.2020.1792850

Neculai, C. (2015). Academic literacies and the employability curriculum: Resisting neoliberal education? In T. Lillis, K. Harrington, M. R. Lea and S. Mitchell (Eds), *Working with academic literacies: Case studies towards transformative practices* (pp. 401–12). The WAC Clearinghouse/Parlor Press.

Nesi, H., & Gardner, S. (2012). *Genres across the disciplines: Student writing in higher education.* Cambridge University Press.

Nixon, J. (2012). Universities and the common good. In R. Barnett (Ed.), *The university of the future: Ideas and possibilities* (pp. 141–51). Routledge.

Nussbaum, M. C. (1990). *Love's knowledge: Essays on philosophy and literature.* Oxford University Press.

Nussbaum, M. C. (2011). *Creating capabilities: The human development approach.* Belknap.

O'Dwyer, S., Pinto, S., & McDonough, S. (2018). Self-care for academics: A poetic invitation to reflect and resist. *Reflective Practice*, 19(2), 243–9. https://doi.org/10.1080/14623943.2018.1437407

Olson, D. (1977). From Utterance to text: The bias of language in speech and writing. *Harvard Educational Review*, 47(3), 257–81. http://hepgjournals.org/doi/pdf/10.17763/haer.47.3.8840364413869005

Olson, D. (1994). *The World on paper.* Cambridge University Press.

Olson, D. R. (2001). *Psychology of Writing Systems. International Encyclopedia of the Social & Behavioral Sciences*, Elsevier Science Ltd.: 16640–11663.

Ong, W. J. (1982). *Orality and literacy: The technologizing of the word.* Methuen.

Ong, W. J. (1986). Writing is a technology that restructures thought. In G. Baumann (Ed.), *The Written word: literacy in transition: Wolfson College Lectures 1985* (pp. 23–50). Clarendon. http://www.ric.edu/faculty/rpotter/temp/ong.pdf

ONS (2019). Participation Rates in Higher Education: Academic Years 2006/2007 – 2017/2018 (Provisional) D. f. Education. https://assets.publishing.service.gov.uk/government/uploads/system/uploads/attachment_data/file/843542/Publication_HEIPR1718.pdf

Orelus, P. W. (2017). Accentism exposed: An anticolonial analysis of accent discrimination with some implications for minority languages. In P. W. Orelus (Ed.), *Language, race, and power in schools: A critical discourse analysis* (pp. 127–37). Routledge.

Orman, J. (2016). Scientism in the language sciences. *Language & Communication*, 48, 28–40. https://doi.org/http://dx.doi.org/10.1016/j.langcom.2016.02.002

Palmeri, J. (2012). *Remixing composition: A history of multimodal writing pedagogy.* Southern Illinois University Press.

Paltridge, B., & Starfield, S. (2020). Change and continuity in thesis and dissertation writing: The evolution of an academic genre. *Journal of English for Academic Purposes*, 48, 100910. https://doi.org/10.1016/j.jeap.2020.100910

Paquot, M. (2010). *Academic vocabulary in learner writing: From extraction to analysis*. Continuum.

Paradis, J. (1987). Montaigne, Boyle, and the essay of experience. In G. Levine & A. Rauch (Eds.), *One culture: Essays in science and literature* (pp. 59–91). University of Wisconsin Press.

Paré, A. (2017). Re-thinking the dissertation and doctoral supervision/Reflexiones sobre la tesis doctoral y su supervisión. *Infancia y Aprendizaje Journal for the Study of Education and Development*, 11–21. https://doi.org/10.1080/02103702.2017.1341102

Paré, A. (2018). Re-writing the doctorate: New contexts, identities, and genres. *Journal of Second Language Writing*, 43, 80–4. https://doi.org/https://doi.org/10.1016/j.jslw.2018.08.004

Parker, K. N. (2017). Response: Never use 'I'. In C. E. Ball & D. M. Loewe (Eds.), *Bad ideas about writing* (pp. 134–8). WVU Libraries. https://textbooks.lib.wvu.edu/badideas/

Parnell, J. E. (2012). Complexity theory. In R. N. L. Andrews, E. Borg, S. Davis Boyd, M. Domingo, & J. England (Eds.), *The SAGE handbook of digital dissertations and theses* (pp. 120–37). Sage.

Paxton, M. (2013). Genre: A pigeonhole or a pigeon? Case studies of the dilemmas posed by the writing of academic research proposals. In L. Thesen & L. Cooper (Eds.), *Risk in academic writing: Postgraduate students, their teachers and the making of knowledge* (pp. 148–65). Multilingual Matters.

Pennycook, A. (1996). Borrowing others' words: Text, ownership, memory, and plagiarism. *TESOL Quarterly*, 30(2), 201–30.

Peters, M. (2008). Academic writing, genres and philosophy. *Educational Philosophy and Theory*, 40(7), 819–31. https://doi.org/http://dx.doi.org/10.1111/j.1469-5812.2008.00511.x

Peters, M. (Ed.). (2009). *Academic writing, philosophy and genre*. Wiley-Blackwell.

Peters, M. (2017). Manifesto for the postcolonial university. *Educational Philosophy and Theory*, 1–7. https://doi.org/10.1080/00131857.2017.1388660

Peters, M. (2018). Academic integrity: An interview with Tracey Bretag. *Educational Philosophy and Theory*, 1–6. https://doi.org/10.1080/00131857.2018.1506726

Peters, M. A., Jackson, L., Hung, R., Mika, C., Buchanan, R. A., Tesar, M., Besley, T., Hood, N., Sturm, S., Farrell, B., Madjar, A., & Webb, T. (2021). The case for academic plagiarism education: A PESA Executive collective writing project. *Educational Philosophy and Theory*, 1–24. https://doi.org/10.1080/00131857.2021.1897574

Peters, M. A., McLaren, P., & Jandrić, P. (2020). A viral theory of post-truth. *Educational Philosophy and Theory*, 1–9. https://doi.org/10.1080/00131857.2020.1750090

Pettersson, J. S. (1994). Evolutionary accounts of writing and the disobedient history of scripts. *Language & Communication*, 14(2), 129–53.

Phillips, R., & Kara, H. (Eds.). (2021). *Creative writing for social research: A practical guide*. Policy Press.

Politzer-Ahles, S., Girolamo, T., & Ghali, S. (2020). Preliminary evidence of linguistic bias in academic reviewing. *Journal of English for Academic Purposes*, 47, 100895. https://doi.org/https://doi.org/10.1016/j.jeap.2020.100895

Politzer-Ahles, S., Holliday, J. J., Girolamo, T., Spychalskae, M., & Harper Berksonf, K. (2016). Is linguistic injustice a myth? A response to Hyland. *Journal of Second Language Writing*, 34, 4–8. https://doi.org/http://dx.doi.org/10.1016/j.jslw.2016.09.003

Postman, N. (1993). *Technopoly: The surrender of culture to technology*. Vintage Books.

Pratt, D. (2011). *Modelling written communication: A new systems approach to modelling in the social sciences*. Springer.

Prinsloo, M., & Breier, M. (1996). *The social uses of literacy: Theory and practice in contemporary South Africa*. Benjamins.

Raimes, A. (1991). Out of the woods: Emerging traditions in the teaching of writing. *TESOL Quarterly*, 25(3), 407–30.

Ramage, J., Callaway, M., Clary-Lemon, J., & Waggoner, Z. (2009). *Argument in composition*. Parlor Press. http://wac.colostate.edu. https://wac.colostate.edu/books/referenceguides/ramage-argument/

Ravelli, L., Paltridge, B., Starfield, S., & Tuckwell, K. (2013). Extending the notion of 'text': The visual and performing arts doctoral thesis. *Visual Communication*, 12(4), 395–422. https://doi.org/10.1177/1470357212462663

Reimann, N., & Jackson, I. (2006). Threshold concepts in Economics: A case study. In J. Meyer & R. Land (Eds.), *Overcoming barriers to student understanding: Threshold concepts and troublesome knowledge* (pp. 115–33). Routledge. Table of contents. http://www.loc.gov/catdir/toc/ecip064/2005034793.html

Richardson, L. (1990a). Narrative and sociology. *Journal of Contemporary Ethnography*, 19(1), 116–35. https://doi.org/10.1177/089124190019001006

Richardson, L. (1990b). *Writing strategies: Reaching diverse audiences*. Sage.

Richardson, L. (1997). *Fields of play: Constructing an academic life*. Rutgers University Press.

Richardson, L., & St. Pierre, E. A. (2005). Writing: A method of inquiry. In Denzin, Norman K. & Lincoln, Yvonna S. (Eds.), *The Sage handbook of qualitative research* (3rd ed., pp. 959–78). Sage Publications Ltd.

Robeyns, I. (2016). The capability approach. In E. N. Zalta (Ed.), *The Stanford Encyclopedia of Philosophy* (Winter 2016 Edition).

Robinson, K. (2001). *Out of our minds: Learning to be creative*. Capstone.

Rodríguez, R. J. (2017). Leave yourself out of your writing. In C. E. Ball & D. M. Loewe (Eds.), *Bad ideas about writing* (pp. 131–3). WVU Libraries. https://textbooks.lib.wvu.edu/badideas/

Roozen, K., & Erickson, J. (2017). *Expanding literate landscapes: persons, practices, and sociohistoric perspectives of disciplinary development*. Computers and Composition Digital Press/Utah State University Press.

Roque, G. (2015). Should visual arguments be propositional in order to be arguments? *Argumentation*, 29, 177–95. https://doi.org/10.1007/s10503-014-9341-3

Rose, M. (1985). The language of exclusion: Writing instruction at the university. *College English*, 47(4), 341–59. https://www.jstor.org/stable/376957

Rose, M. (1989). *Lives on the boundary: The struggles and achievements of America's underprepared*. Free Press; Collier Macmillan Publishers.

Rose, M. (2005). *The mind at work: Valuing the intelligence of the American worker*. Penguin Random House.

Ross, S. (1962). Scientist: The story of a word. *Annals of Science*, 18(2), 65–85. https://doi.org/http://dx.doi.org/10.1080/00033796200202722

Rowland, S. (2008). Collegiality and intellectual love. *British Journal of Sociology of Education*, 29(3), 353–60. https://doi.org/10.1080/01425690801966493

Rüegg, W., & Ridder-Symoens, H. d. (Eds.). (1992–2011). *A history of the university in Europe* (Vols. 1–4). Cambridge University Press.

Russell, D. R. (2002). *Writing in the academic disciplines: A curricular history* (2nd ed.). Southern Illinois University Press.

Russell, D. R., & Cortes, V. (2012). Academic and scientific texts: The same or different communities? In M. Castello, C. Donahue, & G. Rijlaarsdam (Eds.), *University writing: Selves and texts in academic societies*. BRILL. http://ebookcentral.proquest.com/lib/nottingham/detail.action?docID=868547

Russell, D. R., Lea, M., Parker, J., Street, B., & Donahue, T. (2009). Exploring notions of genre in 'academic literacies' and 'writing across the curriculum' approaches across countries and contexts. In C. Bazerman, A. Bonini, & D. Figueiredo (Eds.), *Genre in a changing world: Perspectives on writing* (pp. 395–423). WAC Clearinghouse/Parlor Press.

Said, E. W. (1978). *Orientalism*. Penguin.

Said, E. W. (1993). *Culture and imperialism*. Chatto & Windus.

Said, E. W. (1994). *Representations of the intellectual: The 1993 Reith lectures*. Vintage.

Saussure, F. d., Baskin, W., Meisel, P., & Saussy, H. (2011). *Course in general linguistics*. Columbia University Press.

Sawyer, R. K. (2001). Emergence in sociology: Contemporary philosophy of mind and some implications for sociological theory. *American Journal of Sociology*, 107(3), 551–85. http://iscte.pt/~jmal/mcc/Keith_Sawyer_Emergence_in_Sociology.pdf

Schmandt-Besserat, D. (2001). Evolution of writing. *International Encyclopedia of the Social & Behavioral Sciences*. Elsevier Science Ltd.: 16619–25.

Scott, M. (2000). Agency and subjectivity in student writing. In Jones, Carys, Turner, Joan & Street Brian (Ed.), *Students writing in the university*. John Benjamins Publishing Company.

Scott, M. (2013). *A chronicle of learning: Voicing the text* (pp. 171–91). University of Tilburg. available from http://eprints.ioe.ac.uk/19177/1/Mary_Scott_V1_formatting.pdf

Scott, M., & Lillis, T. (2007). Defining academic literacies research: Issues of epistemology, ideology and strategy. *Journal of Applied Linguistics*, 4(1), 5–32.

Scribner, S., & Cole, M. (1981). *The psychology of literacy*. Harvard University Press.

Sellars, W. (1963). *Science, perception and reality*. Routledge & Kegan Paul; Humanities Press.

Shanahan, D. R. (2015). A living document: Reincarnating the research article [This article is part of the series New ways to publish research findings.]. *Trials*, 16(151). https://doi.org/10.1186/s13063-015-0666-5

Shapin, S. (1984). Pump and circumstance: Robert Boyle's literary technology. *Social Studies of Science*, 14(4), 481–520. http://www.jstor.org/stable/284940

Shor, I., & Freire, P. (1987). *A pedagogy for liberation: Dialogues on transforming education*. Bergin & Garvey Publishers.

Sigmund, K. (2017). *Exact thinking in demented times: The Vienna circle and the epic quest for the foundations of science*. Basic Books, Hachette Book Group.

Smith, R. (1999). Paths of judgement: The revival of practical wisdom. *Educational Philosophy and Theory*, 31(3), 327–40. https://doi.org/10.1111/j.1469-5812.1999.tb00469.x

Sokal, A. D. (1996). Transgressing the boundaries: Toward a transformative hermeneutics of quantum gravity. *Social Text,* 46(47), 217–52. https://doi.org/10.2307/466856

Sokal, A. D. (2008). *Beyond the hoax: Science, philosophy and culture*. Oxford University Press.

Sousanis, N. (2015). *Unflattening*. Harvard University Press.

Sousanis, N. (2016). *The power of images* [Interview]. https://meaningoflife.tv/videos/37781

Sowton, C. (2016). *Contemporary academic writing: A comprehensive course for students in Higher Education*. Garnet Publishing Ltd.

Sperlinger, T., McLellan, J., & Pettigrew, R. (2018). *Who are universities for?: Re-making higher education*. Bristol University Press.

Spivak, G. C. (1987). *In other worlds: Essays in cultural politics*. Methuen.

Street, B. V. (1984). *Literacy in theory and practice*. Cambridge University Press.

Swales, J. M. (1980). ESP: The textbook problem. *The ESP Journal,* 1(1), 11–23.

Swales, J. (1990). *Genre analysis: English in academic and research settings*. CUP.

Swales, J. M., & Feak, C. B. (2012). *Academic writing for graduate students: Essential skills and tasks* (3rd ed.). University of Michigan Press.

Sword, H. (2009). Writing higher education differently: A manifesto on style. *Studies in Higher Education*, 34(3), 319–36. https://doi.org/10.1080/03075070802597101

Sword, H. (2012). *Stylish academic writing*. Harvard University Press.

Tardy, C. M. (2016). *Beyond convention: Genre innovation in academic writing*. University of Michigan Press, Ann Arbor.

Tardy, C. M., & Jwa, S. (2016). Composition studies and EAP. In Hyland, Ken & Shaw, Philip (Eds.), *The Routledge handbook of English for academic purposes* (pp. 56–68). Routledge.

Tarnay, L. (2002). The conceptual basis of visual argumentation – A case for arguing in and through moving images. *ISSA Proceedings 2002 –*. Retrieved 11 November 2017, from http://rozenbergquarterly.com/issa-proceedings-2002-the-conceptual-basis-of-visual-argumentation-a-case-for-arguing-in-and-through-moving-images/

Taub, L. (2017). *Science writing in Greco-Roman antiquity*. Cambridge University Press.

Thesen, L., & Cooper, L. (Eds.). (2013). *Risk in academic writing: Postgraduate students, their teachers and the making of knowledge*. Multilingual Matters.

Thomas, K. C. (2018, 28 April 2018). The accidental cartoonist: Learning the craft of the graphic essay. *The Sociological Review*. https://www.thesociologicalreview.com/blog/the-accidental-cartoonist-learning-the-craft-of-the-graphic-essay.html

Thomson, P. (2013). Do we 'collect' data? or – beware the ontological slip …. *patter*. https://patthomson.net/2013/03/11/do-we-collect-data-or-is-your-ontological-slip-showing/

Thomson, P. (2018a). Getting to grips with 'the paragraph'. *patter*. https://patthomson.net/2018/11/05/getting-to-grips-with-the-paragraph/

Thomson, P. (2018b). Me, myself and I. *patter*. https://patthomson.net/2018/10/01/me-myself-and-i/

Thomson, P. (2018c). Troubling writing as 'representation'. In B. Jeffrey & L. Russell (Eds.), *Writing for ethnography*. Tufnell Press.

Thomson, P. (2021, 5 July 2021). The problem with gap talk. *Patter*. https://patthomson.net/2021/07/05/the-problem-with-gap-talk/

Titscher, S., Meyer, M., Wodak, R., & Vetter, E. (2002). *Methods of text and discourse analysis*. SAGE.

Toulmin, S. 1964 (1969). *The uses of argument*. [S.l.]: Cambridge University Press.

Toulmin, S. (1958). *The Uses of Argument*. Cambridge University Press.

Tribble, C. (2015). Writing academic English further along the road. What is happening now in EAP writing instruction? *English Language Teaching Journal*, 69(4), 442–62. https://doi.org/10.1093/elt/ccv044

Tseronis, A. (22 May 2013). Argumentative functions of visuals: Beyond claiming and justifying. *OSSA Conference Archive, Paper 163*, 1–17. http://scholar.uwindsor.ca/ossaarchive/OSSA10/papersandcommentaries/163

Tuckett, A. (2013, 19 June 2013). *Adult learning in the global university*. mms://resources.lsri.nottingham.ac.uk/haveseminar

Turner, J. (2004). Language as academic purpose. *Journal of English for Academic Purposes*, 3, 95–109. https://doi.org/10.1016/S1475-1585(03)00054-7

Turner, J. (2010). *Language in the academy: Cultural reflexivity and intercultural dynamics*. Multilingual Matters.

Turner, J. (2018). *On writtenness: The cultural politics of academic writing* (1st ed.). Bloomsbury Academic. http://www.bloomsbury.com/9781472514455

Tusting, K., McCulloch, S., Bhatt, I., Hamilton, M., & Barton, D. (2019). *Academics writing: The dynamics of knowledge creation*. Routledge.

Van Noorden, R. (2014, 24 February 2014). Publishers withdraw more than 120 gibberish papers. *Nature: International Weekly of Science*. http://www.nature.com/news/publishers-withdraw-more-than-120-gibberish-papers-1.14763

Van Norden, B. W. (2017, 31 October 2017). Western philosophy is racist: Academic philosophy in 'the West' ignores and disdains the thought traditions of China,

India and Africa. This must change. *Aeon.* https://aeon.co/essays/why-the-Western-philosophical-canon-is-xenophobic-and-racist

Vertovec, S. (2007). Super-diversity and its implications. *Ethnic and Racial Studies*, 30(6), 1024–54.

Vico, G. (1959 (1725, 1730, 1744, 1928)). *La scienza nuova.* Letteratura italiana Einaudi. http://www.letteraturaitaliana.net/pdf/Volume_7/t204.pdf

Villanueva, V. (2015). 3.5 Writing provides a representation of ideologies and identities. In L. Adler-Kassner & E. A. Wardle (Eds.), *Naming what we know: Threshold concepts of writing studies* (pp. 57–8). Utah State University Press.

Vinkers, C. H., Tijdink, J. K., & Otte, W. M. (2015). Use of positive and negative words in scientific PubMed abstracts between 1974 and 2014: Retrospective analysis. *351.* https://doi.org/10.1136/bmj.h6467%J-BMJ

Wardle, E. (2009). 'Mutt Genres' and the goal of FYC: Can we help students write the genres of the university? *College Composition and Communication*, 60(4), 765–89. http://www.jstor.org/stable/40593429

Wardle, E. (2017). You can learn to write in general. In C. E. Ball & D. M. Loewe (Eds.), *Bad ideas about writing* (pp. 30–3). WVU Libraries. https://textbooks.lib.wvu.edu/badideas/

Warner, J. (2018). *Why they can't write: Killing the five-Paragraph essay and other necessities.* Johns Hopkins University Press.

Warnock, M. (1989). *Universities: Knowing our minds. What the government should be doing about higher education.* London, Chatto & Windus Ltd.

Wei, L. (2016). New Chinglish and the post-multilingualism challenge: Translanguaging ELF in China. In *Journal of English as a Lingua Franca*, 5, 1.

Weller, M. (2021, 28 April 2021). Proctorio – Unis as custodians. *The Ed Techie: Martin Weller's blog on open education, digital scholarship & over-stretched metaphors.* http://blog.edtechie.net/edtech/proctorio-unis-as-custodians/

Williams, B. T. (2009). *Shimmering literacies: Popular culture & reading & writing online.* P. Lang.

Williams, B. T. (2017). *Literacy practices and perceptions of agency: Composing identities.* Routledge/Taylor & Francis Ltd.

Williams, B. T., & Zenger, A. A. (2012). *New media literacies and participatory popular culture across borders.* Routledge.

Wimsatt, W. K., & Beardsley, M. C. (1946). The intentional fallacy. *The Sewanee Review*, 54(3), 468–88. http://www.jstor.org/stable/27537676

Wingate, U. (2012). 'Argument!' helping students understand what essay writing is about. *Journal of English for Academic Purposes*, 11, 145–54.

Wingate, U., & Tribble, C. (2012). The best of both worlds? Towards an English for academic purposes/academic literacies writing pedagogy. *Studies in Higher Education*, 37(4), 481–95. https://doi.org/http://dx.doi.org/10.1080/03075079.2010.525630

Wittgenstein, L., & Anscombe, G. E. M. (1953). *Philosophical investigations.* Basil Blackwell.

Wittgenstein, L., & Russell, B. (1922). *Tractatus Logico-Philosophicus (Logisch-Philosophische Abhandlung) … With an introduction by Bertrand Russell. Ger. & Eng.* London.

Wolff, J. (2007, 4 September 2007). Literary boredom. *The Guardian.* https://www.theguardian.com/education/2007/sep/04/highereducation.news

Wongsriruksa, S., Howes, P., Conreen, M., & Miodownik, M. (2012). The use of physical property data to predict the touch perception of materials. *Materials & Design*, 42, 238–44. https://doi.org/https://doi.org/10.1016/j.matdes.2012.05.054

Woodard, R. D. (2001). Writing Systems. *International Encyclopedia of the Social & Behavioral Sciences.* Elsevier Science Ltd.: 16633–40.

Womack, P. (1993). What are essays for. *English in Education*, 27(2): 42–8.

Wright, J. (2011). Causal mechanisms generating writing competency discourses in a radiography curriculum in higher education. *Journal of Critical Realism*, 10(2), 163–91.

Wylie, A. (2003). Why standpoint matters. In R. Figueroa & S. G. Harding (Eds.), *Science and other cultures: Issues in philosophies of science and technology* (pp. 26–48). Routledge.

Yun, S., & Standish, P. (2018). Technicising thought: English and the internationalisation of the university. In S. S. E. Bengtsen & R. Barnett (Eds.), *The thinking university: A philosophical examination of thought and higher education.* Springer. http://ebookcentral.proquest.com/lib/nottingham/detail.action?docID=5376066

Zamel, V. (1998a). Questioning academic discourse. In V. Zamel & R. Spack (Eds.), *Negotiating academic literacies: Teaching and learning across languages and cultures* (pp. 187–98). Lawrence Erlbaum Associates.

Zamel, V. (1998b). Strangers in academia: The experiences of faculty and ESL students across the curriculum. In V. Zamel & R. Spack (Eds.), *Negotiating academic literacies: Teaching and learning across languages and cultures* (pp. 249–64). Lawrence Erlbaum Associates.

Zenger, A., Mullin, J., & Peterson Haviland, C. (2014). Reconstructing teacher roles through a transnational lens: learning with/in the American University of Beirut. In T. Myers Zawacki & M. Cox (Eds.), *WAC and second language writers: Research towards linguistically and culturally inclusive programs and practices* (pp. 415–37). The WAC Clearinghouse Parlor Press. http://wac.colostate.edu/books/l2/wac.pdf

Zgaga, P. (2009). Higher education and citizenship: 'The Full Range of Purposes'. *European Educational Research Journal*, 8(2), 175–88. https://doi.org/10.2304/eerj.2009.8.2.175

Index

academic literacies 10, 12, 20, 93, 99, 100, 116, 119, 122
   see also Theresa Lillis and Brian Street
academic misconduct
   ghostwriting 43, 101
   plagiarism x, 43–4, 76, 99, 101, 117, 123, 138
   proctoring 137–8
academicness 12–13, 70, 73–6, 78–81, 83–5, 87, 99–101, 105, 117, 127, 133, 150–2
Académie Française 61
academy 3, 17, 20, 33–4, 37, 39, 50, 58, 69, 73, 80, 113, 117, 148, 156, 167
Accademia della Crusca 61
access ix, x, xiii, 5, 19, 33–4, 62, 103, 112, 128, 135, 144, 154–7, 169–72
active voice 31, 124
   see also grammar
activism 79–80, 143–4
actual *See* knowledge
affordance 3, 11, 35, 57, 71, 83, 85, 103, 112, 142, 150, 152
agency 2, 15, 27, 29–31, 34, 43, 64, 73, 79, 80–1, 85, 100, 102, 104–6, 109, 114–15, 118–19, 120, 123, 128, 133, 135, 145, 147, 152, 154, 157, 159, 160–1, 165
alienation xi, 25, 56
alphabet x, 17, 35, 45, 47–55, 57, 64, 68, 70, 72–3, 85–6, 136, 163–5
analytic dualism 102, 106
argument
   abductive 110
   clear *See* clarity
   deductive 46, 54, 66, 89–91, 94, 96, 110
   formal 2, 9, 10–11, 18, 26, 32, 39, 78, 90–2, 94, 98, 110, 141–2, 158
   haptic 104
   inductive 12, 89, 91, 93–4, 98, 110, 164
   linear 9–13, 32, 45, 57, 73, 93–4, 115–16, 120–5, 128, 132, 134–6, 145, 147, 152–3
   logical 32, 91
   multimodal 3, 6, 10, 42, 52, 57, 71, 84–5, 93, 97, 100, 134–6, 146, 149–50
   narrative 95–7
   objective 8–12, 18, 35, 44, 56, 60, 64, 69–70, 72, 100, 103, 106–10, 112–18, 125, 132, 139, 141, 145, 164, 167
   propositional 89, 94, 96
   recursive 10, 12, 25, 57, 94, 135–6, 147
   retroductive 109, 110, 116
   rhetorical *See* genre
   substantive 92, 94, 96, 98, 164
   visual 3, 79, 88, 94–5, 104, 127–8, 134, 153
assessment ix, 6, 23, 24, 66, 71, 104, 127, 133, 138, 14–2, 149–50, 152, 160
Athena Swan 144

Bazerman, Charles 15, 57, 62–4, 66–7, 79, 147, 172
Bhaskar, Roy 10, 33, 99, 102–4, 109, 114, 118, 167
Black Lives Matter 144
BLM *See* Black Lives Matter

capitalism 107, 117
CARS *See* genre > create a research space
Carson, A.D. *See* genre > alternative
Cartesian *See* Descartes
censorship 62, 132–3
change x, xi, 3, 4, 12–13, 20, 27–9, 40, 46, 50, 63, 73, 77, 83, 99, 100, 102–6, 108–12, 114, 116, 118–24, 128–30, 133–5, 143–50, 152–61, 165–7, 172
Chinese 47–8, 51–2
clarity 14, 32, 67, 76, 142–3, 150
   see also argument *and* transparency trope
climate change 111, 117–18
commodification 42, 163
composition *See* Rhetoric and Composition/Writing Studies

conventions *See* rules *and* standards
Covid-19 pandemic 2, 138
critical realism ix, x, 3, 6, 13, 18, 99–103, 105–7, 109, 111–17, 119–23, 125–7, 129, 159, 165–6

DBIS *See* Department of Business and Industry (UK)
Department of Business and Industry (UK) [DBIS] 4
decolonization
    colonial 17, 38, 45, 69, 160
    imperial 160
deficit 26, 35, 37–9, 133, 145, 160
    see also remedial
Derrida, Jacques 53, 67, 75–6, 87
Descartes 34, 46, 109
Dewey, John 22, 27, 39–41, 94
disability 4
discipline xi, 5, 9, 10, 14, 24–7, 30, 33–4, 39, 43, 67–8, 81, 91–3, 110, 133, 136, 142, 150–1, 155, 158, 166, 170–2
diversity x, 3, 4, 5, 10, 13–14, 38–9, 40, 42, 45, 72–3, 80, 83, 89, 100, 122, 164, 171

EAP *See* English for Academic Purposes
English for Academic Purposes [EAP] 5, 6, 9, 10–13, 17, 20, 23–4, 32–6, 38–44, 69, 78, 87, 93, 95, 97, 107, 115, 132–3, 137, 155, 158, 163
ecology 41, 72, 135, 139, 145, 153, 160
education ix, x, xi, xii, 3–7, 10, 14, 17, 21, 24, 27, 33, 37, 38–44, 61, 68–72, 77, 80, 93–4, 97, 101, 103, 105, 116–18, 132–3, 142–3, 146, 148, 150–2, 158–61, 163, 166
    see also training
emergence 80, 102, 120, 122, 125–6, 141–2, 161
    weak and strong 126–7, 129
English, Fiona xii, 19, 24
    see also re-genring
epistemic fallacy xi, 11, 108–10
epistemic injustice *See* Fricker, Miranda
epistemology 8, 11, 17–19, 107
EDI *See* Equality, Diversity and Inclusion
epistemic virtue 149–53, 161, 167

Equality, Diversity and Inclusion [EDI] 144
ethics 42–3, 141, 148, 154, 166
    see also values
European statistics agency 4
EUROSTAT *See* European statistics agency

fake 43, 75
    see also hoax
feminism 8, 28, 70, 78–9, 83
Fodor, Jerry 13, 80, 125, 127
    see also Multiple Realizability
Fricker, Miranda 71, 80, 86
    see also epistemic injustice

Galilei, Galileo 62, 78
genre
    abstract 3, 78
    acknowledgments 65
    alternative
        Carson: 78–9, 84, 88, 100–1, 134, 144, 165
        Harron: 78–9, 81, 114, 128, 158, 165
        Sousanis: 15, 37, 79, 88, 127, 131, 144, 153, 165
    biography 57, 147
    blog 3, 38, 137, 158, 160–1, 166
    chronicle 3, 62–3, 91, 147
    citations 66, 129
    comic 3, 91, 145, 152, 154, 174
    commentaries 57
    create a research space (CARS model) 11, 170
    creative non-fiction 70
    dialogue 3, 14, 24, 30, 62, 63, 78, 81, 84, 91, 104, 145, 151–2
    digital 134, 136, 146–7
    dissertations 78, 104, 127, 146, 153
    EdD 134
    essai 60
        see also Montaigne
    essay 1, 3, 6, 10–11, 19–20, 23–4, 27, 32, 36, 38, 40–1, 43, 57, 60–1, 63, 70, 76, 78, 91, 93, 98–9, 101, 104, 107, 117, 128–9, 133, 136, 138, 145, 160, 164, 166
    ethos 10, 86, 89
    experimental article 60, 63, 72, 164

findings 64, 66, 78, 79, 171–2
humour 148
IMRAD 136, 166
infographic (poster) 136
interview 151, 153
introduction 3, 19, 36, 65, 136
journal article 1, 147
letter 57, 62, 63, 91, 147
literature review 95, 170–2
logos 10, 86
main body 3
manifesto 3, 83, 84, 91, 143, 150
memoir 70, 161, 166–7
methods 31, 63–4, 66, 78–9, 88, 95, 97, 108, 136, 172
newsletter 91, 135, 149, 158
pathos 10, 86
PhD 1, 15, 28–9, 75–6, 78–9, 81, 101, 114, 136, 142, 144–5, 147, 153, 158, 165
poem 1, 30, 31, 57, 70, 79, 84, 89, 92, 101, 104, 152–3
  see also poetry
prose 2, 13, 14, 24, 30, 31, 33, 38, 54, 57, 70, 73, 78, 79, 135, 147, 152, 153
rhetoric 14, 36, 60, 64, 67, 70, 100, 107–8, 113–5, 124–5, 149, 170, 172
thesis *See* PhD *and* EdD
ghostwriting *See* academic misconduct
Global North xi
Global South 37, 141, 170–1
grammar 9, 12–13, 17, 20, 33, 55, 67, 79, 82, 98–100, 104
Greek
  eudamonia 80
  phronesis 21, 80
  poiesis 21–2
  praxis 21–2, 27, 29, 133, 159, 167
  technê 21
  γράφω (writing/drawing) 50
Gutenberg Revolution 58
  see also Printing Press

Harris, Roy 47–53, 67, 87–8, 114
Harron, Piper *See* genre > alternative
HEI *See* Higher Education Institution
HESA *See* Higher Education Statistics Agency

higher education ix, x, xi, 4–7, 17, 24, 33, 37–9, 44, 69, 72, 77, 80, 93, 101, 116, 132–3, 137, 142–3, 146, 148, 160
Higher Education Institution [HEI] 4
Higher Education Statistics Agency (UK) [HESA] 4
history 3, 5, 8, 10, 13–14, 36, 45–51, 53–5, 57, 59–61, 63, 65, 67–72, 76, 91, 102, 104, 110, 121, 136, 139, 142, 147, 160, 163
hoax 10, 17, 43, 74–8, 98–9, 108, 112, 116–17, 128, 137, 141, 164
  see also fake
homogeneity 37–8, 107, 148
humanism 14, 41, 46, 60–2, 67
human Rights 144, 148
Hyland, Ken 20, 23, 23, 33–4, 39–40, 66, 125

ideology 4, 6–7, 13, 22–3, 29, 38, 45, 51, 53, 57, 67, 68–73, 80–1, 84, 97, 103, 106, 113, 133, 141–2, 160, 164, 167, 170
IELTS *See* International English Language Testing System
IMRAD *See* genre > IMRAD
intellectual work *See* knowledge
intentional fallacy 76–7
interdisciplinarity *See* knowledge
International English language Testing System [IELTS] 1, 23, 36, 42–3, 78, 98–9, 107, 109, 116–17, 128–9, 158, 164
international students *See* internationalization
internationalization 4, 5, 33, 42, 63, 137, 160, 166

knowledge
  ACTUAL 103–7, 109–12, 118–19, 127–52, 154, 157, 161, 165–7
  data 8, 14, 58, 79, 91–2, 94–5, 124–5, 153
  democratize 3, 9, 14, 38, 57, 69, 101, 141, 154, 170, 172
  dialectic 111, 118–19
  ecologies of 83, 89, 117, 144
  EMPIRICAL 104–9, 112, 114, 119, 127–9, 150–2, 157, 165, 167

epistemology and ontology 8, 11, 13, 17, 18–20, 24, 102, 104–5, 107, 109, 111, 113, 118, 122
essentialist 8, 22, 25, 82
exclusionary 3, 17, 23, 25, 37, 45, 52–3, 69, 71–2, 143, 164
indigenous xi, 156, 160
intellectual work 22
interdisciplinarity xi, 5, 7, 14, 79, 93, 117, 128, 135, 145, 148, 159, 161, 165
(in)transitive 103–4, 106–11, 113–16, 119, 128, 134, 138–40, 144, 146, 154–5, 159, 164
pluralize 8, 14, 170
prediction 2, 7, 92, 115–16, 122–3, 127, 129, 166, 169
procedural 11, 21–2, 26, 107, 133
propositional 11, 21, 26
REAL 103–7, 109–12, 118–19, 127–9, 150–2, 154, 157, 161, 165–7
reflexivity 117
reliability 30, 140, 153
situated 26, 31, 70, 72, 151
stratified 13, 102–4, 109, 111–12, 118, 122, 127, 129, 157
validity 30, 90–2, 153
warrant 80, 91–4, 98
worker ix, 1, 37

language(s)
  alphabetic *See* alphabet
  cuneiform 48, 55
  dominant xi, 135
  English (second and additional) 7, 35, 135
  field-dependent 92–3
  French 15, 31, 32, 50, 61, 69
  Greek *See* Greek
  ideographic 70
  indigenous xi, 84, 146
  isiXhosa 84
  Italian 15, 86
  Latin 12, 49, 50, 59, 61–3, 65, 69
  lingua franca 42, 69, 84
  logographic 48–9, 52–3
  phonetic 48–9, 51–2
  pictographic 48–9, 52
  representational 48
  syllabic 48–9
  symbolic 47, 50
lexis 26, 61, 99
  see also vocabulary

LGBTQ+ 144
Lillis, Theresa 10, 18, 20, 23, 27, 33, 37, 39, 45, 69, 84, 121, 141
linguistics (including sociolinguistics) 3, 5, 38, 48, 53, 67, 87, 120, 121
literacy x, xiii, 2, 4, 6, 12–13, 22–3, 25, 27, 33, 35–7, 41, 45, 47–8, 53–6, 68, 71, 79, 85–7, 90, 99, 100, 133, 141–4, 147–8
Locke, John 34, 142

MacIntyre, Alasdair 27–9, 31, 74, 80
Marxism 103
mechanism x, xi, 100, 103–4, 108–9, 111–13, 118, 120, 129, 143, 167
monolingualism 3, 12, 17, 37–8, 44, 71, 148
monomodality 3, 37–8, 44, 97, 148
Montaigne, Michel de 60, 61, 64, 67
multiculturalism 35, 37–8
multilingualism 12–15, 17, 24, 35, 37–8, 57, 63, 69, 72–3, 134–5, 148, 150
multimodality 3, 6, 10, 13–15, 17, 35–7, 41–2, 52, 57, 71, 73, 84–5, 93, 97, 100, 134–6, 145–6, 148–50
Multiple Realizability 124–5, 128, 159
  see also Fodor, Jerry
myth of transience 11, 24, 26, 118
  see also skill *and* Rose, Mike

Newton, Isaac 63–4, 97, 139

objective *See* knowledge
Olson, David 45, 47, 50–1, 53–4, 65, 67, 114
Ong, Walter 55–6, 79, 90
ontological complicity 57, 141, 164
  see also Turner, Joan
ontology 11, 13, 17–20, 24, 102, 104–5, 107, 109, 111, 113, 118, 122
open system 3, 13, 50, 91, 101, 112, 119–20, 122, 128, 130, 153–4, 165–7

paragraphs 6, 11, 19, 22–3, 36, 53, 82, 95, 108, 127, 129, 133, 136, 146
passive voice 2, 13, 18, 20, 31, 35–6, 74, 107–8, 124
  see also grammar
pedagogy 13, 22, 24, 41, 115–18, 125, 131, 133–5, 137, 139, 141, 143, 145, 147, 149, 151–5, 157–61, 165–6

emancipatory 38, 118, 166
performativity
   Lunsford 43, 83
   Macfarlane 43, 83, 99, 137–8
personal pronouns 2, 19, 34, 36, 117, 124–5, 132
   see also grammar
Philosophical Transactions (Royal Society) 63, 92, 171
philosophy
   hard problem of science 126
   of mind 13, 80, 125
   of sociology 10, 13–14, 30–1, 89–91, 97, 102, 159
plagiarism *See* academic misconduct
power x, 6, 8, 19, 27, 29, 33–5, 38, 40, 46, 67–9, 79, 82–3, 86, 100, 102–3, 109, 112
practices (social) 14, 20–1, 23, 46, 68, 83, 143
Printing Revolution 181
   see also Gutenberg Revolution
proctoring *See* academic misconduct

readers (audience) 23, 60, 63–4, 67, 71, 74–7, 79–81, 84, 87, 91, 94, 108, 112, 138, 140, 149–52, 158, 170
reality ix, x, xi, 8, 30, 46, 64, 67, 87, 89, 91, 98–104, 106–14, 116–19, 122, 124, 127, 129, 138–40, 146, 153–5, 157, 159, 161, 164–6
reduction/ism 12, 100
   see also essentialism
re-genring 24
   see also English, Fiona
relativism ix, 99, 100, 110, 115
   see also Relativist Turn
Relativist Turn 67
   see also relativism
remedial 25–6, 33
   see also deficit
representation *See* language
rhetoric
   logos, ethos, pathos *see* genre
Rhetoric and Composition Studies 5, 17, 113–14, 136
Richardson, Laurel 2, 23, 26, 29–31, 70, 92, 97, 113, 141, 152–3, 167
Rose, Mike 11, 21, 24
Received Pronunciation 37–8, 141, 148
   see also Writtenness

RP *See* Received Pronunciation
rules 1, 21, 23–4, 29–31, 35–8, 43, 46, 51, 78, 80, 100, 103–4, 132, 156–7, 163
   see also standards

Said, Edward 46
Socio-academic practice [SAP] 74, 77, 80–1, 83, 85, 87, 91, 98, 111, 127–9, 133, 137, 143–4, 147, 149, 151–4, 161, 163–4, 167
scholarship xi, 3, 7, 43, 68, 93, 106, 123, 133, 142–3, 150–2, 154, 155–8, 160–1, 165, 170–1
science 8, 21, 57, 62–3, 65–8, 70, 91, 97, 103, 126–7, 134, 139–40, 159
scientific paradigm *See* science
semasiography 51, 53
semiotics 3, 25, 35, 41, 53, 71, 80, 87–8, 97–8, 104, 134–6, 149–50, 152, 154
service industry 33, 36, 38–9, 43–4, 107, 132, 137–8, 155, 158
shallow consensus 9, 10, 12
skills
   autonomous 22, 56, 69, 70, 133
   Myth of transience *see* Myth of transience
   transferable x, 6, 7, 12–13, 17, 20, 31, 39, 41–2, 93, 118, 133, 146, 155, 158
social justice ix, x, xi, 3, 5, 8, 33, 46, 74, 80–1, 101–3, 111, 116, 127–9, 143–4, 158, 161, 166
SoTL *See* scholarship
Sousanis, Nick *See* genre > alternative
standardization *See* standards
standards 1, 3–4, 11–12, 19, 24, 28–31, 35–8, 41–4, 51, 57, 60–2, 66–74, 78, 83, 91, 93, 100–1, 103–4, 109, 129, 132, 141–3, 146, 149, 155, 172
   see also conventions *and* rules
standards of excellence 27–31, 74–5, 79–80, 88, 100–1, 128, 143, 146–7
Street, Brian x, 20, 22, 38, 45, 69, 99, 121, 165
structure x, 2, 13, 31, 102–4, 106–7, 109, 111, 113, 117–22, 129, 154, 158–9, 161, 165
student ix, x, xi, xii, 1–7, 9, 11–12, 15, 18–19, 22–5, 32–43, 58, 65–6, 68, 70, 72, 75, 77–8, 81–2, 84, 93, 106–7, 109, 115–23, 135–8, 141–3, 146, 148–9, 151, 154–61, 171

subjective *See* knowledge
success ix, 37, 42, 129, 148, 171
supervenience 126–9
supervenient base *See* supervenience
supervisor 1, 3, 34, 75, 157, 160
Swales, John 11, 24, 133, 170, 172

teacher xi, 3, 5, 11, 13, 28, 32, 34, 36, 41, 58, 81, 89, 113, 114, 116, 122–3, 153–7, 160–1, 165–6
text x, 2–5, 11–12, 17–18, 23, 30, 32, 35–6, 40, 43, 51, 54, 57, 65–7, 70, 73–87, 89, 95, 99, 100–1, 104, 108, 112, 114, 116–17, 128–9, 134–9, 141–54, 157–9, 161, 163, 172
   see also textual environment
textual environment 7, 15, 79, 80–5, 87, 91, 98, 100–6, 111–12, 128, 150–2, 163–5
theory
   Cartesian 34, 46, 109
   cognitive 5, 22, 24, 55, 86, 109, 115–16
   complexity 10, 25, 66, 76, 80, 95, 99, 120–6, 128, 154, 159, 169
   constructivism/constructivist 106, 108, 115–17, 119
   expressivist 99, 100, 115–17
   idealism 109, 115
   macro 13–14, 131, 133, 164
   positivism 89–90, 97, 106, 115, 142
   standpoint 8, 10, 26, 104, 160
thinking
   consciousness 34, 39, 56, 68, 72, 86, 90
   critical 24, 158–60
   higher order x, 17, 45, 57, 72, 86, 163
Thomson, Pat xii, 6, 7, 22, 26, 28, 93, 124, 157
threshold concept 73, 80–5, 91, 98, 104, 128, 145, 150–1, 159, 164, 167
training 39–40, 138
   see also education *and* Dewey, John
translanguaging 24, 72, 88, 135, 149
transparency trope 87
   see also clarity

truth 8, 30, 33, 42, 46, 64, 74–5, 77–8, 80–9, 91, 96–8, 109–12, 117, 125, 127, 139, 147, 164, 167
Turner, Joan 6, 22–4, 28, 35, 37–8, 42–3, 45, 57, 64–5, 67, 69, 94, 141–2
   see also Writtenness *and* ontological complicity

university
   Enlightenment 45, 93, 142
   Humboldtian 65, 68, 144
   Mediaeval 58, 61
   Renaissance 58–9, 61

values 5, 6, 21, 27–8, 38, 45, 70–1, 73, 79, 80
   see also ethics
vocabulary 13, 25–7, 75, 96, 104, 125
   see also lexis
voice 2, 10, 14, 18, 23, 31, 39, 49, 63, 74, 79, 107–8, 124, 129, 134, 143, 146, 151, 153, 169–70, 173

West (The) 8, 21, 45, 48–9, 51–5, 57–8, 65, 68, 76, 85, 99, 142–4, 147, 170–2
Wittgenstein, Ludwig 67, 75–8, 87–8
writer xi, 1–7, 11, 13–15, 23, 25, 27–9, 34–9, 41–4, 63–4, 67, 71–4, 77–88, 91, 96, 98–101, 103–23, 125, 128–9, 132–5, 137–8, 140, 145, 147–50, 152–66
Writing Studies 10, 73, 82–3, 103, 133, 136, 145
   see also Rhetoric and Composition Studies
writing
   academic *see* academicness
   creative 93, 156
   method of enquiry 103–5, 107–11, 113–14, 118, 128, 133–4, 138–40, 144, 153, 157, 159, 164, 166
Writtenness 28, 37–8, 141–2
   see also Received Pronunciation, Turner, Joan *and* ontological complicity

www.ingramcontent.com/pod-product-compliance
Lightning Source LLC
Chambersburg PA
CBHW062227300426
44115CB00012BA/2252